The Punishment of Pirates

The Punishment of Pirates

INTERPRETATION AND
INSTITUTIONAL ORDER IN THE
EARLY MODERN BRITISH EMPIRE

Matthew Norton

THE UNIVERSITY OF CHICAGO PRESS
CHICAGO AND LONDON

The University of Chicago Press, Chicago 60637
The University of Chicago Press, Ltd., London
© 2023 by The University of Chicago
All rights reserved. No part of this book may be used or reproduced in any
manner whatsoever without written permission, except in the case of brief
quotations in critical articles and reviews. For more information, contact the
University of Chicago Press, 1427 E. 60th St., Chicago, IL 60637.
Published 2023
Printed in the United States of America

32 31 30 29 28 27 26 25 24 23   1 2 3 4 5

ISBN-13: 978-0-226-66788-1 (cloth)
ISBN-13: 978-0-226-82311-9 (paper)
ISBN-13: 978-0-226-82310-2 (e-book)
DOI: https://doi.org/10.7208/chicago/9780226823102.001.0001

Library of Congress Cataloging-in-Publication Data

Names: Norton, Matthew, 1976– author.
Title: The punishment of pirates : interpretation and institutional order in the early
modern British empire / Matthew Norton.
Description: Chicago : The University of Chicago Press, 2023. | Includes
bibliographical references and index.
Identifiers: LCCN 2022020185 | ISBN 9780226667881 (cloth) |
ISBN 9780226823119 (paperback) | ISBN 9780226823102 (ebook)
Subjects: LCSH: Piracy—Great Britain—History—18th century. | Piracy—
Prevention—Law and legislation—Great Britain—History—18th century. | Trials
(Piracy)—Great Britain—History—18th century. | Social change—Great Britain—
History—18th century. | BISAC: HISTORY / Maritime History & Piracy | HISTORY /
Europe / Great Britain / Stuart Era (1603–1714)
Classification: LCC DA16 .N67 2023 | DDC 364.16/4—dc23/eng/20220506
LC record available at https://lccn.loc.gov/2022020185

♾ This paper meets the requirements of ANSI/NISO Z39.48-1992
(Permanence of Paper).

"What's real is family."
This is for them!

Contents

INTRODUCTION
Meanings and Mass Executions 1

1: INSTITUTIONS AS CULTURAL SYSTEMS 11

2: THE TRANSFORMATIONS OF EMPIRE 36

3: VAGUENESS AND VIOLENCE ON THE
MARITIME PERIPHERY 53

4: THE CLASSIFICATION OF PIRATES 82

5: GUNS, GALLOWS, AND INTERPRETIVE
INFRASTRUCTURES 110

6: "HUNG UP IN IRONS, TO BE A SPECTACLE,
AND SO A WARNING TO OTHERS" 140

7: AMBIGUITY LOST
Temporality and Fatalism on the Edge of Empire 158

CONCLUSION
Pirates, Adverbs, and Institutions 177

Acknowledgments 185   *Notes* 187
References 207   *Index* 219

INTRODUCTION

Meanings and Mass Executions

Two ships wage battle off the western coast of Africa; it is February of 1722, and they are pounding each other with cannons and grapeshot. One ship is an echo of the English Empire's unruly maritime past. The other represents the new empire: more orderly, oriented to trade, and more intensively state governed. In this struggle between men and their boats, one crew has the clear upper hand—it is better equipped and has the better position against the wind. Moreover, its adversaries, drunk after days at loose ends, are surprised to find themselves confronting not the easy merchant prey they expected but the armed and ready HMS *Swallow*. The *Swallow*, commanded by Captain Chaloner Ogle of the British Royal Navy, grasps this advantage and wreaks a largely unanswered carnage on its enemy. That enemy is the *Royal Fortune*, a pirate ship that under its captain, Bartholomew Roberts, had plundered more than four hundred ships in a career beginning in 1719 and crisscrossing the Atlantic. As of this day, it will go no further. Minutes after the battle begins, a round of grapeshot fired from the *Swallow* tears out Roberts's throat and he dies on the deck. Yet the crew of the *Royal Fortune* battles on for hours. What else are these men to do? Their prospects have narrowed to the cannon or the noose, neither much to hope for.

The battle ends with the surrender of the *Royal Fortune*'s crew. The men of the *Swallow* bring their captives to Cape Coast Castle on the Gold Coast of West Africa, a center of the English slave trade. Between March 28 and April 20, 1722, seven British officials under the direction of the piracy tribunal president, Captain Mungo Herdman of HMS *Weymouth*, set out to try some 169 prisoners, 4 of whom will die before their cases can be heard. Perhaps 70 more men from Roberts's crew, all African, are not tried at all but sent or returned into slavery. The tribunal ultimately acquits 74 men after hearing convincing evidence that they had been forced to turn pirate by Roberts and the more vicious and enthusiastic members of his crew. It convicts the rest, sentencing them to be executed for the crime of piracy, though in the end it will commute 39 sentences to lesser punishments. The tribunal has 52 men hanged on a beach between the floodmarks of low and high tides during those early days of April: 6 on the third, 6 more on the ninth, 14 on the eleventh, 4 on the thirteenth, 8 on the sixteenth, and on through a final 14 on the twentieth, with the most incorrigible further sentenced to have their bodies hung in chains.[1]

If we take the battle between the *Swallow* and the *Royal Fortune* as a reflection of the broader confrontation between piracy and an empire rising to global hegemony through maritime trade and naval mastery over the seas, then its grisly end in the waves off Cape Coast Castle is fitting. Beginning around the same time as Roberts's career and ending in the mid-1720s, the English Empire through various agents and methods contrived a concentrated bloodletting against pirates. Across the empire, hundreds of these marauders were killed in battle or tried by piracy tribunals and hanged, with their grisly remains displayed as warnings. By the end of the 1720s, the outcome of this broader struggle had been decided, and piracy no longer represented a systemic threat to England's maritime empire.

The eradication of this threat to the political and economic foundations of the British Empire is the end of the story that is the focus of this book. Our story begins in the far murkier maritime social order of the previous century. In the seventeenth-century colonial maritime world, even the humblest merchant vessel was well advised to go armed, and the boundary between lawful and unlawful violence routinely blurred in encounters at sea. Privateers, buccaneers, and other men of violence who took English colonies as their bases ferociously seized the opportunity provided by this legal ambiguity; they engaged in ambitious acts of private warfare and theft as they plundered foreign empires. They operated under no effective authority but that holding their loose coalitions together. The Spanish were the ideal targets of this lawless and entrepreneurial maritime violence based in English and French colonies. Though the decline of the Spanish Empire had been already under way by the early seventeenth century, it remained an object of fantastic wealth compared with England's paltry colonies clinging to survival around the Caribbean and the East Coast of North America. Spain's cities were near the sea, and its political-economic structure involved extensive maritime trade, including the transport of bullion from the New World to the Old. And the Spaniards were Catholic, providing many of the mariners gathered in England's colonies a hardly necessary religious justification for their predation. Throughout the mid-seventeenth century, ships and crews of all sizes and in all national combinations sailed from English ports to visit erratic violence and predation on Spanish towns and shipping.

As the century wore on, developments in the political economy of the English Empire made many of its colonies less hospitable hosts for such private pillage. In a broad sense, these developments involved displacing the freebooting adventure capitalism that characterized parts of the empire's periphery through the mid-seventeenth century in favor of a merchant capitalist empire of trade. The barely governed crews of armed men bent on robbery by sea responded to this new environment by enlarging their range. Still sailing from New England and the Caribbean in many cases, they added new hunting grounds off the west coast of Africa and in the Indian Ocean where their predation continued to disrupt the efforts of the English privileged class to put its empire on a more savory, more predictably profitable footing. Despite the turn of English elites from around 1670 onward against what they now saw as unwanted piracy, it retained a foothold in their empire. That piracy continued with periods of greater and lesser intensity contingent on international war, developments in maritime trade, and the whims of colonial governors. The brutality of merchant ship captains, the isolation that was their usual state as they plied the high seas, and the propensity to violence of some among the mariners who manned this crucial maritime network holding the empire together meant that ships were always available for men willing to cast off the law and sail freely and violently for their own fortune.

From 1717 to 1725, the war against the pirates—in its naval and legal dimensions, and with its accompanying spectacle of rotting bodies displayed at ports throughout the British Empire—marked a dramatic turning point for this social system. It was the bloody flourish ending a decades-long process that in fits and starts made the maritime world safer for trade and more dangerous for those who would turn pirate. This process replaced the vista of an open world where men of violence could make their own fortunes with a world defined by the promise of rapid, deadly punishment in support of the state's strengthened claim to hegemony over violence at sea. This book focuses on this pacification process, asking how the English produced coercive power over piracy and why the violence deployed against piracy took the form that it did. To answer these questions, it examines the efforts of English elites to define and punish piracy throughout the empire between 1670 and 1730. Its first goal is to analyze the social processes and the constellation of actors who reshaped the early modern English colonial maritime world by imposing a state-centric order on the ambiguous violence endemic to it for much of the seventeenth century.

The sociolegal category of piracy was at the center of this consolidation of state control. This category was not new; it had ancient roots, and England had a well-developed piracy jurisdiction that was central to controlling waters close to home. But the way the English defined piracy as a matter of law and practice was poorly suited to the new geographical context of its empire during the later seventeenth century.

The new powers of punishment that the English used to bring the pirates to heel during the early eighteenth century were not automatic or obvious. They were the outcome of an extended definitional struggle waged across the English Empire, on the lonely high seas, in governors' mansions, in the directorates of trading companies, at slaving forts, on Caribbean islands, in the East Indies, and all along the Atlantic coast of America. Violent encounters like that between Ogle and Roberts were just the most dramatic eruptions of a social struggle that ultimately transformed piracy from an ambiguous, ill-defined social and legal category into a well-defined one that agents of the English state could use to label and slaughter pirates and exert control over the maritime reaches of their empire. To follow this story, the book moves through a sprawling network of gun battles, executions, jailbreaks, parliamentary maneuvers, and courtroom dramas. It shows that the heart of the struggle to pacify the pirates pestering the foundations of England's new empire of trade is to be found not only in cannon shot and hangman's ropes but also in the genesis of a coordinated collective capacity to define piracy, to bring it into being as a social category, if only to better destroy it. As Foucault puts it, "visibility is a trap" (1977, 200); and once the trap was sprung and the pirates could be seen, all that was left for them was the fighting.

Pirate stories have the potential to be pretty good stories. They capture in dramatic tableaux the contours of a long-gone world formed differently in many respects from our own. They stage small dramas of social power that pit elites against social outcasts. Picturesque coves, tense standoffs, and dastardly betrayals abound in this history, and for those of a grislier disposition the annals of early modern piracy include a graphic record of inventive torture. Fifty-two men hanged on a beach by the Cape Coast slavers' fort is a hard image to forget, and there is a doubtless frisson to tales centered on vulnerable and often oppressed seamen rising up violently to seize fate in their own hands. In addition to these evident fascinations of pirate stories, there are two other motivations for recounting the historical narrative of the pacification of piracy that give these tales more social scientific heft and resonance. First, the disablement of the pirates was historically important, helping lay the foundations of long-distance trade on which the British Empire would eventually rise to rule the waves.

The apotheosis of the pirate threat occurred at an inflection point in the political-economic history of the British Empire and thus of the political-economic history of the world. To be clear, pirates were not the main stumbling block between the English and global maritime supremacy. But the story of the eradication of the systemic threat to maritime commerce and diplomacy posed by piracy provides a window through which we can examine the inner workings of the British Empire as its agents mobilized around a threat gnawing at its maritime foundations during one of the most important periods of its consolidation. Second, the issue of piracy is a good one to observe up close because it was entangled in fundamental questions about the viability of long-distance commerce for the empire; its political economy; its relations of authority and systems of sovereign delegation; how the law would work in an imperial context; the epistemological frameworks through which different actors sought to know their empire and make it "legible" (Scott 1999); and the state's monopoly on legitimate violence in a territory that was vast, isolated, and central to the birth of the modern world. This second aspect of the piracy case extends its interest beyond tales of derring-do: it brings together a cluster of questions of social scientific interest, from matters concerning institutions and economic order to questions concerning the consolidation of a monopoly on violence by state actors; and because of the peculiarities of the case, it helps shed new light on them.

Most notably, the story of the pacification of the pirates is part of a genre of similar stories of the disarmament, demobilization, discipline, "civilization," and settlement of unruly peoples. This recurrent theme of human history includes episodes such as the taming of samurai and the taming of duels, the disciplining of the mad, the relegation of threatening disruptions to outside the walls, the enclosure of territories, the monopolization of violence by agents of the state, and the disarming of lords, pirates, bandits, and others who would challenge that monopoly (Barkey 1997; Elias 1969; Gorski 2003; Ikegami 1995; Merriman 1991; Scott 2010; Shoemaker 2002; Thomson 1994; Tilly 1990). The prevalence of such similar pacification stories across such great swaths of time and space points to another goal of this book: to use piracy as a case that can shed its specific light on the more general social scientific question of how groups create, maintain, and enforce social orders. It is in pursuit of this theme that the book turns to an idea as old as the social sciences but nonetheless still at the center of a vibrant line of current inquiry: the power of institutions to remake the social world. The premise of the argument that I will be making in the following pages is that the piracy case, though interesting and important in its own right, and though indeed particular in the twists and turns of the events marking its historical course, has something more general to tell us about the sources of institutional order. More specifically, the empirical particulars of the piracy case make it well suited for advancing our understanding of the relationship between institutions and social meaning.

The next chapter goes into greater detail about what institutions are. Essentially, though, they are social rules. The thrust of the institutions literature is to argue that the rules, formal and informal, about how things are done in different domains of social life are uniquely powerful in explaining outcomes of great interest, because they enable humans to act in collective, patterned, and durable ways. The content of piracy laws—and laws are an important sort of formal institutionalized rules—had much to do with the proliferation of nonstate maritime violence in the later seventeenth-century English Empire and with its curtailment during the early eighteenth century. People trying to impose order on their social world as well as people trying to analyze and understand how and why their ordering takes the forms and has the effects that it does—that is to say, both social actors and social scientists—turn to institutions. The former do so because rules are basic tools of social coordination and control. For their part, social scientists from economics, management, political science, history, and sociology have turned to the idea of institutions because the rules adopted by different social groups and the social orders resting on them are essential to answering big questions: Why are some countries rich and others poor? Why are some states strong and others weak? Why do some states fail and others persist for hundreds of years? How do democracy and autocracy intersect with state strength? Why do some social orders inspire trust and long-term planning and others inspire distrust? How do any social orders persist over time? We can say something about all these questions and many more by examining both general and specific features of the institutions, the rules, created and enforced by the human communities involved.

But for all its breadth and power as an analytical tool, most institutional scholarship relies on a limited palette when it comes to the mechanisms through which institutions explain action. Most lines of institutional analysis focus on interests and incentives such as rewards and punishments as the central mechanisms for explaining institutions' power. People act out of self-interest, these approaches note, and institutions play a powerful role in shaping where their interests lie. They focus, that is to say, on who gets what for explaining individual action and therefore institutional outcomes. The piracy case is a paradigmatic example of this point: hanged by the neck until dead, as the sentences of pirates often read, is a pretty ultimate incentive. But institutional actors also need to determine how the rules fit the specific circumstances of the actual situations they face. Rules do not apply themselves, and so in addition to the importance of who gets what for understanding institutional order, we also need to pay attention to how actors in institutions answer questions about what *is* what. These questions are often bypassed or glossed over by scholars of institutions.

In order to reduce piracy through institutionalized violence and coercion, British imperial elites first needed to create the collective, practical, and symbolic capacity across a global empire during the age of sail to answer the question, What is a pirate? in a coordinated manner. This was not just, or primarily, an intellectual or a conceptual problem but a practical question of social meaning. It was a question of how to bring the semiotic category of piracy into being as a bloody, real social fact. In the following pages, I will show that the ability to collectively, authoritatively, and consequentially *interpret* in this way was necessary for creating the power to *punish*. Guns and gallows, elementally brute material incentives rooted in state violence, only became effective—indeed, only became possible—when deployed in support of the semiotic boundary dividing the lawful from the lawless, the pirate from all the other practitioners of violence and commerce who plied the early modern seas. Powers of collective, coercive violence depended on powers of collective interpretation that worked across a far-flung maritime empire.

The core theoretical argument of this book is that these interpretive aspects of institutions, so important to the story of the pacification of piracy, play a greater role in the production of all institutional orders than the theoretical attention they have received suggests. It is through such interpretive institutional infrastructures that actors bring into concrete, situational being the symbolic universes addressed by the institutionalized rules that undergird all institutional orders. They play such an outsize role because the interpretive aspects of institutions operate as metarules determining how other rules apply, whom they apply to, who decides, and other aspects of how institutional rules will work. Their operation is not purely conceptual or ideal. Rather, these interpretive infrastructures bridge the symbolic and the material, translating systems of semiotic relations into situated social facts and realities by powerfully shaping how institutionalized rules will be, can be, incorporated into the making of meaning in the unique circumstances posed by the concrete social situations that institution-oriented actors face. It is only in such situated circumstances, and through meaning-oriented social action, that rules become real.

The theoretical argument that I will advance in the following pages draws new connections between culture, institutional order, and institutional outcomes. It contributes to a school of thought that takes meaning to be one of the foundational sources of all institutional orders and an inevitably important mechanism for understanding the power of institutions to shape and reshape the social world. But my aim in putting meaning and interpretation front and center is not to relegate other mechanisms of institutional order from the prominent theoretical and analytical positions they currently occupy, nor do I intend to encourage a return to tired debates that oppose meaning and incentives, culture and rationality, or ideas and materials. In fact, I intend the opposite: to explain the *interplay* of meaning, incentives, culture, and rationality in explaining the outcomes of institutional orders (Adams 1996, 1999; Spillman and Strand 2013). Game theory, for instance, works better as a tool of social analysis when it is integrated with a theory of social meaning that accounts for the coordinated collective performance of values, identities, and powers which form social life in playable ways. I describe this approach in detail in the following chapter.

The piracy case has a number of advantages for examining theoretical questions beyond those already mentioned. For instance, the demands of communication in a global empire during the early modern period accentuated the problems of coordination and the deliberate, explicit attention that contemporaries gave to developing their interpretive infrastructures. Other more contingent details are also helpful, such as the long-standing conflict between common law and admiralty law in England that traveled with its colonists and helped set the scene for one of the sites of struggle in the making of a new piracy jurisdiction. This and other factors stretched out the process of developing the interpretive infrastructure of English piracy institutions, leading to the long gap between the turn against piracy by English elites beginning around 1670 and the actual pacification of piracy by the mid-1720s. Much of the analysis to come focuses on this period of political, military, legal, and social struggle over how piracy would be defined and how state power would be organized in support of empire.

I have found the case of early modern English piracy so captivating a context for thinking about institutions and interpretation because it is marked by both stark contrasts and long-lingering ambiguities. As for contrasts, this is a story about the imposition of human order on a part of the earth that perhaps epitomizes the opposite. The ocean vigorously resists us. It is impermanent: in flux; stormy; deadly calm, peaceful and mild, with lovely sun and good wind. It is a site of starvation and of caloric abundance; "water, water, every where, / Nor any drop to drink."[2] It is also a place that under the best of circumstances is hard to survive on for very long. The ocean is virtuosic at breaking down human social systems, human technology, and human bodies. One of the defining features of piracy as a social system, wherever and whenever it occurs, is that it is never a purely maritime matter. All pirates must land to refresh and refit, collect food and water, fix rot, scrape barnacles, and turn what they have stolen into what they need—which the sea would not always, or even very often, provide.

The case of piracy is also ambiguous. The pirates whom I am writing about here are not, in my view, sympathetic heroes of class-based resistance, though they often were victimized by class-based oppression and violence.[3] Inventively sadistic scenes of violence frequently mark the historical record of this period, and the pirates' victims were not limited to their oppressors. Many people were tortured and killed as the price for the freedoms that others sought to seize. On the other hand, mariners of the period lived in an abusive social system that put them at the mercy of captains and merchants who often thought nothing of cheating them of their pay, leaving them in ports far from home when their services were no longer needed, or lashing them to disability or death if they deemed circumstances to warrant it when on the high seas. Then there is the ambiguity that is the empirical focus of the book, filled in by men of violence with chaos and risk, reflecting a fundamentally different vision of social order than the state-dominated merchant capital system that supplanted it, not to mention the even more entrenched state domination of violence of the present. Counterposed to this morass we have the effort of a human community to wrap webs of significance around an unruly, often unreachable, and complex social world, a society attempting to establish a measure of control at its physical, political, technological, and semiotic limits. This is not to blindly valorize either ambiguities or social orders, for indeed such spaces still exist, and the ways they are filled in by violence, oppressive control, and always the play of power in our own day remind us of the risks on all sides of the social order equation. Rather, it is to appreciate ambiguity and efforts to order it as an analytical opportunity to observe the sometimes sharp remaking of social worlds.

The first chapter of the book is devoted to the detailed development of the aforementioned theoretical argument about culture, meaning, and institutions. The second chapter chronicles the early modern English maritime world, focusing on the transformations that set the stage for efforts to limit, control, and eventually eradicate English piracy. Chapter 3 describes the ambiguity of piracy in the seventeenth-century English maritime world, focusing on the difficulties English metropolitan elites faced in trying to define piracy. This was in crucial respects an interpretive problem rooted in the inadequacies of the existing interpretive infrastructure of English piracy institutions. The elites' early efforts to remedy these issues left them tied in knots made of law, politics, divergent interests, and questions about the basic structure of state power, given the inadequacies of the distribution of interpretive authority in the empire that the persistence of piracy laid bare. Chapter 4 analyzes the effort to resolve these issues, documenting the trials and errors of the later seventeenth century with respect to piracy that culminated in the creation of a new interpretive legal structure, the Act for the More Effectual Suppression of Piracy of 1700. The fifth chapter documents the ensuing translation of this new structure into the concrete realities of colonial maritime, legal, and political situations faced by English state agents. The sixth chapter examines how the new interpretive infrastructure comprising the 1700 piracy law and the state-oriented performances of social meaning that actuated it led to the integration of the new meanings of piracy into the lives and worldviews of English colonial society; this integration was achieved through spectacular public executions and the enlistment of religious fervor against piracy as a newly clarified social category. Chapter 7 discusses how this new interpretive infrastructure and the powers of coercion it created impacted seamen and pirates, reshaping their actions even when opportunities for predation arose far from the coercive clutches of state agents. By shifting the meanings of piracy, the interpretive infrastructure described here managed to bring coercion to bear even in remote and lonely places. It was this power that ultimately broke the back of piracy as an endemic and at times intense threat to Britain's merchant capitalist empire.

CHAPTER ONE

Institutions as Cultural Systems

BORDER STORIES

Cross a border and you are somewhere else. Depending on the border, the experience of being elsewhere can range from one of gentle novelty to deep disorientation. Many border crossings further confront us with questions about how to behave. We may know perfectly well how to do something at home, but as North notes, "we would readily observe that institutions differ if we were to try to make the same transaction in another country" (1990, 4).

Borders aren't the only place where such questions and confusions confront us, but in the modern world they offer dramatic demarcations of places where the rules differ. In addition to explaining many of the pleasures and pains of traveling, this feature of borders has been helpful in developing an important social scientific insight: differences among human groups in the rules they use to govern, control, and organize behavior can be crucial for explaining the differences in outcomes experienced by members of those groups. Different places, different rules; different rules, different lives is the institutionalist's slogan, suggesting that if we want to explain the divergent fates of human communities, states, societies, and civilizations, we need to look at the systematic differences in the rules that define in an enforceable way how they govern themselves, appease their gods, and run their economies. Recent books have made the case for institutional answers to questions of the greatest significance: Why are some nations rich and some poor? Why does political order emerge in some situations and collapse in others? What are the consequences of colonial rule for colonized societies and why? and How have groups over time managed the constant human struggle to control violence? (Acemoglu and Robinson 2013; Fukuyama 2011; Mahoney 2010; North, Wallis, and Weingast 2009) Institutions, according to these books and the voluminous literatures they are part of, are among the most important analytical tools for answering some of the biggest social scientific questions.

So we should be sure that we understand what institutions are. This is a deceptively simple requirement, and later in this chapter I will argue that we do not understand some aspects of the institution concept as well as we should. North's classic definition is a good place to begin, though. He writes that "institutions are the rules of the game in society or, more formally, are the humanly devised constraints that shape human interaction. In consequence they structure incentives in human exchange, whether political, social, or economic" (North 1990, 3). North makes the further point that his definition includes both formal institutions, a written legal code, for example, and informal institutions such as unwritten customs. In everyday language, an institution is roughly synonymous with an organization, but its social scientific meaning is more general. Formal organizations—firms, states, teams, agencies—are certainly places where we will find institutions, but they are hardly the only place where we would expect to find rule-based social orders. A playing field, a schoolhouse, a wedding, a courtroom, an intersection, these are all places where we would also expect to find systems of rules shaping interaction in interesting, observable, and powerful ways.

Since comparisons are useful if we want to be able to figure out anything of significance to say about how institutions shape social outcomes, it is no surprise that institutionalists like to tell border stories. Go to Nogales, Arizona, and then cross the border to the adjacent city of Nogales, Sonora, Acemoglu and Robinson write, and you will notice that "life south of the fence, just a few feet away, is rather different" (2013, 7). The differences they go on to note in the Mexican Nogales include lower household income, lower education, higher infant mortality, poorer public health conditions, lower life expectancy, inferior infrastructure, more threats to law and order like higher crime rates, and more political corruption and ineptitude (7–8). Another prominent contemporary institutionalist, Francis Fukuyama, suggests an even more ambitious comparative itinerary in *The Origins of Political Order*, inviting us to think about the intractability of the differences between Somalia, Haiti, Nigeria, Iraq, Afghanistan, and Denmark (2011, 14). Mahoney (2010) uses a carefully structured comparative analysis to tell a complex border story that he uses to disentangle indigenous, precolonial social order, colonial rule, and postcolonial developments in explaining the divergent fates of Latin American societies. Border stories, when systematically told, are an important comparative tool that allows us to draw the connections between rules and outcomes: the point and the promise of institutional analysis.[1]

But there is a problem of complexity inherent to these border stories. Nogales and Nogales are just cities, not whole societies or nations, but at the institutional level they each contain great knotted systems of rules tangled with other social structures and processes in the myriad interactions of millions of people, both within and between each city and through the further entanglements of life in the two cities with national, international, and global institutions, all complicated still further if our analysis requires our examining these institutional orders as they develop and change over time. A good border story—and by "good" I mean one that captures something noteworthy and extracts it from the sheer complexity of life without damaging so much of its context that its reality slips away in the telling (Schelling 1960, 162–63)—must cut through this complexity. This is indeed a problem, but it is a typical social scientific problem. As with all our efforts to pull order from complexity, it is *theory* that guides us in making our cuts in defensible places. It is through theory that institutionalists typify the elements of the complex institutional tangles that confront them and focus their inquiries on the aspects of institutional order that matter most for outcomes of interest.

The border stories of the institutionalists are meant not just to tell us that things are different over there, "another country heard from" (Geertz 1977b, 23), but to develop generalizable findings about the aspects of institutional order that make the greatest difference in how people live their lives. Acemoglu and Robinson, for example, far from finding the detailed empirical complexity of the two Nogales daunting, proceed to add aspects of dozens more cases and historical episodes to their analysis before drawing the general conclusion that patterns in the prosperity and poverty of societies depend on whether political and economic institutions are arranged in ways reflecting the interests of a wide range of people or only social elites. They then go a step further, arguing that inclusive political institutions create the conditions for inclusive economic institutions, and inclusive economic institutions create the conditions for economic prosperity. With this account, Acemoglu and Robinson adeptly take us from border stories and comparative complexity to a general theory of how institutional order shapes social life.

But we should not forget the role of theory in structuring what we compare and what we draw from those comparisons. I want to dwell on some questions about institutional theory in this chapter and to consider how it has shaped the questions we ask and the answers we get in institutional analysis. I will argue that some of the most prominent contemporaneous institutional theories cast a predictable empirical shadow because of how they theorize culture. Though culture has been part of institutional analysis from the beginning, I will argue that the depth of its significance for institutional analysis has not been adequately incorporated into many variants of institutional theory, even though it observably affects the processes and outcomes that they analyze. The cultural aspects of institutional order are often relegated to explaining irrational conundrums or the humdrum mechanics of interaction, or to background conditions so general that they have only faint causal significance for explaining actual outcomes and the social processes that produce them. On the other hand, a robust research tradition into the interactional foundations of institutional order, especially when combined with analytical techniques from historical institutionalism and cultural sociology, can lay down a marker for a more generally relevant theory of culture and meaning in institutional analysis. This book contributes to these theoretical developments through an approach that integrates the cultural sources of institutional order with its other sources rather than holding culture and meaning out as either special problems with distinct applications or background conditions without much specific empirical significance. To achieve this goal of bridging between often opposed ways of looking at the social world—game theory and cultural analysis, incentives and semiotics, behavioral equilibria and social meaning—I will focus on a specific set of mainly cultural mechanisms that structure two important parts of institutional order: coordination and what I call the interpretive infrastructures of institutions. The value of this approach lies in its capacity to connect meaningful interaction in concrete settings and situations with transsituational cultural systems and institutionalized incentives, and through that nexus to help explain culture's impact on institutional forms and outcomes, including material manifestations of institutional power.

To develop these ideas further, though, first we need to return to the question of how institutions work.

HOW INSTITUTIONS WORK

Why do people follow the "rules of the game" in any given field of social life? One well-developed answer to this question is that incentives explain rule following. People are motivated to follow rules because they are rewarded if they do and punished if they don't. For this answer to make sense, though, the rules need to be enforced, raising the ancient question of who watches the watchmen.

We might answer that other incentives and enforcers of their own motivate institutional enforcers. For instance, let's say that the rules in a labor market forbid employers from discriminating in a certain way and that most employers comply. An incentives approach to institutional theory says that the durable pattern of incentives associated with the no-discrimination rule causes this pattern of behavior. But this incentive structure is itself a pattern of behavior that must be explained through other incentives. Say an employer violates the rule and becomes the target of a discrimination suit. The judge allows the suit to proceed, the attorney for the plaintiff smells blood in the water and insists on a stringent settlement, the attorney for the employer recognizes the same risk and recommends that the employer come to terms, and the employer does. The sequence reaffirms the institution by reaffirming the existence of its rule-associated incentive structure. That reaffirmation, though, depends on the actions of a network of people all doing different things that, taken together, support this aspect of the labor market's institutional order. In this example, the enforcement of the rule depends on a subsidiary network of institutional rules and their enforcing incentive structures. Judges and lawyers are paid and treated as judges and lawyers by other actors in the legal system only if they show up to work and do the tasks associated with their positions roughly in the manner expected; the company trusts that its attorneys are not colluding with the plaintiffs because of the stringent criminal and professional penalties supporting institutionalized expectations for conduct in the legal profession; the defense provides discovery because of the potential penalties for failing to do so; and so on— incentives as a tower of turtles, both cause and effect, all the way down.

The problem with this picture is not that its causality is circular but that it is partial. We can see this in how it overlooks what should be a mysterious, unsettling coalescence of the actions and incentives of so many different people coming at the issue from so many different positions, with so many different interests. Before we even get to *why* they do it, we need to ask how they even know *what* to do to prevent the tower from collapsing. From a complex intersection of action and actors comes a rule system that is relatively stable across the perspectives and actions of different people with different organizational and social positions and across space and time. To be sure, there are gaps, breaks, inconsistencies, and interruptions, but what is most striking is that the overall pattern survives these and exhibits a remarkable persistence, like a standing wave in a turbulent stream (Abbott 2001b, 263, 274). The problem that an incentives-only approach is poorly suited to answer is how this system of incentives and actions becomes and remains organized enough to observably operate as a system of related rules distributed across time, space, and a multitude of actors.

What I take from this observation is that a focus on incentives is important for understanding the contribution of *distribution*—what people get and what they suffer—as a mechanism involved in the production and reproduction of institutional order. But it is poorly suited to account for another foundational aspect of institutional order: the *coordination* of complex networks of people, things, ideas, and actions in ways that bring the world contemplated by institutional rules into being. Another way to put this idea is in terms of the questions we should ask. Instead of asking, Why do people follow rules? as a way to think about the explanation of institutional order, we need to ask something more comprehensive: Why do people follow the rules that they do, in the ways that they do? This second question has a double meaning. It asks about both motivation (*Why* do they do that?) and coordination (Why do they do *that*?).

Many social scientists from economics, political science, anthropology, and sociology have understood coordinated, collective action to be a key part of how human communities survive, generate power, engage with the physical and social worlds, and solve (or, for that matter, create) social problems (Bowles and Gintis 2011; Lewis 1969; Schelling 1960; Chwe 2013; Alvard and Nolin 2002; Sterelny 2012). This study contributes to that long-term social scientific focus through its investigation of a suite of mechanisms connecting coordination to culture and the power of institutions to shape and hold social worlds. A focus on the problem of coordination adds to the repertoire of institutional theory by requiring us to explain more carefully where rules come from; how they are collectively produced and sustained in ways that give them their specific forms and thus shape their outcomes; and how individuals configure their behavior in light of the social forms and meanings that define institutional orders. It is when we try to answer these sorts of questions about how coordinated social action occurs that we run squarely into the otherwise hidden thicket of the cultural sources of all institutional orders.

THE CULTURAL SOURCES OF INSTITUTIONAL ORDER

Culture is a famously baggy concept that can be defensibly defined in many ways. But how it is defined has consequences. In some prominent recent works of institutional scholarship, for example, culture has been defined in ways that inexorably push it to the margins and background of empirical institutional analysis. Acemoglu and Robinson are among those who consider and discard the "culture hypothesis" that major features of national culture drive patterns of prosperity and poverty. Their argument is with views such as "Latin America will never be rich because its people are intrinsically profligate and impecunious" (2013, 57).[2] Culture in this sense should indeed not be taken seriously. North, Wallis, and Weingast's

Violence and Social Orders (2009) advances a different argument, understanding the problem of culture through the lens of what they call causal beliefs. The result, however, is the same, as they fold culture into the analysis of preferences, entirely avoiding questions of social meaning and its connection to coordinated social action. Even in works more committed to culture in its broad sense as an important aspect of institutional order, the ways that culture matters can be left vague. Fukuyama, for example, insists that "institutions reflect the cultural values of the societies in which they are established" (2011, 14), but he never specifies reflection or values in the analytically precise way necessary for taking them to matter empirically, and culture inexorably becomes a general background to his analysis rather than an active part of it.

The cultural theory that this book adopts, on the other hand, takes culture to revolve around the twin poles of symbols and social meaning. It is that aspect of all social orders involving not merely or mostly how people think, but how we individually and collectively experience and act within a meaningful social world. We find this symbolic dimension of social life anytime meanings arise that cannot be attributed simply to the immediate, self-evident physical circumstances of the situations in which they occur but are instead due to what things and circumstances physically present stand for. Culture in this view is "the semiotic dimension of human social practice," as Sewell puts it (2005a, 164), and it is often the case that we need to think in semiotic terms and adopt semiotic modes of analysis to get at how culture enters into the causal mechanisms and contingent eventfulness of history's unfolding (Wagner-Pacifici 2010). As Geertz describes the focus of this semiotic and meaning-centered approach to cultural theory, "Human thought is basically both social and public— . . . its natural habitat is the house yard, the marketplace, and the town square. Thinking consists not of 'happenings in the head' . . . but of a traffic in what have been called, by G. H. Mead and others, significant symbols—words for the most part but also gestures, drawings, musical sounds, mechanical devices like clocks, or natural objects like jewels— anything, in fact, that is disengaged from its mere actuality and used to impose meaning upon experience" (Geertz 1977a, 45).

The approach to cultural analysis that I adopt understands culture as the great coordinating engine of human collective action centered on the public, interactive conjuration of symbolic aspects of social life into concrete being as meanings that synthesize the semiotic and the merely actual. It builds on the symbolic interactionist tradition with its focus on situations and the definition of situations through interaction by associating these mechanisms with the manifestation of transsituational cultural systems, thus combining interactional and structural tools of cultural analysis. In a sense, the approach to culture that I adopt here grafts the analysis of cultural structures onto the interactive mechanisms that define symbolic interactionism, thereby tugging structuralism in an interactionist direction and interactionism in a semiotic one (Norton 2011, 2014b, 2019).

Behind this approach is the observation that for humans, the symbolic meanings of situations, things, people, and relationships are not an overlay that they use to make sense of what is happening; they *are* what is happening. Culture is not the lens we use to understand the real, because what humans perceive and treat as real is inseparable from symbols and from meaning. From this perspective, we do not experience the world and then use culture to interpret it. Rather, our experience of the world is in the first place an experience of meaning, symbolic and nonsymbolic. Humans grasp the world as a synthesis of symbols and "mere actuality" (Geertz 1977a, 45; Norton 2019). For instance, in Gilbert Ryle's well-known example, a wink is not a blink plus some additional other action; a wink might be a contracting of the eyelids, but that is not all it is (1968, 5). Culture is what winking is beyond that "mere actuality"—its meanings and the symbolic systems that those meanings are oriented toward and derive from. To use a dramatic example, and one central to the case of piracy, consider a hanging. How do we know whether it is a murder or an execution? Killing is central to both. But they are killings with different cultural orientations reflected as different patterns of meaning that in turn anchor different patterns of practical consequences—a payment for the executioner on the one hand and a trial for a murderer on the other. The mere actuality is similar, but the meaning is not. The task and contribution of cultural analysis in this case are to examine, understand, and ultimately explain the interwoven system of symbolic, cognitive, performative, ideal, material, and practical features that differentiate the two into categories of killings that mean very different things. In reality, we can say, they are different because reality for social scientific purposes is always a synthesis of the merely actual and the webs of signification that are its semiotic circumstance.

This idea that culture fundamentally forms the social world is intimately tied to the idea that culture is just as much an intersubjective and collective phenomenon as it is a cognitive and mental one. As Geertz puts it, "Cultural acts, the construction, apprehension, and utilization of symbolic forms, are social events like any other; they are as public as marriage and as observable as agriculture" (1973, 91). This public and interactive character of culture is valuable for institutional analysis, because symbolic forms play a central role in human coordination. *We* define what is real in situations, but *I* don't. If I call an encounter at sea piracy and nobody else supports that symbolic orientation, it won't matter much. On the other hand, when this orientation is picked up by others, repeated, enacted as real by them, and transmitted to other institutional and organizational settings, eventually leading to a hanging, it becomes an intersubjectively enforced definition of the situation and of the identities of the people, things, and relationships within it. It aligns the concrete situation to a cultural system, in this case a legal code, that defines piracy as a particular, perhaps demonized, certainly punishable sort of violence. It also aligns the situation to an *institutionalized* cultural system in which are encoded the procedures, organizational forms, rewards, and punishments that define piracy institutions as a nexus of rule-ordered human action and make the coordinated, collective production of incentives possible. Incentives, in this sense, are meanings too, and they are made real social facts through coordinated, collective, meaningful action and interaction oriented toward a cultural system.

It is worth explicitly noting that this public, interactive, and meaning-centered understanding of culture is an answer to the puzzle of coordination as a core aspect of institutional order that is far removed from any associations with a reductive idealism, a tendency that takes culture to be primarily a matter of mental forms like ideas, beliefs, and values (Geertz 1981, 135–36). The premise of thinking about culture in the way I have described is that humans were, are, and will be a "cooperative species" (Bowles and Gintis 2011) that achieves a capacity for collective action by orienting itself not just to the world but also to other humans and the ways *they* are oriented to the world (Geertz 1977a, 47–48). An important aspect of how we achieve this intersubjective coordination, this reflexive, collective world making, is through the establishment of symbolic systems establishing identities, relationships, and meanings that we fuse with the mere actuality of the world, turning it into a real part of the social environment of action and consummating a primordial alchemy that is elemental to both individual and collective human being.

SWORDS AND SEMIOTICS

Indeed, the thrust of the argument of this book is in the opposite direction from the school of thought that relegates culture to ideas, beliefs, and values. It is a contribution to what Isaac Reed has dubbed the "lawyers, guns, and money" approach to cultural and historical analysis (Adams 1996, 2007; Reed 2013, 2019, 2020, 355–58; Norton 2014a, 2014c, 2015). The distinguishing analytical preoccupation of this approach has been to connect the semiotic dimensions of social life with the dimensions that, for a few decades in the most prominent strands of political, institutional, sociological, and economic theory, were seen as furthest from it: the material, the violent, the coercive, the calculative, the filthy lucre. It contributes to the argument that reducing culture to the ideal or the epiphenomenal is an analytical error (Alexander and Smith 2003) by examining that claim at its extreme, where culture structures in strong and analytically important ways even the bluntest manifestations of power.

Generally speaking, this approach seeks to identify promising ways forward for thinking about the relationship between state formation, state capacity, and culture. Instead of discarding the material emphasis of classic "bellicist" (Gorski and Sharma 2017) analyses of state formation and state capacity that emphasize the demands of preparing for and waging war as a prod to state formation but relegate culture to a modest role (Brewer 1990; Downing 1992; Ertman 1997; Evans et al. 1985; Mann 1986; Skocpol 1979; Tilly 1975, 1990), this approach aims to better understand the integration of symbolic and material dimensions of state power. In doing so, it builds on a now-estimable counterpoint to the bellicist tradition where culture and meaning play an important role as both an object of state formation and as its means (Gorski 2003; Loveman 2005; Adams 2007; Steinmetz 2007; Go 2008; Wilson 2011; Loveman 2014; Reyes 2019).

My analysis picks up the lawyers, guns, and money argument through a focus on how institutions link social performances—actions that assert symbolic meanings—to chains of reinforcing action that propagate the performed meanings, ratify them, and make them real.[3] Coordination of this sort plays a particularly important role in linking the cultural and material dimensions of state and institutional power. In his book *Negara* Geertz notes that in many variants of cultural theory, "the semiotic aspects [of social life] . . . remain so much mummery. They exaggerate might, conceal exploitation, inflate authority, or moralize procedure. The one thing they do not do is actuate anything" (1981, 123). This is a good way of putting the problem with some of the approaches to culture, states, and institutions described above: culture is present, but it doesn't do much. In contrast, in the cultural theory that I adopt here the effects of culture are not primarily decoration or distraction; nor does culture enter into the causal chains and conjunctures of social explanation through some sort of osmotic magic, through processes exclusively hidden away inside peoples' heads, or as a context connected to action through underspecified mechanisms. It is not the ideal drapery laid on the real structures of power. Rather, it is one of the most important *sources* of the real structures of power. Coordination plays a key role in explaining this theoretical claim.

One of the reasons that culture and meaning are such important aspects of sociological analysis and explanation is because they are primal aspects of human collective action. As Geertz has argued, humans have an "extreme dependence upon a certain sort of learning: the attainment of concepts, the apprehension and application of specific systems of symbolic meaning" to get by in the world and to act on it, individually and collectively (1977a, 49–50). One of the main reasons that symbolic systems are so important to all forms of anthropocentric social order (including institutional order) is because of the role that symbolic meanings—significant symbols, Mead calls them (2015, 78)—play in creating intersubjective references for coordination. Mead writes that "symbolization constitutes objects not constituted before, objects which would not exist except for the context of social relationships wherein symbolization occurs. Language does not simply symbolize a situation or object which is already there in advance; it makes possible the existence or the appearance of that situation or object, for it is a part of the mechanism whereby that situation or object is created" (78). It is through mechanisms involving symbolic meaning that we bring into being the social objects and relationships that form the circuits of life, power, money, goods, people, and signs which constitute the real in our intersubjective social worlds (Norton 2017). Pirates are not an ontologically distinct category of beings—they need to be brought into existence through coordinated definitional and boundary work, and their existence is necessary for their punishment. Institutional order, like any other sort of social order, does not just depend on this sort of coordinated collective world making. It is never anything *but* collective world making, a collective bringing into being of the social world and its enforced contours.

Coordination is thus an important mechanism in accounting for how and why institutions work as they do. For actors in search of, as Mary Douglas puts it, "some practical basis for projecting forward . . . a version of the world that works" (1986, 62; Goodman 1983), options are limited by the symbolic orientations of other actors in the situation. They face, to use Wagner-Pacifici's phrase, a "resistant reality" (2000, 148). What works depends on what others are doing, and what others are doing in turn depends on the cultural systems that they are oriented toward and that help define their positions, perspectives, and possibilities for action. Because institutions are constructs dependent on coordination, and therefore tied to the symbolic systems defining the forms and relations that make institution-related action meaningful and intelligible, they work in specific ways shaped by the cultural systems that ground them and only in these ways. They are not generic structures of power but specific ones empowered and constrained by their cultural form. Cultural systems and the forms of coordination that they make possible are therefore crucial to explaining how and why institutions work as they do.

INTERPRETIVE INFRASTRUCTURES

The significance of interpretation to institutional order has a long pedigree in institutional analysis. Meyer and Rowan, for instance, argue that among other things, we should understand institutional rules to be "classifications built into society as reciprocated typifications or interpretations. Such rules may be simply taken for granted or may be supported by public opinion or the force of law. Institutions . . . often enter into social life primarily as facts which must be taken into account by actors" (1977, 341). But this sentiment focuses too much on the deep, quiet structuring of the taken for granted. The concept of interpretation that I have in mind is much more active in accounting for how culture enters into life as fact. In this sense, it is closer to the emphasis placed on classification by scholars such as Lamont and Bourdieu. Lamont, for example, has shown the power of enforced social boundaries and boundary-making processes in enshrining inequality and hierarchy (2002; Lamont and Molnár 2002). Bourdieu (1985, 1999b, 1999a, 2015) has written extensively about the social power that derives from "principles of vision and division," showing how the way that we divide up the world ties what we classify to systems of power that reify and entrench those classifications. These approaches to classification are useful in that they highlight the proximity of classification rituals to the implementation of social power. Through interpretive acts, actors locate themselves, others, and the physical world in the symbolic world of the institution and its enforced network of rules and relations. Institutional interpretations are like "hinges" (Adams 2007, 8) made of social meaning that can be swung to mobilize coordinated patterns of action and other social forces in support of the definitions and designations put forth by actors empowered by the institution to interpret.

We can productively think about the character of interpretation in this power-actuating sense through its relationship to that other tent pole of institutional order, enforcement. Enforcement, as Schelling has argued, depends on two things: "some authority somewhere to punish or coerce and an ability to discern whether punishment or coercion is called for" (1960, 131). We can adequately understand neither of these unless we equip ourselves with a robust theory of interpretation linking culture to patterns of concrete action. Authority as an empirical reality has to do with whether actors will ratify the enacted assertions of meaning of those who claim it through culturally appropriate reciprocal action supplied by the institution (i.e., coordination). The second of Schelling's requirements, the capacity to decide whether a rule has been violated, likewise shows the dependence of institutional order and power on a capacity to interpret even in this clearly incentivizing mode.

The idea of the interpretive infrastructure of an institution is meant to help conceptualize what is involved in the creation of this collective capacity to interpret and to link interpretations to coordinated chains of action that ratify and propagate them and that make institutions real social facts. Institutionalized power, achieved through enchained, coordinated performances of meaning propagated and ratified through collective action both within and across situations, is always dependent on an institutionalized capacity for saying "what is what." It is this interpretive infrastructure of the institution that determines how classification can occur, when, by whom, and with what limits, vocabulary, and purported consequence, and it is this infrastructure that claims to activate further chains of action that ratify and propagate the inciting interpretation. Interpretive infrastructures are the aspects of institutional orders involving interpretation and the coordinated propagation and enforcement of institutional interpretations as real social facts. They are how actors can answer "what is what" in a way that summons institutionalized, coordinated powers in support of those classifications by motivating other people to act in ways that support the inciting interpretation. If institutions are in one sense stabilized systems of coordination that can be activated with a greater degree of consistency than novel coordination claims, interpretive infrastructures are the stabilized ways that those powers can be called on through the activation and invocation of institutional signs, classification procedures, and associated lines of action.

How this capacity is achieved has no generic answer. Different institutions have different interpretive infrastructures, some more formal, some baroquely veiled, some easy to change, some poorly understood even by those enmeshed in them. Interpretive infrastructures are components of all institutionalized, rule-like social orders. They can be constituted in many different ways. In a charismatic cult, for example, the leader may simply say what is what, and across some limited space of possibility has the ability to command the enchained responses of adherents to make that classification real. Different ways of establishing a coordinated interpretive capacity lead to different social dynamics and outcomes, depending on their empirical specifics. Because they are crucial to the creation and continuation of institutionalized social orders and because the details of the interpretive infrastructures of institutions differ in significant ways, describing them and how they work is one of the fundamental questions in the analysis of any institution. They hold the key to understanding how interpretations become transsituational and interpersonal social facts and institutional rules become realities that can incentivize, mobilize, and otherwise shape outcomes.

I hope that readers will find the concept of the interpretive infrastructures of institutions intuitively accessible. We deal with these interpretive aspects of institutions all the time, and we routinely experience the social power leveraged by these institutionalized interpretive capacities. Loan officers, for instance, who "evaluate, authorize, or recommend approval of loan applications,"[4] are part of the interpretive infrastructure of mortgage institutions, playing an important role in a rule-based system for lending money by classifying those worthy of credit and those unworthy. Law, as another example, is widely taken to be a fundamental part of modern institutional orders. What are laws if not rules? But likewise, what is law if not an epistemic machine, a semiotic device that makes acts meaningful—known, legible, cognizable, or commensurable—by translating them into the semiotic categories and related enforcement mechanisms that comprise state power? The legal system itself can and often does act as a powerful interpretive infrastructure with a wide scope of action. Courts, laws, juries, bailiffs, and judges are tied together in a web of relationships collectively capable of coordinated interpretation. English piracy law during the seventeenth and eighteenth centuries plays an important role in this study, because it was at the heart of an interpretive infrastructure that created and wielded significant social powers to define piracy and to implement that definition pragmatically through classification rituals and procedures establishing guilt and innocence. The meanings that it created and enforced played a crucial role in establishing a durable, transsituational, rule-like social order.

Bank loans and law courts are just a few examples of interpretive infrastructures. We can find other examples wherever we see collective, coordinated classification happening that is tied to the rule-based distributional aspect of institutions: financial aid officers and forms and the laws that give categories of meaning and power to them; water resource boards, administrative rule making, agency staff, permits, and treaties; immigration adjudication and enforcement; tenure and promotion committees; inspectors general; adoption agencies and Child Protective Services; ratings agencies; prize juries; school dress code enforcement. Through classification and the propagation and enforcement of those classifications and the boundaries they establish by institution-oriented actors, all these patterns of interaction operate to define situations and social objects in alignment with institutionalized meanings and link those interpretations to institutionalized powers of social control (Smith 2008). They are interpretive infrastructures (or parts of more involved interpretive infrastructures) that say what is what and are empowered to swing the hinges of coordinated, rule-based institutionalized power to make their classifications real. The question that this book focuses on is what we can make of this interpretive dimension of institutional order if we focus on it specifically.

Though interpretive infrastructures come in many different forms, and attention to the details is necessary to characterize them in any specific case, for analytical purposes it is useful to have at least a basic description of their common elements. They have three common, interrelated parts. First, interpretive infrastructures draw from a network of codified signifiers, an analytically identifiable system of signs that are related to other signs and signifiers to form a relational system of connotations, antinomies, intersecting signifiers, and semiotic identities. A legal code is an obvious example of this, but it is not necessary for codification to take such a formalized, explicit form. The imagery and narratives of a holy text could, for instance, form the codified symbolic substrate of interpretive judgments. The code that interpretations draw from can be formal or informal, rigidly fixed or somewhat flexible. *Codified* here simply refers to the existence of conventional (i.e., socially constructed) relations between signs that establish their meanings and angle of entry into specific situational contexts.

Second, interpretive infrastructures need classification rituals. These are the procedures, the apparatuses, the recipes, the scripts, the mechanisms for how to classify in an institutionally embedded and hinge-activating way. Following Austin (1976, 45), they are the specific conditions for actually and successfully calling on chains of coordinated, institutionalized ratification and propagation in a specific institutional context. Really, classification rituals are just a specialized part of the codified sign system specifically defining the forms, aesthetics, magic words, and other conditions that make institutionally oriented interpretation a social act that commands collective, coordinated ratification.

Third, institutionalized interpretive infrastructures require performative enactment of the classification rituals. To become situational realities (and ultimately social-structural realities), codes and classification rituals must be translated into action in some concrete circumstances. Someone somewhere needs to do something that actuates the infrastructure or that propagates the interpretations it generates. These specific enactments are the social performance dimension of interpretive infrastructures. Through such social performances, actors "display for others the meaning of their social situation" (Alexander 2004, 529; Goffman 1990), just as they display those meanings for themselves. In doing so, they bring into being the forms and relations of cultural systems, synthesizing them with situational circumstances and making them real. "Acts are performative in the sense that the essence or identity that they otherwise purport to express are *fabrications* manufactured and sustained through . . . discursive means" (Butler 1989, 136; emphasis in the original). By the same token, actors perform classifications as situationally specific assertions of trans-situational, institution-oriented meaning.

These three basic elements operate together to create institutionalized systems of interpretation. One of the broader arguments of this book is that these are more important to understanding institutions than is often recognized and that social scientists could do better in recognizing that these systems range across artificial divisions like those between materiality and culture or individual acts and relational systems. While it is important to recognize that institutionalized interpretive infrastructures are heterogeneous in ways that take empirical work and creativity to chase down, so is identifying the limit of an interpretive infrastructure.[5] That limit can be clearly drawn at the actions of people and other parts of the institution that have a designated (i.e., institutionally recognized) role in making and enforcing classifications. For institution-oriented actors, it is often the goal of classification to see those interpretations propagated by actors within the institution and also outside it as they accept institutionalized interpretations as symbolic realities (Sahlins 1981), but this onward, extra-institutional propagation is an effect of an interpretive infrastructure rather than a part of it.

More generally, the goal of an interpretive infrastructure is the achievement of an interpretive act that asserts a claim about the meaning of a specific situation or circumstance by locating it in a codified system of institutional signs. The interpretive act, and interpretation more generally, as I conceptualize it here, is a synonym for what Peirce called semiosis, "an action, or influence, which is, or involves a cooperation of *three* subjects, . . . a sign, its object, and its interpretant. . . . [Semiosis] in Greek of the Roman period . . . if I remember rightly, meant the action of almost any kind of sign" (1990, 394).[6] Often, the best way to conceptualize that action of semiosis, or interpretation, is as a translation (Liszka 1996, 20–34) of the relationship between some signifying thing (the sign: "he is a pirate") and the object that it signifies (the object: a relationship between a man, his history of action, and a criminal category) into some effect (the interpretant: seize him, try him, hang him).[7] *Interpretation*, as I use the term in this book, can range from the grand gesture of a verdict, to the mundane action of everyday this-is-that speech, to the construction of social structures and even physical environments into which interpretive translations of purported sign-object relations are encoded and stored, and from public pronouncements to cognitive graspings of salience and significance.

The analysis of the following chapters will move about in the analytical space described by these elements in an effort to understand the interpretive infrastructures that defined English piracy institutions, how they changed over time, and why this layer of institutional order played such a significant role in the pacification of piracy during the early eighteenth century. As I argued above, the analysis of interpretation and interpretive infrastructures becomes particularly important when it comes to institutions because institutions are so dependent on the conjunction of rules and patterns of coordinated action. In the context of institutional analysis, the framework that I have just described becomes a tool for understanding the production of potentially large-scale and far-reaching forms of social power and social organization.

There is also an analytical argument about interpretive infrastructures twined around this theoretical one that I want to make explicit. The interpretive aspects of institutional orders involve mechanisms and processual dynamics different from those suited for the analysis of other aspects of institutions. This has two important implications. If the mechanisms through which interpretive infrastructures work are distinct, then we need to adopt analytical concepts and techniques that allow us to address those mechanisms. The techniques that I adopt here are a fusion of interactionist and structural-hermeneutic (Alexander and Smith 2003) cultural analysis linked to concepts of coordination that tie culture to institutional order through a series of mechanisms involving social meaning. These or other approaches are necessary, not to better balkanize the cultural dimensions of institutional order, but to better understand how they work and are connected to other aspects of institutions. If the processual dynamics relating to interpretive infrastructures are distinct, then we need to devote specific analytical attention to them, because they are at least potentially autonomous from other aspects of institutional order. This means that the interpretive aspects of institutional orders may be associated with different causal processes, and they may impose developmental trajectories that are contingent on the specificities of the interpretive infrastructure and its associated cultural systems. Moreover, these trajectories may exhibit and impose their own temporality on processes of institutional change. This dynamic is important in the piracy case. As I will show in subsequent chapters, the pace of change in piracy institutions in the English Empire was contingent on the entwined temporalities of piracy outbreaks and processes of legal contestation and change that extended the question of the interpretive infrastructure available for defining piracy over decades.

Once we start looking, we can find interpretive infrastructures throughout all institutional orders. Indeed, wherever we can observe institutionally oriented interpretive acts, we should expect there to be an interpretive infrastructure that makes collective interpretation possible—as well as legible, sensible, manifest, real—and defines the costs of making it. It is this essential aspect of interpretation that leads to the central theoretical argument of this book: that interpretive infrastructures play an outsize role in shaping all institutional orders. This is so because cultural structures and mechanisms that constrain and afford all symbolically oriented definitions and classifications are a central aspect of what rules are and how they enter into social action in a consequential way.

On that note, we have arrived back again at the question of what institutions are.

WHAT ARE INSTITUTIONS?

The approach to culture I have just outlined, far from relegating it to the analytical margins, puts it at the center of institutional analysis. But how should it be reflected in our understanding of what institutions are? North's definition, again, starts out by saying that institutions are "rules of the game." But he immediately clarifies this idea, stating that institutions, "more formally, are the humanly devised constraints that shape human interaction" (North 1990, 3). But are rules and constraints the same? They are in power-distributional, incentive-focused understandings of the mechanisms at the core of institutional theory. Constraints are the effect of incentives, and incentives are a good, if incomplete, general-purpose tool for explaining why people do what they do. But my argument in this chapter insists that incentives, based on collective action, are invariably undergirded by cultural systems and their associated mechanisms of interpretation and meaning making. Institutionalized constraints and incentives, in addition to being causes in their own right, are outcomes produced in part by specific interpretive infrastructures and the forms of coordinated meaning making that they make possible.

But how does this set of ideas about the cultural sources of institutional order and the meaningful character of institutional rules translate into a definition as manageable as North's? I would add to his definition that in addition to being constraints, institutional rules are "models of" and "models for" (Geertz 1973, 93–94) how things ought to be done in some specific aspect of social life and what ought to happen if they are not. Thinking about rules as models puts us in a better position to analyze the contours of the social world presumed by the rule that defines its operation across situations and from different perspectives and social positions. Incentives are an outcome, in part, of the content of the models that constitute rules, of the social objects, interactional routines, categories, classificatory systems, and other elements that constitute the model as a transposable, enforceable social order.

A definition of rules as incentivizing constraints and a definition of rules as cultural models are ultimately complementary visions of institutional order that ought to be integrated rather than set at odds. Nevertheless, they suggest different analytical strategies and possibilities. In particular, the idea that rules are "models of" how things are and "models for" how things ought to be done suggests two distinct pathways through which institutions as cultural systems that work through the master mechanism of social meaning can produce and shape institutional order and its outcomes. The "model for" sense of rules has to do with symbolic-performative action, with the provision of scripts that model how to do things in institutionally oriented ways. Rules are what the institution calls for and calls forth, playing a key role in chains of propagation and ratification of institutional interpretations and other meanings. This is the aspect of institutions that shapes social action, bending it to the form of institutionalized meanings (Geertz 1973, 93). In this sense, rules are models for institution-oriented thought and action. This aspect of institutional order is found in things like the sense of rightness of action that institutionally embedded people have in institutionally relevant circumstances, in documents describing behavior such as the scripts provided to English colonial piracy tribunals during the early eighteenth century, in habits, in roles, and any other mechanisms that guide action. This aspect of institutions is relevant even if the main reasons that people want to act in institution-oriented ways have everything to do with incentives, because we need to be able to explain how people know, or are able to figure out, what to do. Not just *Why* do they do that? but also Why do they do *that*?

In the "model of" sense, rules represent the world as institutionally meaningful. They translate the happenings and doings of the world into the institution's "imaginative universe" (Geertz 1977b, 13). Doing so provides the ground for institution-oriented actors to classify, interpret, and judge the institutional significance of what has happened and what has been done. In this sense of translating the world into the symbolic structure of the institution, cultural models are the foundation for the classification of action and other aspects of situations. They are a crucial part of the apparatus of enforcement of institutional rules, indeed a precondition for enforcement.

OTHER APPROACHES TO THE PROBLEM OF
CULTURE AND INSTITUTIONAL ORDER

Friedland has argued that "we need to stop the dance of angels and grain prices" (2009, 62) in institutional analysis—that is, to end the tedious zero-sum back-and-forth between cultural and distributional, sociological and economic, incentivized and meaningful understandings of institutional order. The theoretical approach I have just described provides an analytical framework that takes angels—culture—and grain prices—incentives—to be fundamentally interrelated in institutional orders. It rejects the "modern worldview [that] presents instrumental institutions as nonsymbolic" (Dobbin 1994, 117) in favor of a view that sees instrumental institutions and their incentives as enmeshed in meaning and culture; incentives are produced in part by cultural mechanisms, but just as importantly, incentives are also signifiers that work simultaneously through the mechanisms of interests and meanings. Such an approach necessarily has analytical implications. Theory, after all, tells us where to make our cuts and where to focus our energies, and this theory proposes a different way of thinking about the cultural sources of institutional order that has analytical consequences.

This theory of institutions and of the cultural sources of institutional order is not radical. Rather, it combines influences from several affiliated ways of thinking about cultural, historical, and institutional analysis and moves away from some other approaches that share nominal interests but advocate more abstract modes of analysis. The early new institutionalism in sociology laid an important marker for thinking in sophisticated ways about the role of culture in the creation of institutional order. Deploying concepts like myth, ritual, and institutional logics, these approaches described institutions as macrocultural systems. Sometimes those systems seem to soar above the heads of the people who enacted them, and the ways that institutional cultures actually entered into reality through action remained hazy.

Two more recent approaches have come to the fore in shoring up this line of analysis. The institutional logics perspective that built on the early work of Alford and Friedland and was championed by Thornton, Ocasio, and Lounsbury approaches this problem of cultural theory unmoored in individual action. It does so through the construction of an elaborately detailed metatheory that loops energetically from the entwined symbolic and material dimensions of all institutional orders to action to specific institutions to the interinstitutional system; from the micro to the meso to the macro and back again; from schemas to identities to practices to mobilization, all in service of a vast theoretical enterprise that finds a space for nearly everything—syntheses for all. The most prominent definition of institutional logics, the core concept holding this enterprise together, is revealing about the ambitions of this grand effort to embrace the entirety of institutional theory. Institutional logics, write Thornton and Ocasio, "are the socially constructed, historical patterns of cultural symbols and material practices, including assumptions, values, and beliefs, by which individuals and organizations provide meaning to their daily activity, organize time and space, and reproduce their lives and experiences" (Thornton, Ocasio, and Lounsbury 2012, 2), leaving little out. In saying it all, though, this approach loses the specificity I am after in the approach to integrating the interpretive and the coordinating mechanisms I have just described into institutional analysis. For instance, the specification of vast interinstitutional "logics" is of little help in constructing explanations at the midrange, of specific institutions and the ways that actors can and cannot mobilize them to make meanings in concrete situations. Indeed, the most important overlap between the approach to institutional analysis that I adopt here and the institutional logics perspective, besides a generic perception that culture is important and we have yet to sort out a really compelling way of handling culture in institutional analysis, is its commitment to identifying specific mechanisms to explain the "partial autonomy of actors from social structure" (Thornton, Ocasio, and Lounsbury 2012, 7).

Another recent branch of sociological institutionalism offers a more straightforward way of developing these arguments: the inhabited institutions approach. Pioneered by Hallett and Ventresca, this perspective forges a meaning-centered institutionalism by focusing on interaction. In contrast to "the contemporary institutionalist concern with meaning [which] is more implicit and treated in the abstract, as public culture" (Hallett and Ventresca 2006, 227), the inhabited institutions approach adopts the tenets of symbolic interactionism (broadly understood to include predecessors like Mead and Cooley as well as the works by Blumer and Goffman, among others) as a way to "people institutions," as Hallett, Shulman, and Fine put it (2009), and to resist approaches to institutional theory that turn institutions into "disembodied structures acting on their own volition while depicting actors as powerless and inert in the face of inexorable social forces" (Colomy 1998, 267). At the heart of the inhabited institutions approach is the claim that meaning, and even macroinstitutional meaning, is primarily made in social interactions (Hallett and Ventresca 2006, 223).

Drawing inspiration and direction for the analysis of this book from inhabited institutionalism is in a sense a strange fit. The focus of the book is on explaining macrohistorical change at the scale of decades and centuries in a global empire when travel time made effective distances further still. Even with such macro-level analytical goals, though, I have found it essential to anchor the analysis in the specificities of situational interactions to understand the powers in play at a level granular enough to support sociological explanation. A further theoretical tradition has helped me integrate the different levels of analysis of this study. Alexander and Smith describe a method for cultural sociological analysis that they call structural hermeneutics (2003). This approach adopts the view that the microsociological analysis of utterances, actions, and interactions and the transsituational analysis of durable social structures (Sewell 2005b) must often be conducted in conjunction because these levels of analysis operate as important causes for one another (Norton 2014b). The method involves moving back and forth between these contexts to trace the patterns of mutual influence that make them both part of the same sociological stories. The movement of the evidence and argument of this book between the specific and the structural reflects this approach.

Structural hermeneutics also makes it possible to adopt an approach that echoes the concerns of inhabited institutionalism while pursuing a research agenda that reflects the tradition of institutional analysis in historical sociology and its focus on large-scale questions (Adams, Clemens, and Orloff 2005; Mahoney 2000; Thelen 1999). This tradition includes some different methodological options, from formal comparative methods to case studies. The kind of argument that I pursue here that dives deep into the sui generis details of a particular case is not ideally suited for comparative analysis, as comparison seeks to generalize across cases rather than to particularize. Instead, the approach to historical sociological analysis that I take here examines a single case of the genesis of coercive power through the closely historicized analysis of its specific causal trajectories that I then tie to more general arguments about culture, meaning, institutions, and power through theory (Mahoney 1999, 1155, 1170; Sewell 1996). Such an approach contributes to what Wilson identifies as "efforts to downshift the analysis of colonialism from abstract universals into the concrete political, institutional, and cultural processes in particular places and times" (2011, 1468). It is an ethos that attempts to integrate the situated, interactional focus of inhabited institutionalism and the movement between the active performance of meaning and the analysis of historical and semiotic structures that shape environments of action (Alexander 1987) advocated by the structural-hermeneutic approach to cultural sociology.

Another advantage of the combination of historical institutionalism and inhabited institutions–style attention to people acting in situational contexts that I adopt is its capacity to explain institutional change. Interaction orders are not rigidly scripted workings-out of structure by cultural dupes but rather sites of struggles over meaning, locations of contestation, polysemy, and interpretive conflict. North's metaphor presents itself again as apt here: "rules of the game" is a better way to think about institutional order than some concepts overly focused on the "order" part, because it reminds us that the rules and the playing are distinct parts of the outcome as well as interacting parts. A concept of institutions that does not do a good job accommodating winners and losers, crushing defeats and surprising victories, cheats and referees and loopholes, or the relative autonomy of actual outcomes from the transposable system within which those outcomes are made, loses the blood of institutionalism in favor of its forms. On the other hand, an approach grounded in the meaning-material synthesis that comprises human situations is well suited to developing explanations that can account for institutional change in ways that challenge more order-centered and static forms of institutionalism.

Finally, it is likewise through intentional efforts to trace the circulation of meaning from semiosis through situations to a specific historical trajectory that the theoretical approach adopted in this study differs from Bourdieu's emphasis on the role of classification processes in asserting state power (1999a, 2015). The approach adopted here insists on the preeminence of situations as the nexus for tracing meaning as it circulates between individuals and social structures. This circulation plays a vital role in the constitution of social power. To pursue this idea, this approach provides an account that specifies the mechanisms linking microsociological contexts such as interactions, conversations, and relationships to empirically observable outcomes in patterns of state power and to the hermeneutic engagements of situated individuals. In doing so, it aims to more explicitly account for the causal significance of cultural forms like semiotic structures, social performances, and interpretive infrastructures as well as of mechanisms like coordination and the propagation of meanings. Bourdieu's approach to microsociology, on the other hand, typically focuses on socialization and individual-level cognition (Lizardo 2004) as the foundations of institutionalized social structure. Bourdieu speaks of the "mysterious" character of the exercise of state power (1994, 10–12). That mystery can only ever be partially adduced unless we turn to a more robust and heterogeneous account of the microsociological foundations of state power that includes an account of how semiotic mechanisms fill in the mystery of power's situated production and operation. As Bourdieu puts it, the question of classification has been raised in the context of several theoretical traditions (13), and the different angles of each provide a valuable widening of the view on this complex and involved question of classification and state power.

PIRATES!

The case of early modern English piracy institutions is also a good one in other ways for thinking about the issues of culture and institutional theory that this chapter has described. For one thing, it is a case that does not fit with the assumption that cultural theories of institutions will emphasize the irrational and value driven. Indeed, in many respects it was driven by the rational pursuit of enrichment by merchants and of political power by state officials throughout the English (then British) Empire. Elites pursued these goals through the deployment of massive violence in support of imperial maritime institutional order, a highly material form of incentive mongering. Institutional order in this case depended on coercive threats and reduced the uncertainty posed by piracy to the public goods of trade and empire. This is a case that is about power, control, distribution, materiality, and the creation of incentives: the heart of distributional, incentive-driven variants of institutional analysis. It turns on not irrational idealism or persistent inefficiencies of organizational form attributable to culture, but the incentives created by guns and blood deployed in a manner that made piracy a more dangerous choice than it had been before.

But the creation of coercive institutional power over pirates was nonetheless a demonstrably interpretive cultural achievement. It took decades to assemble the interpretive infrastructure that allowed English state agents to bring piracy into being as a bounded category of social meaning that could be predictably and remorselessly targeted for punishment. The following pages tell the story of the bringing into being of piracy as a social category through the creation of an interpretive infrastructure that could define it through public, symbolic, interpretive acts spread across space, time, and social circumstances. The infrastructure that made this possible had multiple parts and was assembled over decades, eventually becoming a central tool in the imposition of state-centric institutional order on the empire's anarchic, violent maritime reaches.

The story of the pacification of piracy in the early modern British Empire thus needs to account for the struggles over meaning that went into the creation of piracy institutions and the way the resulting institutional order handled the problem of classifying piracy. It shows that even brute, material incentives rooted in state violence—guns and gallows—could only be effective when they were linked to interpretive infrastructures that made it possible for a far-flung network of people to coordinate their answers to an apparently simple question: What is a pirate? Changing the collective answer to this question, and changing how it could be legibly answered, was not just an abbreviated technical exercise but an ongoing, active process of dividing the social world anew and redefining the boundaries of the objects that inhabited it. Participants in this process, including merchants, lawyers, investors, audiences to executions, members of the Board of Trade (a body charged with coordinating matters relating to trade and the colonies), kings, queens, and pirates, all reflected different interests, perspectives, and social positions. And they also reflected the ways that their desires, strategies, and experiences were embedded in the cultural systems defining early modern state power: law and politics, written codes and practical powers, justice and commerce, the use of violence and the management of risk, and the relationship between the empire's center and its periphery. The content of these cultural systems powerfully influenced the interpretive systems of the changing piracy institutions. So, too, did the actors who breathed life into the emerging institutional order, making it manifest through their words and actions in the concrete situations and settings where the new social meanings of piracy were made.

The case that I describe in the following chapters is a specific one, and my account will sometimes travel through arcane details of long-gone institutions. It is specificity in support of a general point, though: that the cultural sources of institutional order are there whether or not we look. By examining the role of interpretation in this institutional system, I hope to help bring these sources out of the theoretical shadows and into clearer analytical view. We need the details to find the devil.

CHAPTER TWO
The Transformations of Empire

English overseas activity during the early seventeenth century was both tentative and violent. Its social and economic foundations were of such a fragile character that, to an observer during this period, it would likely have been a shock to know that within a century, England would be the dominant European commercial and colonial power (Andrews 1984, 1–2; Israel 1998). Much of this overseas activity took the plunder of Spanish shipping as its principal objective. The emergence of the English Empire during the seventeenth century, first as a going concern and then as a crucial aspect of English economic and political power, depended on a series of transformations. In aggregate, these transformations made the empire's colonies more self-sustaining, reduced the importance of violent plunder as an economic activity, and greatly increased the direct involvement of the metropolitan government in the management of its seaborne empire. One of the particularly important developments for the study of piracy was the transition in some especially unsettled and unruly pockets of the overseas English Empire from what Weber calls "adventure capitalism"—characterized by opportunistic plunder—to "merchant capitalism," profiting from long-distance trade and the exploitation of economic opportunities created by the political structure of empire (Adams 2007, 22–28; Gerth and Mills 1958, 66–67). This transition, along with others, contributed to the rise of the colonial, maritime English Empire in the later seventeenth and eighteenth centuries. As Pincus writes, "The key factor in accounting for English and Dutch prosperity in the face of crisis elsewhere in Europe, is the growth of long-distance trade and the development of overseas colonies" (2009, 82).

This consolidation of trade and colonies pursued by English state agents and merchant capitalists is the crucial context for understanding the transformation of English piracy institutions. During England's war with Spain at the end of the sixteenth century, private maritime plunder of various degrees of legality became entrenched as a valuable technique of English overseas expansion and a central economic activity for many of its fragile overseas settlements. The rise of merchant capital and the consolidation of a maritime empire, however, created a new economic and political environment within which private maritime plunder posed increasingly large risks and costs and decreasingly obvious benefits. The patterns of social action that comprised the English Empire were changing in fundamental ways that made the private, violent pursuit of maritime plunder and the ambiguous legal space it occupied targets for the regulatory gaze of state agents.

Piracy has existed for as long as people have gone out sea in ships. The analytical question about the production of coercive power against piracy by English state agents during the seventeenth and eighteenth centuries, however, can only be answered in the context of empire. The legal reforms of 1536 created a regime for fighting piracy around the British Isles that proved durable, because it was effective. Pirates were routinely tried and hanged, and the specially commissioned piracy court remained busy and active. Piracy became an acute problem again during the late seventeenth century, because the new geography of the empire and the scale of piracy posed fundamental challenges to the existing regime of legal classification. The logistics of shipping an accused pirate from Cornwall to London were straightforward compared with sending the accused from the Bahamas. The opportunities for piracy in an increasingly rich but still inconsistently governed empire were also great, and so the scale of the piracy problem required not just a different geography of interpretive power but an overall greater capacity for making authoritative legal classifications. Both geography and case volume rendered the 1536 legal infrastructure ineffective in the context of the later seventeenth century.

Multiple transformations in the seventeenth-century English Empire created the conditions for the collision between pirates and empire, and they are the focus of this chapter. I will first describe several important aspects of the English Empire's maritime character during the early seventeenth century for understanding the context of early modern piracy. I will then describe the transformations that occurred in trade, colonial society, governance, and international relations, and finally in how contemporaries regarded trade and empire. It is through the conjuncture of these transformations that we can understand the rapid increases in the scale, complexity, and vulnerabilities of English trade and the increasing desire of metropolitan state agents to strengthen their control over violence at sea.

THE EARLY SEVENTEENTH CENTURY

From the late sixteenth through the early seventeenth century, English merchants and colonists designed multiple schemes for exploiting the New World. Their failures were many, their successes mostly marginal. It was no accident that the colonial exploit of the period viewed as the greatest success in England was Francis Drake's spectacular pillage of the Spanish Empire and circumnavigation of the globe from 1577 to 1580—essentially a piratical assault on the Spanish Empire that Queen Elizabeth retroactively authorized (Kelsey 2000). When we examine the beginnings of the English Empire during this period, we are liable to smuggle in an anachronistic sense of inevitability about the eventual maritime, commercial, free, and dominant English Empire of the eighteenth century. As Andrews argues, however, "Looking back with knowledge of the success which ensued, one can see that between 1550 and 1630 the path of English history did turn in the direction of seaborne empire, but to contemporaries this was by no means an obvious fact even at the close of the period. The nascent empire was struggling for survival in the 1620s" (1984, 2).

The establishment of colonies with permanent populations capable of participating in commerce is a long-term, capital-intensive, and always uncertain process. Colonization of this sort was part of how the English imagined their empire from the beginning. This is reflected in the work of propagandists for empire such as Richard Hakluyt[1] as well as in early English efforts at colonization, including failed attempts to settle such as those that occurred in Guyana and Newfoundland, and eventual successes such as those in Virginia and Massachusetts. But during the late sixteenth and early seventeenth centuries, opportunities for immediately profitable violent plunder often took precedence over requirements for the establishment of stable colonies. Parts of the empire during this period well exemplify Weberian adventure capitalism, organized around the efforts of private English ships and crews to intercept and violently expropriate as much as possible from the Spanish colonial trade. Plunder of this sort thrived in an environment of legal ambiguity that made the lawfulness of any given act of plunder a question both uncertain and unlikely to ever be answered by a court.

This "new social pattern of maritime force" (Andrews 1984, 235) involving private ships took shape during England's war with Spain during the late sixteenth century, and it flourished during the early seventeenth as agents of the two states ground against one another in the West Indies. In the late sixteenth century, for example, hundreds of ships set out as privateers from English ports to raid Spanish shipping.[2] Merchants as well as nobles invested in these voyages as profit-making activities. The social boundaries around this sort of private maritime plunder were so loosely drawn that even lord admirals of the navy were known to invest in privateering voyages. The life of Henry Mainwaring demonstrates the flexible acceptance that English state agents in practice showed toward piracy (Harris 2008). Mainwaring was assigned to suppress piracy in 1612 but shortly thereafter himself turned to piracy against the Spanish in the Mediterranean, using one of the principalities of the Barbary Coast as his base of operations. He enjoyed spectacular success and was a source of complaints from the Spanish to James I of England. Finally in 1616 James forced Mainwaring to accept a pardon. He then served in various official naval capacities, most notably as a vice admiral in 1639. Mainwaring's case is particularly striking because it was clear to contemporaries that his attacks against Spanish ships in the Mediterranean were indeed piracy, and he nonetheless was readily able to return to the English navy.

Many acts of plunder during this time, however, were more ambiguous. The concept of privateering was central to this ambiguity. Privateers engaged in personal plunder, but first they obtained a commission or some other form of authorization from a legitimate sovereign power. The three main forms that this took during the seventeenth century were general commissions allowing all subjects to raid against an enemy power during wartime; letters of marque licensing a particular ship and crew to raid enemy shipping, again during wartime; and letters of reprisal, issued when a merchant or shipowner could demonstrate economic loss suffered at the hands of a subject of a foreign sovereign, allowing the aggrieved party to seek reprisals from any ships sailing under the offending nation's flag.[3]

Privateers were principally motivated by the opportunity for rich profits, but for their part, sovereigns also found the system to have benefits. Given the ruinous expenses involved in building, maintaining, and staffing a regular navy relative to the fiscal resources that state agents could mobilize, privateering allowed cash-strapped sovereigns to meet the challenge of projecting naval power on the cheap. No less importantly, the encouragement of privateers allowed for the development of English human resources concerning shipping, navigation, and maritime warfare. Privateering provided a way for Englishmen to become mariners, developing skills critical for the defense of an island nation, the prosecution of its maritime wars, and the servicing of its expanding network of trade (Appleby 1998, 68).

The weakness of state support for colonial economic development also made plunder an important economic model for some colonies (Appleby 1998, 68; Zahedieh 2010, 177), with privateering filling a critical gap in the availability of capital for colonial settlements. For example, Zahedieh clearly demonstrates the central role in colonial economic life played by privateers and their profits in mid-seventeenth-century Jamaica. She argues that "the role of plunder in financing colonization has been underplayed" (1990, 145) and that privateering was the dominant economic activity for the island through the 1670s, yielding much of the capital that island elites used to establish plantations and eventually the Jamaican sugar economy. The capital requirements for outfitting a privateering vessel were low, joint ownership was common, and the potential for profits was high,[4] making privateering an ideal activity for English West Indian colonies with good access to Spanish trade routes.

The price of this capacity to greatly expand naval power, maritime human resources, and colonial capital with no direct outlay of royal or state funds was the loss of control over the royal prerogatives of war and international relations. In the English maritime system, privateering became particularly chaotic in practice, because letters could be issued by English colonial governors of charter and proprietary colonies as well as by agents of trading companies, in addition to any foreign sources of letters. This made commissions easy to come by. Due to the easy availability of privateering commissions, trade and warfare were closely intertwined at this time. Merchant ships, especially English merchant ships, were often heavily armed. While prepared to engage in trade, they were also often legally authorized and prepared to turn violent if an appropriate opportunity presented itself. The allure of plunder and adventure capitalism as ways to reap the benefits of empire was partly due to this permissive system of sovereign delegation that made it easy to have the right to steal.

In order to understand the importance of privateering in the formation of the English Empire, however, its niche in the political economy of the New World needs to be developed further. Most important in this regard was the relative position of Spain and England as imperial powers and the religious character of their competition. Spain's empire grew during the early sixteenth century, flourished through the end of the century, and then began a slow decline that left it eclipsed in the mid-seventeenth century by the Dutch, French, and English (Elliott 2007). During the period when privateering began to crystallize as a "new social pattern of maritime force" (Andrews 1966, 235) in the late sixteenth century, Spain remained the dominant world colonial power, giving it the strength and confidence to assert, and attempt to defend, a monopoly on all trade and navigation in the West Indies. Spanish sovereigns and diplomats promoted this claim in various ways over time. It had two basic elements. The strongest was a claim based on discovery and possession, a rationale for colonization generally shared by the English (Elliott 2007, 11). The problem with this argument was that the Spanish had only ever succeeded in occupying part of the territories that they claimed. The other basis for Spanish claims, which even the Spaniards knew would carry little weight with the Post-Reformation English, was a series of papal bulls, issued between 1493 and 1494, through which Alexander VI purported to grant the Spanish Crown dominion over all lands discovered in the West. While the English indignantly rejected the authority of the "Bishop of Rome" to grant what he did not own (Mattingly 1963, 153–54), the Spanish nonetheless took the view that any English ships in the West Indies were interloping on the Spanish Empire and could be treated as pirates (Andrews 1984, 9; Zahedieh 1990, 148).

This dispute over papal authority and colonial dominion highlights the importance of religion as an aspect of Anglo-Spanish rivalry. The early English propagandists for empire explicitly make the case that it was England's duty to provide a vigorous response to the spread of religion disparaged as papist by engaging in a Protestant civilizing mission among the Native peoples of America (Canny 1998a, 4; Mancall 1998, 335). This religious framework for understanding what was at stake in the Anglo-Spanish War and subsequent struggles influenced how contemporaries viewed the privateering war against Spain. Henry Morgan, whose career is discussed in later chapters, invaded Spanish colonial possessions on a number of occasions with significant private military forces and little or no legal authority, but many contemporaries saw him as a heroic figure in the struggle with Spain.[5] This view of privateering as a patriotic, Protestant activity continued in some form or other through most of the seventeenth century.

In this context of political-economic and religious competition, privateering and other forms of private plunder became entrenched in parts of the developing English Empire. English shipbuilding reflected this entrenchment (Rodger 1998, 2005). English ships by the early seventeenth century were hybrid craft. They sacrificed much in terms of tonnage and carrying capacity—in which areas, for comparison, the Dutch merchant fleet excelled—for the sake of lots of cheap but effective iron cannons and excellent seaworthiness that gave them great advantages of speed and maneuverability in battle. The English preference for privateering, that is to say, was encoded in the material stock of their fleet, and this further entrenched privateering as a key competence of English colonial enterprise while giving privateering a relative advantage over other approaches to empire, such as trade-based colonization. As Rodger writes, the English fleet was "excellently adapted for defensive and piratical war at sea. It was not, in this period, at all suitable for founding or sustaining a colonial empire overseas. It was not fit for peaceful trade on competitive terms. It was a predatory fleet developed to profit from other people's colonies" (1998, 96–97).

It is a common refrain in the historiography of the English Empire during the early seventeenth century that state support for colonial endeavors was erratic and weak. This increased the salience of private military and commercial enterprises. The role of the state, however, should not be underestimated. Throughout this period, metropolitan state actors successfully claimed certain forms of sovereign authority over the activities of English subjects in the New World. English state agents met the challenge of enforcing sovereign claims during a period of fiscal strain and with an extremely limited capacity to act directly by developing a system of "government by license" (Braddick 1998, 305) where sovereign authority was "parcellized" (Adams 2007, 17) in various ways among colonial state agents. The great English trading monopolies of this period, such as the East India Company, the Royal Africa Company, or the Levant Company, all enjoyed an exclusive trading concession that allowed them to exploit certain elements of the king's prerogatives and powers. Similarly, proprietary and charter colonies such as Pennsylvania and Massachusetts were given charters that licensed them to establish a civil government and exercise a wide range of state powers, including the power to issue commissions and, under certain circumstances, make war. Privateers similarly enjoyed their own form of state license that granted them the authority to plunder the shipping of other states, especially Spain; on this basis they could create a profitable business model that gave early English colonization in the New World a highly aggressive dimension that was beneficial in many ways.

The idea of government by license is easy to misread through modern eyes as a sort of diminishment of state power in favor of private entities. But in many respects, it was a way to maintain some degree of state control in places and circumstances where state agents had no capacity to govern directly. It was a way of expanding the scope of government by harnessing the capacity and capital of private actors (Erikson 2014; Norton 2015). Certainly in the case of privateers it reflected a certain weakness on the part of the English state with respect to direct control over violence at sea. But the fragility of the English Empire of the early seventeenth century should not be misunderstood. What was fragile was its future trajectory. English overseas presence was so strongly influenced by an aggressive posture of armed competition with Spain, pursued largely by private actors bent on plunder and quick profits, that in some colonies the long-term foundations of colonization were often only haphazardly laid. It was, in other words, a fragility characterized by a ferocious armed presence and an entrepreneurial willingness to engage in plunder of dubious legality. As Rodger notes, however, at this time "the English advantage lay largely in the disordered and dangerous condition of the seas (disorder which they and their countrymen had done a great deal to generate)" (1998, 90). In these conditions, armed English merchants could do very well through both trade and plunder.

This conjunction of a violent and chaotic maritime order with an English fleet and colonial presence well suited to benefit from this sort of disorder began to unravel as the seventeenth century progressed, however. Transformations in trade, international relations, the colonies, governance, and the meanings of empire fundamentally changed these dynamics. Increasingly, the disorder of the seas and the actors who profited from it were eclipsed by those promoting a more lawful and orderly empire organized around the merchants' regular trade rather than the privateers' sporadic bloodshed and profits.

THE TRANSFORMATION IN TRADE

From the beginning, commerce comprised one of the main motives for English imperial expansion. Even during the early seventeenth century, when plunder played such a prominent role in English overseas endeavors, Sir Walter Raleigh saw trade (albeit trade often intertwined with violence) as the real prize. He famously wrote, "Whosoever commands the sea commands the trade; whosoever commands the trade of the world commands the riches of the world, and consequently the world itself"[6] Over the course of the seventeenth century, however, the character and importance of trade to England and the English Empire changed so drastically that it can be usefully characterized, following Davis, as a revolution in trade or, as others have it, a commercial revolution (Braddick 1998, 292; Clay 1984, 177–78; Davis 1954, 162–63; Pincus 2009, 83; Zahedieh 1998, 399; 2010, 31). As far as its impacts on piracy go, this revolution can be described as having three main parts: an increase in the scale of trade, an increase in its economic significance, and an increase in its complexity. All these factors helped put commercial interests on a collision course with the chaos of plunder and adventure capitalism.

From a modest start, English overseas trade grew rapidly during the seventeenth century. Andrews estimates that the tonnage of English shipping doubled between 1570 and 1630 (1984, 8), and Pincus estimates that it doubled again between 1640 and 1686 (2009, 83). Long-distance trade on the transatlantic and East Indies routes comprised 20 percent of English imports by the 1660s and around 30 percent by 1700 (Clay 1984, 163–64; Zahedieh 1998, 399). This great increase in the scale of imports from the plantations and the East Indies had a further impact in that it created the potential for the emergence of the previously nonexistent re-export trade: colonial and East Indian commodities were shipped from England to the rest of Europe, especially sugar, tobacco, and Indian calicoes (a kind of cotton textile). Over the course of the second half of the seventeenth century, these re-exports came to comprise around a third of total English exports (Davis 1954, 162). The increasing scale of English long-distance maritime trade translated directly into an increase in its significance. While still only part of the bigger picture of English trade in the later seventeenth century, Pincus argues that colonization and long-distance trade account for English and Dutch economic success in this period, compared with economic turmoil in the rest of Europe (2009, 82). The colonies furthermore represented a new and captive market for English manufactures, and in conjunction with the raw materials that they provided for the re-export trade, the internal economy of England began to develop in ways shaped by aspects of the maritime trading system, as did colonial economies and societies. Another aspect of the significance of these trades was the increasing influence of merchants, especially the East India Company, on politics—a key vector of pressure in the political transformations that ultimately brought about the end of piracy.

As the scale and significance of England's overseas trade increased, so did its complexity. The main pieces in this aspect of the trade story are the development of significant import trades in tobacco from North America (valued at £141,606 by 1686), sugar from the West Indies (£586,528), and textiles from the East Indies, especially cotton calicoes (£259,498) (Zahedieh 1998, 410, 413). But these trades cannot be properly understood in isolation. They were, as were the colonies and commercial enterprises which made them possible, embedded in an increasingly complex network of ancillary trades and maritime transport (Canny 1998a, 28–29). Indeed, the English Empire was progressively becoming an interdependent system of specialized regions.[7] For example, the West Indian sugar trade depended on coerced enslaved labor and the transportation of captives from West and Central Africa to the New World by the Royal African Company, the bearer of the English monopoly on slave trading through the later seventeenth century (Norton 2015). England's West Indian colonies were likewise dependent on a wide range of manufactured goods exported from London and on produce, foodstuffs, and shipping from New England. The trades of the East India Company were similarly embedded in a network of mutual dependencies spanning the imperial system. While low

The Transformations of Empire | 45

production costs made Indian textiles extremely competitive in England, its colonies, and Europe, the company never succeeded in creating an Indian market for English goods. The trade, therefore, involved textiles moving from east to west, and bullion moving from west to east. The bullion for this trade mostly came from the Americas through either plunder or trade with the Spanish (Clay 1984, 179; Zahedieh 1998, 401). An excerpt of the exports Zahedieh finds moving from London to the West Indies helps give a sense of the diversity of the sorts of items circulating in the imperial commercial system in the later seventeenth century. In 1686 silks, woolens, hats, shoes, iron, nails, barrel hoops, books, candles, glasses, gunpowder, saddles, beer, biscuits, and flour were all loaded on ships in London for the transatlantic trip to the West Indies (Zahedieh 2010, 263). London played a central role in this network as the preeminent English, and later European, entrepôt. This resulted in rapid developments of trading culture in the capital, as merchants increasingly sought one another to work out deals in coffeehouses (Pincus 2009, 77–78), and the available shipping infrastructure rapidly developed.

The growing complexity of trade also drove financial innovation. Among the most important innovations of the early modern empire, driven by the risks and capital requirements of long-distance trade, were the joint stock companies. These entities, such as the East India Company, the Levant Company, and the Royal African Company, were often given trading monopolies, purportedly as an inducement to take on the risks of uncertain commerce. As the seventeenth century wore on, however, the rationale for monopolies of this sort increasingly came under attack; and while the Royal African Company and East India Company maintained their monopolies through the century, the new Atlantic trades were "open to all . . . and large numbers participated, including manufacturers, retailers, gentlemen, and widows" (Zahedieh 1998, 403). There were also important developments in systems of payment and credit. Bills of exchange had long been the main way of making payments without shipping specie, but in sparse trade networks they were often unwieldy or simply unavailable. This was no longer the case by 1700, when, as Clay writes, "merchants of virtually every trading city, not only in western and southern Europe, but also in the North, the Levant, the Americas and even the Far East, were able to transmit funds to those of any other without the need to ship specie" (1984, 179). At the same time that systems for making payments were becoming more flexible and readily available, in London maritime insurance was becoming a standard and increasingly trustworthy part of the maritime shipping business (Steele 1986, 227). Then, in 1694, the Whigs successfully passed legislation creating the Bank of England. To its proponents, the bank represented a major advance in the management of state debt as well as in the creation of credit for the most productive sectors of the economy, such as manufactures (Pincus 2009, 390–92).

The increasing scale and significance of English long-distance trades on the one hand and the growing complexity of these trade networks on the other posed significant problems for the chaotic plunder that was the specialty of pirates, privateers, and adventure capitalists. The increasing scale and complexity of English trade networks made them more vulnerable to counterattack and reprisal. Of perhaps greater importance, however, was the increase in the wealth created by trade. While the English looked to Spain and its bullion-based empire as their models in the earlier seventeenth century, by the middle and later part of the century the benefits of routinized, regular, and predictable trade supported by sophisticated financial and legal technologies and defined markets became increasingly clear to a widening circle of metropolitan and colonial imperial elites. Plunder, however, had little to contribute to such a system. Despite its early importance as a source of capital, military capacity, and human resources, the bet it placed was on extracting profit from a perpetual cycle of reciprocal violence by being better at navigating chaos than those it would prey on. Adventure capitalism, even if pursued by only a fraction of mariners and supported by a fraction of colonial officials, by its nature created serious systemic risks that were costly and destabilizing for the emerging merchant capitalist trade regime.

THE TRANSFORMATION IN COLONIAL SOCIETY

Meanwhile, other transformations of empire were helping shape these developments in trade, even as they were being shaped by them. It is easy but wrong to see colonial developments as responses to the real action of empire formation emanating from London. But this metropole-centric vision achieves its tidiness by ignoring the real character of imperial governance and formation as multidirectional patterns of circulation (Norton 2017). During the seventeenth century, colonial societies were also undergoing rapid and fundamental changes, and they were remaking the empire as they did.

In a sense, though, the issue here is less the transformation of colonial society than its invention. In the 1620s the population of all England's American colonies numbered in the low thousands. By 1700, the number was some four hundred thousand (McCusker and Menard 1985, 218; Zahedieh 2010, 281). Colonial societies developed in very different ways, partly in response to very different demographic and environmental conditions, but it is still helpful to identify some general trends that help specify the changing colonial context of piracy (Greene 1988).

By the later seventeenth century in the West Indies, the Chesapeake and New England affluent planter and merchant society had emerged. The freedom of colonists to engage in trade with other colonies and the metropole, combined with the rapid development of tobacco and sugar plantations and the continued influx of enslaved African and indentured European labor, laid the foundation for the accumulation of wealth. Canny, for example, characterizes the West Indies at the close of the seventeenth century as supporting "a wealthy planter plutocracy and an affluent commercial community that was the essence of Britishness in its composition and outlook" (1998a, 30). This issue of outlook was critical, for the ultimate demise of English piracy was partly dependent on the attitudes of colonial elites to relations of authority within the empire, and in this regard they were clearly of the view that they were Englishmen (Bilder 2008). Already by the late seventeenth century, the convergence of diverse colonial societies and cultures into a hybrid British Atlantic culture was well under way (Greene 1988).

This consolidation and convergence of Atlantic culture depended on the movement of goods through the trade networks described above but also of people and ideas. Key to these movements were the sea and the ships as well as the mariners who acted as the great connective tissue of a global empire in the age of sail. Canny notes that it was a "remarkable passage of boats" that made the sense of a single British Atlantic community possible. Ships traveled along various routes and engaged in trade patterns made propitious by seasonal changes in the winds and tides, but these seasons were just periods of greater average travel. In fact, throughout the year a constant passage of ships sailed back and forth from England to its colonies in the west and to its factories in the east (Canny 1998a, 28). Steele provides a rough estimate of 500 departures from England for America per year in the 1680s, rising to more than 1,000 by 1730, and estimates another 500 voyages a year in the intercolonial trades of the 1680s, rising to 1,500 voyages annually by 1730 (1986, 92).

Mariners themselves played an important role in drawing the geographically disparate colonies together by disseminating information and representations of the empire as a meaningful frame of reference and by providing regular reminders of the immediacy of the connections between its constituent parts (Hatfield 2005, 140–41). The exchange of information throughout the Atlantic World also increased rapidly during the seventeenth century as newspapers and packet ships carrying mail became routine (Steele 1986). Bilder's (2008) account of the role of Atlantic legal culture in seventeenth-century Rhode Island gives a good sense of how strongly colonial societies were oriented toward one another and to the metropole, with migrants bringing legal culture to the New World through their experience and knowledge, through their libraries, and importantly through continued movement back and forth. The movement of colonists from metropole to colony was often not a single voyage, especially not for wealthy elites, but instead involved multiple passages back and forth. This consolidation of colonial society would prove essential in the eventual emergence of new imperial piracy institutions.

THE TRANSFORMATION OF IMPERIAL GOVERNANCE

As Braddick writes, while it is a "commonplace of the historiography of early modern England that the national government was weak," its trajectory was toward "increasingly direct responsibility for war, trade, and colonization" (1998, 286). By the mid-seventeenth century, government by license was in retreat, at least when it came to what contemporaries saw as the core functions of the imperial state. This transformation in the governance of the empire depended on the increasing capacity of the English state to directly pursue its objectives both at home and in the colonies. Charles II, for example, upon his restoration to the throne in 1660, sold the right to collect customs revenues to a group of tax farmers but in 1671 reassumed direct control, sending the first customs agents to America (Barrow 1967, 10–11). Indeed, the Restoration marked an important point of transition in the governance of the empire. While the protectorate had largely left the colonies to govern themselves, Charles II was interested in colonial trade as a source of revenue, and he and other actors at the center of English state power saw the governance of trade and of the colonies as linked objectives (20). One striking manifestation of this renewed effort to administer the colonies directly was the Restoration Privy Council's plan to revoke the charters of proprietary and company colonies and to place them instead under direct royal rule, though this did not come to pass (Mancke 2005, 250).

The most visible and ambitious manifestation of this centralizing ambition of English state agents in the latter half of the seventeenth century was the Navigation Acts. These were a series of laws enacted in 1651, 1660, 1673, and 1696[8] that represented a major state intervention in the system of overseas commerce. It is important to note that while these laws did have direct consequences for revenue, they were not designed primarily with revenue gain in mind. Instead, they were designed to reshape the structure of the commercial system (Barrow 1967, 7).[9] The Navigation Acts were a response to the perceived threats to English trade posed by foreign shipping and by foreign markets for colonial goods. They required that colonial goods be exported in English (including colonial) ships, restricted the export of certain colonial goods—the so-called enumerated commodities, a list that was occasionally updated and included items such as tobacco and sugar—and created new regimes of enforcement that extended the reach of state classifications deeper into the fabric of commercial life.

The customs service epitomized this insinuation of the state into colonial commerce. Agents of the Crown began collecting customs in the colonies in 1671, when Dudley Digges was appointed royal customs officer in Virginia (Barrow 1967, 12). Parliament lent its authority to this development in the Navigation Act of 1673, laying the foundations for a permanent new administrative agency. Customs officers were quickly appointed, particularly in the colonies with the most lucrative trades (14). It was under the auspices of the 1696 Navigation Act that an inspector general of customs was appointed, a historiographically as well as governmentally important moment, because it is from that appointment that a regular series of English trade statistics becomes available (McCusker and Menard 1985, 73; Zahedieh 1998, 398). The same act created a licensing system requiring that ships register to ensure that only English ships were used for English cargo.

This same will to govern was also visible in other areas, such as the governance of colonies and the recurring pressure to revoke the charters and assume direct control of places like Massachusetts (Mancke 2005, 248–54). The Royal Navy likewise increasingly came to reflect the contraction of government by license and the expansion of direct control. While, as Rodger writes, in the early seventeenth century the "Navy Royal was so much under the control of private merchants and shipowners that it was in great measure absorbed into their private naval warfare" (1998, 96), at the time of the Restoration the division between merchants, the national navy, and privateers was clear (Davies 1991). The state of the navy in the early 1680s, however, was bad. A series of reforms emerging from James II's conviction that the navy was central to his ambitions for establishing a modern state, funded by revenues from vigorous, long-distance commerce with colonies, improved matters beginning in 1686. The navy overhauled its dockyards, refitted its ships, and reorganized its administration, making it a more formidable force by the late 1680s (Pincus 2009, 149; Rodger 2005, 110–11). In a good example of the feedback loops involved in the increasing capacity for direct action by agents of the central state, the enhancement of the navy contributed to revenues as well through its involvement in customs enforcement (Barrow 1967, 17).

THE TRANSFORMATION OF INTERNATIONAL RELATIONS

From the late sixteenth through the seventeenth century, the slow collapse of the Spanish Empire and the rise of the Dutch, French, and English Empires were the background reality for political, social, and commercial developments throughout the colonial world. As the seventeenth century progressed, Spain's vast claims of territorial dominion extending far beyond its capacity to settle or police faltered. Under continual assault from privateers targeting its trade and settlers from competitor nations carving out footholds on the coast of North America and in the West Indies, the Spanish determined that they needed to begin negotiating international agreements that would be binding across the Atlantic. Before the mid-seventeenth century, European powers—in part influenced by the Spanish assertion of a right to punish as pirates and interlopers those it seized in waters it claimed—adopted a dual approach to international relations, captured in a phrase invented much later: "no peace beyond the line" (Mattingly 1963). The line in question seems to have been the Tropic of Cancer, and what the famous later phrase captures is that European treaty agreements were not generally understood to pertain to relations in the New World unless this was specified.[10]

This exclusion of the New World from the states of war and peace in Europe created a situation where war, peace, and neutrality had no clear legal or political definition there (Andrews 1984, 27). Privateering thrived in this environment, because it made Spanish colonies and Spanish shipping a perennially legitimate target for plunder. But as Spain's claims to exclusive rights to shipping and colonization beyond the line became obviously untenable, its stance against negotiating peace treaties applicable in the New World withered. The Treaty of Münster in 1648 concluding the Eighty Years' War and securing Dutch independence from Spain was the first crack in the absolute claims made by the Spanish to all the New World territories south of the Tropic of Cancer. The treaty acknowledged the right of the Dutch, including Dutch trading companies, to retain possession of their New World landholdings. In 1667 and 1670 the crack in Spanish claims to dominion over much of the New World split wide with the Treaties of Madrid, acknowledging the sovereignty of England over the islands it had seized in the Caribbean and the right of English ships to navigate those waters.

With these developments, the European social categories of war and peace were extended to the New World. As Steele writes, "Peace was an innovation [in] Europe's New World, transforming colonial warfare from an endemic local condition into a transatlantic event to be declared by monarchs on behalf of all their subjects" (1986, 189). This redefinition of colonial politics as a theater of European international relations, rather than as a zone characterized by ambiguity and chaos, shifted the structural conditions that previously favored privateering and piracy. Mancke argues that these Spanish concessions rested partly on "an understanding that England, France, and the Netherlands would start to eliminate the use of privatized force overseas, particularly the licensing of privateers" (2005, 256). Sections 3 and 4 of the 1670 treaty reflect this international ambition to subordinate private maritime violence to state control and to states of war and peace as decided by metropolitan European political elites:

> 3. . . . For the future all enmities, hostilities, and dissensions between the aforesaid lord kings and their subjects and inhabitants shall cease and be abolished; and both parties shall wholly forbear and abstain from all pillage, depredation, hurt, and injury and any sort of molestation, as well by land as by sea or in fresh waters in whatever part of the world. 4. Also that the said Most Serene kings shall take care that their subjects abstain from all violence and injury, and they shall revoke all commissions and letters containing powers either of reprisal or marque, or of making prizes in the West Indies . . . and they shall declare them null, void, and of no effect, as by this treaty of peace they are declared null, void, and of no effect. Whoever shall contravene this shall be punished.[11]

In fact, English concerns over the lack of control over privateers began earlier, but by the 1670s, a desire by metropolitan authorities to rein in the haphazard plunder of the privateers and their colonial backers becomes obvious. Letters of marque become harder to get—in part because they could no longer be justified by a perpetual condition of war with Spain— and governors were increasingly taken to task for issuing them at will. The nearly lawless circumstances that pertained in parts of the overseas English colonial maritime world in the earlier seventeenth century were changing in fundamental ways, but it was still not clear to any involved exactly what those changes would mean in practice.

THE TRANSFORMATION IN THE MEANINGS
OF TRADE AND EMPIRE

As the complex, diversified commercial system described above began to develop on the substrate of English colonies, a transformation in the older view of trade and empire was also under way (Erikson 2021). Where the justification for colonization had originally drawn strength from religious arguments and hopes of discovering gold, commerce itself became the most urgent justification for empire (Canny 1998a, 32). By the end of the seventeenth century, as contemporaries became aware of "the transformative impact of overseas trade on England" (Pincus 2009, 83), this new, commercial vision of the sources of wealth had solidified and anchored a fundamentally different image of empire from what had prevailed during the earlier part of the century (Pagden 1998).

This transformation in the meanings of trade and empire can be seen most clearly in the evolution of arguments about empire in the metropole. William Blathwayt put this transformation most starkly in 1685, writing that "those plantations which heretofore were looked upon as desperate adventures are now become necessary and important members of the main body" (Pincus 2009, 84). By the 1680s, Pincus shows, debates about trade and empire had become central to English politics (368–69). Perhaps more striking than these debates, however, is the consensus that had emerged that England's was a commercial empire. "Again and again," Pincus writes, "the English described themselves as a trading nation in the later seventeenth century" (90). This understanding of the meaning of empire and the English nation in terms of trade and the idea that trade was essential to economic prosperity and state power (Erikson 2021) were the impetus for England's vigorous attempts to rein in its privateers and to turn on its pirates beginning in the later seventeenth century. Together these developments marked a stark contrast to the vision of empire and overseas activity as a semiprivatized and unpredictably profitable assault on Spanish imperial riches that had previously dominated in the earlier seventeenth century. Not only was there no place for pirates in this new vision of trade and empire, but their presence posed a fundamental challenge to that system and the national, economic, and military ambitions it promised to deliver. In this new vision of empire, private plunder was at the periphery. Where it had once been a purpose of empire, elites now saw it as posing a disruptive threat and moved to confront it.

CHAPTER THREE
Vagueness and Violence on the Maritime Periphery

A streak of audacious lawlessness runs through the maritime history of the western Atlantic during the sixteenth and seventeenth centuries. It persisted through periods when European sovereigns and their agents sought to curtail their violent seagoing subjects and flourished when those claims receded, with pirates, privateers, buccaneers, and other men of violence taking what could be taken and living to tell the tale. Making this lawlessness even more interesting and instructive from a social scientific perspective is the fact that it persisted and even flourished—for a time—in the face of elite-driven efforts to pacify the seas. Though pirate captains and their crews often died while they attacked rich prizes and towns, it was far rarer in the seventeenth-century English maritime world for them to become victims of coordinated powers of state violence.

Throughout this period, piracy was an intransigently ambiguous social practice. English state agents routinely, if unintentionally, displayed their inability to authoritatively classify pirates and thus to interpolate them into their institutionalized powers of violence. Or to put it in the theoretical terms developed in earlier chapters, the interpretive infrastructure available to English state agents in their attempts to direct the imperial state's institutionalized powers of violence against pirates was incapable of achieving what state agents in the later seventeenth century wanted to do with it. Even when pirates were caught, the ambiguity over how to define them and what to do with them persisted, because they could not be easily or efficiently interpreted in an institutionalized, authoritative way. Pirates remained at not just the maritime periphery but also the interpretive periphery of the English state, and it was in the shadow of the sheltering social ambiguity they found there that they thrived, even as the agents of state power railed impotently against them.

CATHOLIC POWER, PROTESTANT
PLUNDER: AMBIGUITY FOSTERED

In the late sixteenth century, plunder, patriotism, and Protestantism were fused in England's long struggle with Spain (Andrews 1966; Appleby 2009; Elliott 2007). These motives undergirded the ambiguous mix of violence and commerce that English mariners used to break into the eastward flow of wealth from Spain's New World colonies, laying the foundations of sustained neglect and avariciousness that, with some exceptions, defined the attitude of English state agents to private maritime violence through the mid- to later seventeenth century. The careers of a few of these famous sea dogs exemplify this pattern as well as its limits.

John Hawkins's efforts to enter the slave trade in Spain's West Indian colonies provides an apt example of this fusion of commercial and coercive methods and motives. Particularly along the outer rim of Spanish colonies far removed from the centers of Spanish imperial authority and action in Lima and Mexico City, there was constant, sometimes desperate demand for enslaved people and trade goods. Hawkins and others saw this as a valuable crack in their exclusion from trading with Spanish colonial possessions. In three boldly loathsome voyages, Hawkins sailed from England to the Canary Islands and then to the west coast of Africa, where he kidnapped and purchased as many captives as his ships would bear. In each voyage he then sailed west to sell his prisoners as slaves to Spain's New World settlements. Spain, however, forcefully prohibited such transactions, insisting that it alone could license trade to its empire and routinely claiming that all interlopers were pirates. As Andrews describes the significance of Hawkins's voyage, "[In the 1560s] it remained to be seen whether an Englishman could in fact conduct trade in the West Indies and whether the king of Spain had sufficient real authority in the region to scotch the attempt" (1984, 119–20).

Hawkins, intent on forcing the question, always embarked on his excursions well armed. While his first voyage involved violence only against the three hundred captives he took from the western coast of Africa to sell in Hispaniola, it alarmed Spanish elites and raised real questions about their capacity to control interlopers trading to their empire. On his second and third voyages, this conflict came to a head. These voyages had a higher profile, with significant financial backing from Queen Elizabeth, other prominent members of court, and English merchants. Once in the Caribbean, Hawkins sailed south to the Venezuelan island of La Margarita, but the governor refused to trade. Hawkins then sailed for Borburata, where a protracted dispute ensued over whether the English could receive a license to trade and over the price for their human cargo. Finally, Hawkins, displeased with the terms and delays concerning the question of whether he would be permitted to trade at all, landed a hundred of his men and marched on the Venezuelan town. Under this threat of violence, the governor allowed trade to proceed on terms more favorable to Hawkins. This ambiguous blend of violence and commerce proved to be the key that allowed Hawkins to circumvent Spanish prohibitions on this interloping trade.

His third voyage had an even higher profile. As Andrews writes, "This venture bore more emphatically the aspect of a national undertaking, combining private and public investment by way of a joint-stock. Although no object other than slaving is apparent, it may be that the queen wished to impress the king of Spain by a veiled threat, a demonstration of her own power and his vulnerability" (1984, 125). This voyage was also more violent than the previous ones, during both the acquisition and the sale of enslaved people. Hawkins's fleet seized some of these captives from Portuguese ships that it encountered, and it seized others as it participated in a war between nations on the African coast. To sell the captives into slavery in the West Indies, at one point Hawkins resorted to burning and pillaging part of Rio de la Hacha to persuade the locals to overlook questions of trading licenses. The settlers of Santa Marta seem to have devised a better strategy. They requested that he engage in a kind of pantomimic invasion to give them cover for engaging in illegal trading with interlopers (though Spanish colonial officials were well versed in such tricks and could not be relied on to turn a blind eye). As the fleet began to make its way home, however, it was hit by bad weather and forced onto the Spanish fortress of San Juan de Ulúa guarding the harbor at Veracruz, Mexico. To make matters worse, the next day a Spanish fleet arrived, commanded by the viceroy of New Spain. After a brief standoff, the Spaniards attacked and drove Hawkins and his men off the island. Only two ships survived the attack and made their separate ways back to England.

The commander of the first of those ships to have returned home, Francis Drake, is another of the Elizabethan sea dogs who so iconically captured the ambiguity of the maritime violence defining their times. Hawkins was well known to contemporaries for his demonstration of the vulnerabilities of the Spanish Empire and the possibilities for plunder and trade in the West Indies—and the ways in which the two could be hard to distinguish. Drake, however, would ultimately eclipse his former master in demonstrating the ambiguity of private maritime violence in the New World, at least insofar as it related to English law and policy.

Though his career was varied and long, Drake's notoriety is largely due to one outrageous voyage of plunder that established him as the iconic figure of a generation of swashbuckling, semi-state Elizabethan seamen who sailed from England to punch holes in Spain's imperial carapace and steal what booty they could. After participating in the African leg of Hawkins's first trading voyage, Drake signed on again for the second voyage, this time crossing the Atlantic. As Kelsey puts it, "It was a perfect training voyage for young Drake, with attacks by land and sea, intricate navigational problems, and diplomatic and business negotiations of every kind" (2000, 19). After the successful and profitable completion of the voyage, Drake sailed again with Hawkins on his disastrous third voyage, eventually limping home after the Veracruz debacle. There followed a series of voyages he undertook with Hawkins's backing that in their purposes fell somewhere between reprisals and outright piracy. On those voyages, Drake probed and prodded the Isthmus of Panama to great Spanish trepidation, and he pioneered one of his characteristic strategies by striking up an alliance with the Cimarrones, escapees from slavery who combined intense antipathy to the Spanish with deep local knowledge, making for a formidably threatening collaboration.

Drake's circumnavigation of the world began in 1577 in this spirit of freebooting violence at the margins of the law. After piratically seizing a number of Spanish and Portuguese ships—including that of Nuno da Silva, a Portuguese navigator with extensive knowledge of the southern coastline of South America and unlawfully executing one of his co-commanders, Drake's fleet headed west. Over the course of the next three years, the fleet pillaged many towns and Spanish ships, threatening the entire Pacific coast of Spain's empire. In 1579 Drake captured two Spanish treasure ships in rapid succession, a fantastically rich haul that he ultimately returned to England via the second known circumnavigation of the globe. The audacity of his predation and seamanship generated tremendous fame. But Drake's voyage is noteworthy also because he had no authorization to wage what was essentially a single-handed private war against the Spanish Empire. Yet upon his return, Queen Elizabeth knighted him on the deck of his ship the *Golden Hind*, conferring her retroactive authorization on the whole affair. Moreover, the knighthood cemented Drake's position as one of the most prominent and influential of his generation of explorers, mariners, and privateers who turned their attention and ambitions westward to the Spanish Empire and all it offered in trade, plunder, and the ambiguous space between.

It is important to note, though, that what voyages like those of Hawkins and Drake demonstrated was not that plunder was legal and acceptable. Rather, they expressed its essential ambiguity. The life, and especially the death, of Walter Raleigh punctuates this point. Raleigh was a favorite of Queen Elizabeth's and a veteran of multiple maritime adventures and efforts to plant English colonies in the West Indies and North America, including the Roanoke expedition. Upon Elizabeth's death in 1603 and the ascension of James I, Raleigh found himself on the wrong side of the new, more conciliatory approach to Spain and its imperial claims. He was accused of treason and convicted, but then in 1616 James allowed Raleigh to undertake a further exploration in the New World for the hypothesized El Dorado on the condition that he avoid hostilities with the Spanish. After members of his expedition engaged in a violent attack on Santo Tomé in Guyana, Raleigh returned to England, where James reinstated his death sentence under Spanish pressure to punish what they viewed as a piratical attack. The executioner beheaded Raleigh at the Palace of Westminster in October 1618.

Raleigh's case emphasizes the essential ambiguity of private maritime violence in this era: it was neither fully illicit nor fully acceptable, neither permitted nor prohibited. In some cases, like that of the unfortunate Raleigh, state agents could still authoritatively classify piracy and illicit plunder occurring in the New World and act on those classifications, but that interpretation was rare and situational rather than systematic and widespread. As a result of this ambiguity, the question of whether voyages like Drake's, Hawkins's, Raleigh's, or others undertaken by Elizabethan mariners are best understood as trade, plunder, warfare, or settlement misses the point. The ambiguity demonstrates that such distinctions are dependent on patterns of consistent classification and coercion that did not exist at that time and place, leaving the ultimate meanings of these episodes of maritime violence up in the air for contemporaries. Their interpretation was subject more to factors like notoriety, bad timing, and local politics than to a rule-based institutional order. Raleigh's execution, for example, is less a function of what he did, which was similar to the actions of others from his era, than of the embarrassment his raiding caused James I as he sought to end Elizabethan hostility with Spain and pursue a closer relationship. James, in his turn, was subject to significant popular scorn for what was perceived as his intemperate submission to Spain's will in the Raleigh matter; Raleigh had been, after all, one of the great maritime heroes of the Elizabethan age, pirate or not.

BUCCANEERS OF THE CARIBBEAN? AMBIGUITY ESTABLISHED

James's efforts to rein in piracy against the Spanish were to prove fleeting. The assembly of England's own colonial empire during the early and mid-

58 | CHAPTER THREE

seventeenth century complicated the character of private maritime violence established by the Elizabethans but did not fundamentally change it. Indeed, many new English colonies actively fostered privateering, allowing an expansion in scale and scope of the autonomous predation of the previous generation of freebooters. Providence Island, Barbados, Jamaica, and other possessions were ideally suited to threaten Spanish trade, and they were also desperate for the capital and protection that privateers would afford. This synergy of geography, economic need, and political authority allowed privateering from English possessions to flourish.

None better exemplify this thriving lawlessness than the buccaneers who sailed against the Spanish from Port Royal, Jamaica, between 1655 and the 1670s. Henry Morgan, the most famous of these men, came to Jamaica as part of Oliver Cromwell's Western Design in 1655. He received a privateering commission in 1662 and participated in Christopher Myngs's raid on Santiago de Cuba and possibly Campeche. He cruised as a privateer for the next few years. The new governor of Jamaica, Thomas Modyford, demanded a halt to attacks on Spanish possessions from his island, but Morgan and several others ignored this order and sacked the city of Villahermosa de Tabasco in 1665. Their ships were taken in the assault, and the group of buccaneers proceeded to fight their way up the coast to Lake Nicaragua, where they sacked Granada. A contemporaneous source recounts how Morgan and his men "marched undescried into the center of the city, fired a volley, overturned 18 great guns in the Plaza de Armas, took the [commander's] house wherein were all their arms and ammunition, secured in the great church 300 of the best men prisoners, abundance of which were churchmen, plundered for 16 hours, discharged all the prisoners, sunk all the boats, and so came away" (Marley 1994, 263). The next six years involved nearly constant fighting as Morgan and a variety of crew members, soldiers, and allies raided towns throughout the Spanish Caribbean, at one point leading a force of one thousand against the mighty Cartagena de India, though the attack did not come to pass. His exploits at this time were intensely violent, predatory, and sadistic. Exquemelin writes that when Morgan and his men found Maracaibo, Venezuela, abandoned,

> they sent a troop of 100 men to seek for the inhabitants and their goods. These returned the next day following, bringing with them to the number of thirty persons, between men, women, and children, and fifty mules laden with several good merchandize. All these miserable prisoners were put to the rack, to make them confess where the rest of the inhabitants were and their goods. . . . Others had burning matches placed betwixt their fingers, which were thus burnt alive. Others had

slender cords or matches twisted about their heads, till their eyes burst out of the skull. Thus all sorts of inhuman cruelties were executed upon those innocent people. . . . These tortures and racks continued for the space of three whole weeks.[1]

This relentless campaign of violence and plunder took advantage of the same ambiguities exemplified by the Elizabethan sea dogs like Hawkins and Drake. On the one hand, the doctrine of "no peace beyond the line," decoupling states of war and peace in Europe from violence in the West Indies (Mattingly 1963), gave latitude for making private war on England's adversaries, even if there was no formal state of war declared. On the other, there were sporadic efforts to rein in these private wars for plunder, though such efforts were often half-hearted. Governor Modyford of Jamaica, for instance, ordered a stop to assaults against the Spanish using Jamaican ports and ships, but he also issued the commission that Morgan used to justify his assault on Panama. Morgan left Jamaica on August 11, 1671, and would later make the dubious claim that word of the Treaty of Madrid superseding his commission failed to reach him in time to forestall his attack. After marching around twelve hundred irregular troops and buccaneers across the Isthmus of Panama, he sacked Panama City and made it his own for the next month. In November of 1671, the new governor of Jamaica, Thomas Lynch, received an order to arrest Morgan for the sack of Panama and the trouble it had caused between the Spanish and the English, though Lynch delayed until March of 1672 in an effort to avoid alienating the privateering interests on the island. Once returned to London, Morgan remained under threat of trial, but apparently due to his ill health he was not imprisoned. After an intercession from a friend at court, he reentered the good graces of Charles II, who knighted him in 1674. The king also made Morgan lieutenant governor of Jamaica, a position he retained until his death in 1688 and a symbol of the impunity enjoyed by all but the unluckiest who engaged in private maritime plunder at this time.

This impunity that the sociolegal ambiguity of piracy often afforded is on stark display in the career of another of the era's most notorious and, from an elite state and merchant capital perspective, most troublesome seamen. While Morgan's entire career occurred on the margins of legitimate state power, Bartholomew Sharpe's activities were more marginal still. The Franco-Dutch War of the 1670s had ended with a series of treaties made in the Dutch city of Nijmegen between 1678 and 1679, and the Third Anglo-Dutch War had ended a few years earlier. In a familiar dynamic, the end of war meant the contraction in the supply of privateering commissions, and many found their livelihoods now technically unlawful. At the outset of their voyage of plunder, Sharpe and his comrades had received "Letpasses to goe into the bay of Hundorus, to cut logwood [a kind of wood used to make dyes], from his Maj'ties Reall subject the Earle of Carlisle."[2] That is to say, they had permission to go logging and nothing more, and they seem to have simply pretended that this commission was sufficient legal authorization for plunder. In Sharpe's case, however, it was clear that this was mere pretense. One of his men, when asked for his commission by the Spanish governor of Panama, told him, "We would . . . bring our commissions on the muzzles of our guns, at which time he should read them as plain as the flame of gunpowder could make them."[3] The group sacked Portobelo in Panama in early 1680 and then crossed into the Pacific, where they attempted to sack Panama City. Sharpe eventually took over as the commander of a fleet of pirate ships that took many prizes in the Pacific before disbanding back in the West Indies in 1682. He then returned to London laden with a fantastic treasure, the most valuable part of it being not gold but the *derrotero* he had captured from the Spanish ship *Santo Rosario.* The derrotero was a collection of maps and charts of Spanish American waters and ports that Sharpe had captured before the crew could throw it overboard. Back in London, he was arrested and tried under a commission of oyer and terminer for piracy. He appears to have swung the verdict in his favor by making a gift of the derrotero to Charles II (Baer 2007, 2:100–101), so he, too, avoided punishment for piracy.

THAT SWEET PLUNDER: AMBIGUITY ENDURES

Beginning around 1670, the first serious challenge to the entrenched networks of private plunder and piracy emerged with the turn of metropolitan English political and merchant elites against the chaotic and bloody vision of the colonial maritime world. As the vision of a prosperous, orderly empire of trade and the attendant vision of orderly seas free of the threat of random violence began to take hold, they started to insist on challenging the buccaneers, privateers, freebooters, and other piratical sorts having their way with the colonial maritime system. And yet private maritime plunder and pillage persisted and even thrived. The Treaty of Madrid in 1670, with provisions calling for England and Spain to restrain their privateers, serves as a useful marker of this change in the orientation of English elites toward piracy, though in reality the change occurred over a longer period of time.[4] In the decades following the treaty, English metropolitan political elites, some colonial elites, and merchant capitalists increasingly turned against piracy and toward long-distance trade as their favored political-economic model of empire. This turn brought them into conflict with the long-standing ambiguity of colonial maritime violence and revealed that this ambiguity had sources beyond the simple lack of will on the elites' part. The first of these sources was the deep integration of private violence and plunder into colonial states, societies, and economies.

Key metropolitan and colonial actors may have lost their taste for the chaos created by such a loosely regulated and entrepreneurial system of maritime violence, but the integration of this system and its steady supply of plunder into the social, economic, political, and military spheres of colonial life provided it with a source of support that muted the impact of elite efforts to crack down on it. And plunder was at the heart of the ongoing support that private maritime violence received from English colonial officials and subjects. The blending of violently and often illicitly acquired goods into colonial economies echoes throughout the correspondence passing between England and its colonies during the later seventeenth century. At various times, Jamaica, the Bahamas, Rhode Island, Massachusetts, New York, New Jersey, Pennsylvania, the Carolinas, and Virginia were all accused of trading with pirates, giving them refuge and protection, and even aiding them in retiring with their loot.[5]

Piracy occurs at sea but depends on access to ports where goods can be converted into money, ships refitted, and money spent. Colonial port cities were often welcoming of this influx of commercial activity (Ritchie 1986). (Pirates also brought hard currency with them, which was particularly prized in colonial economies that were, in the 1690s, starved of specie.)[6] Rhode Island, for instance, was known as a place where deserters from naval and other ships could go to join a "piratical voyage,"[7] and as a result some reported that the entire colony had become a "nest of pirates."[8] By this time, Pennsylvania was well known for harboring pirates[9] and, as the Board of Trade heard, "pirates, against whom warrants had been issued, walked through the streets of Philadelphia in perfect safety."[10] New York was perhaps the most notorious of all the colonies of this period for aiding and abetting pirates, providing a notorious refuge under Governor Benjamin Fletcher, while Nicholas Trott was explicitly removed from his position as governor for "entertaining pirates at the Bahamas."[11]

One of the persistent themes of this era of private maritime violence is that it was often fostered by colonial authorities who saw the privateers as essential to colonial survival and thus supported them even against metropolitan wishes.[12] For example, from at least the time of Edward D'Oyley in the late 1650s, Jamaican governors handled prize matters in a manner reflecting the perception that the island's security was contingent on the community of buccaneers who made Port Royal their base.[13] Governor

Thomas Modyford received instructions from England to restrain privateering but instead mastered the practice of adapting legal categories to the demands of the privateering interests on the island. In one case, he tried fourteen pirates, condemned them to death (though he had no clear legal power to do so), but then, "having shown the law and force, changed [his] copy, pardoned all the pirates but three," and proceeded to grant them commissions against the Dutch—an accounting for piracy turned into an inducement to privateering that puts the porous distinction between the two on fine display.[14] Regardless of the state of relations between England, Spain, France, and the Netherlands, Modyford could always find a pretext to authorize violence.

Colonial merchants also became involved in outfitting ships and providing other support services for pirates. New York merchants, for instance, were accused of ferrying Madagascar-based pirates and their loot from the East back to the American colonies for a fee. Pirate ships would also use the Atlantic colonies to outfit ships, recruit, head out for the Indian Ocean, and then return. As Jeremiah Basse, new governor of West Jersey, wrote to William Popple, secretary of the Council of Trade and Plantations, the principal coordinating body for colonial policy at the time,

> You cannot be insensible of the dishonor as well as damage suffered by this nation through the increase of piracies under the banner of England in any part of the world. . . . The Colonies in the Islands and Main of America have not a little contributed to this increase. In my time several vessels, suspected to be bound on this design, sailed from one province or another of the continent . . . and I am advised that four or five vessels are expected to return within these few months, which have on board them men belonging to New England, New York, the Jerseys, & c. They will be emboldened thereto by the good entertainment that they have formerly met withal in those provinces.[15]

Basse captures the sense running throughout the council correspondence that colonial ports saw real benefits from welcoming pirates and in turn played a critical role in perpetuating piracy.

Basse was somewhat unique in opposing piracy, for many colonial state agents deliberately and profitably used state power to encourage and support maritime predation. As the Council of Trade and Plantations wrote to King William III in 1697, pirates routinely received "favourable encouragement . . . in several of the Colonies . . . both in fitting out from thence and in returning thither as a secure receptacle."[16] One of the most pervasive ways this occurred was through governors offering privateering commissions to provide some legal cover to captains whose intentions were otherwise purely piratical. Governors could also simply neglect to pursue alleged pirates in their territories. Governor Fletcher of New York notoriously welcomed and supported Thomas Tew with both protection and commissions:

> Captain Tew had a commission from the Governor of New York to cruise against the French. He came out on pretence of loading negroes at Madagascar, but his design was always to go into the seas, having about seventy men on his sloop of sixty tons. He made a voyage three years ago in which his share was £8,000. Want was then his mate. He then went to New England and the Governor would not receive him; then to New York where Governor Fletcher protected him. Colonel Fletcher told Tew he should not come there again unless he brought store of money, and it is said that Tew gave him £300 for his commission. He is gone to make a voyage in the Red Sea, and if he makes his voyage will be back about this time. This is the third time that Tew has gone out, breaking up the first time in New England and the second time in New York.[17]

Tew's career in the 1690s is a good indicator of this impunity even in the face of its gross violations of elite pretensions to sovereignty and authority over the use of violence at sea. Tew headed from the West Indies to the Red Sea in 1693, with the intention of seizing one of the heavily laden and lightly armed vessels that carried much of the Indian Ocean trade. He captured one spectacularly wealthy ship and returned to Newport, Rhode Island, in 1694, with shares for the crew of £1,200 to £3,000 each (Marley 1994, 389), a rich sum. After being refused a commission from the governor of Rhode Island, Tew went to New York, where he befriended Governor Fletcher, renowned for the friendly welcome he gave to pirates and his willingness to provide them with commissions for a price.[18] Tew received his commission and returned to the Red Sea, where he was killed by a gut shot during a battle with a Mughal ship.

Despite the chaos Tew wreaked in one of England's most lucrative trade relationships, he was never subjected to legal scrutiny of any kind and even managed to receive state authorization for his further exploits. A somewhat similar fate appears to have been in store for Henry Every, another Indian Ocean pirate, who was inspired by Tew's incredible first voyage (Marley 1994, 143). Every led a mutiny on a privateer and took the ship to the Indian Ocean, where he encountered and sacked one of the grandest and most controversial of all pirate prizes. The ship, *Gunj-i-suwaee*, was owned by the Mughal emperor Aurangzib. In addition to treasure, it was filled with courtiers, whom Every's crew brutalized and tortured. The sack of the *Gunj-i-Suwaee* became a crisis for English relations with the Mughal emperor, and throughout the English Empire the search for Every and his men was on. They left the Indian Ocean and in 1696 arrived in the Bahamas. Every and his men paid Governor Trott

> twenty pieces-of-eight *per* man besides two chequeenes of gold, on which he allowed them to come on shore, and gave them a treat at his house, at which one of the men broke a drinking glass, and was made to pay eight checqueenes for it. The men also presented the Governor with the ship and all on board her, including some elephants' teeth. The Deputy-Governor, Richard Tallia, shared with Trott in the booty. Here the Captain changed his name from Every to Bridgeman, and went ashore with about eighty men, who dispersed to several ports and bought sloops there.[19]

Several of Every's men were eventually caught, tried, acquitted, retried, convicted, and executed in London. But despite a hue and cry raised throughout the empire for his capture, Every disappeared and perhaps inevitably became a figure of romantic legend.[20]

CLASSIFICATION PROBLEMS: THE ESSENCE OF AMBIGUITY

These cases show how the integration of plunder and piracy into colonial states and societies afforded some protection for private maritime violence, even when metropolitan elites began to work against it. But intransigent and malfeasant local officials are hardly a unique problem for these elites. Also hampering their efforts to bring maritime violence under state control was an easily missed factor that shielded the pirates from scrutiny and state coercion. Piracy was continually defended, and elite English state agents' efforts at coercive power to subdue the pirates continually undermined, by the interpretive infrastructure the agents had available to them for both classifying pirates and directing the powers of institutionalized state violence against them. At their disposal was a sixteenth-century interpretive infrastructure for defining and deterring piracy that had been rendered obsolete by the expansion of the English Empire over the course of the seventeenth century. In their frustration we can see the power of interpretive infrastructures to channel, direct, and make real the social power that comes from institutionalized coordination. The effects of these structural interpretive problems on the persistent ambiguity of piracy are best seen in the shambolic handling of cases where hostile state agents actually managed to get accused pirates in their grasp, cases where the outcome should be most consistent and clear in its coercive consequences.

In particular, a trio of Jamaican pirates well exemplifies this interpretive chaos and how it perpetuated the ambiguity the pirates so exploited. In 1676 John Deane, the first of the three, seized an English ship, the *John Adventure*, took wine and a cable from it, and then brought the ship to Port Royal, Jamaica. There he was accused of piracy and of flying Dutch, French, and Spanish colors without authorization. Deane was tried that same year by Lord Vaughan, the governor of Jamaica, supposedly acting in his capacity as vice admiral by using a civil law procedure in which he and the other judges determined guilt. Vaughan found Deane guilty and sentenced him to death. When the Lords of Trade and Plantations received word of the trial and verdict, they requested that the High Court of Admiralty review Vaughan's legal procedure. Sir Richard Lloyd, judge of the court, determined that Vaughan "had not regularly proceeded" in the case and was not in fact authorized as vice admiral to try pirates. Indeed, "the Lord Admiral himself cannot . . . try piracy,"[21] wrote Lloyd, except as the chief of a commission of oyer and terminer. This legal form had been created by Henry VIII's 1536 piracy law, Act for Punishment of Pirates and Robbers of the Sea, which combined civil law judges with grand and petit juries for indictments and determinations of guilt.

Though the facts of Deane's violent maritime pillage were not in dispute, and the Lords of Trade and Plantations faced political pressure to regulate piracy, the admiralty judge's opinion authoritatively undermined the legitimacy of Vaughan's process for classifying Deane as a pirate. The Lords of Trade and Plantations wrote immediately to Governor Vaughan, ordering him to halt the execution. They meanwhile petitioned King Charles II for commissions of oyer and terminer to be sent to Vaughan and other governors—a measure that itself later ran into legal problems, and in any case it required a fundamentally different legal procedure for determining guilt based on a jury verdict—and any jury in Jamaica was likely to acquit. The classification of Deane thus began in a colonial court that followed one procedure; was referred to a metropolitan political body for its consideration; was referred in turn to a centralized maritime legal authority; and then on the basis of its interpretation of the rules and procedures for the exercise of judicial coercion, the High Court of Admiralty used its authority to reverse the decision and order a new trial using procedures unlikely to result in a successful conviction.

Meanwhile, back in Jamaica, Governor Vaughan had in fact pardoned Deane, and he had been freed. Such great uncertainty and legal complexity in a case where the facts of Deane's unlawful violence were never in dispute demonstrate the weakness of piracy as a hinge for the coordination of coercive power at this time; it was very hard for state agents to use the classification of piracy to bring force or the threat of force to bear. Deane's career also represents a frequent trajectory for mariners in the English maritime system of the mid- to late seventeenth century, moving into and out of the ambiguous legal and political margins of maritime predation and of governmental maritime authority (Benton 2010).

What Deane's case shows is that English state agents who sought to address the piracy issue in the later seventeenth century had a problem beyond the vast expanse of the area they sought to control, its isolation and lack of naval forces as well as the collusion of colonial governors and merchants. The interpretive infrastructure for coordinated, legitimate classification of maritime violence had not kept pace with the geographical expansion of the territory of the English state, nor had it kept pace with the political-economic demands placed on an empire built on merchant capitalism. The emergence of piracy as a social object and as an object of coercion depended on actors having the ability to collectively and violently enforce the boundaries of the category and to make it a highly consequential reality of state-imposed social order. Deane's case typifies the late seventeenth century in that it revealed that English state agents did not have an interpretive infrastructure that could support such a coordinated, consistent display of state meaning and social power, even when state agents had the will and coercive resources at hand to use violence in support of this vision of maritime order.

Like Deane, James Browne sailed out of Jamaica. He had a commission from a French governor, but it had become invalid by the time he looted a Dutch slave ship in 1677. Browne landed his captives surreptitiously on Jamaica, but when the governor, Lord Vaughan, heard of this, he sent a naval vessel that managed to capture one hundred enslaved people, several crew members, and Browne himself. Browne was tried by Vaughan and found guilty. The "trial" was entirely illegal, however, for the power to try pirates had been explicitly denied Vaughan by the Board of Trade and the High Court of Admiralty. The Jamaica Piracy Act of 1681 would give governors new powers to try pirates, but it was four years off.[22] Vaughan was, in effect, inventing legal powers of classification and assigning them to himself. Despite this lack of legal authority, the end result was clear enough in practice. Learning his lesson from the Deane debacle, Vaughan rushed through the execution despite the objections of the Jamaican Assembly; Browne's attempts to secure the benefits of the recently passed Privateering Act, which would have allowed him amnesty; and a writ of habeas corpus delivered minutes too late.[23]

Vagueness and Violence on the Maritime Periphery | 67

Despite the bloody outcome, Browne's case and the uncertainty of the legal status of the verdict, along with the questions until the last of whether it would be carried out, reveal not the strength of the interpretive infrastructure for classifying piracy but its weakness. In order to execute Browne, Vaughan had to feign legal powers he did not have and on the basis of that fraudulent verdict order an execution to be carried out with enough speed to beat the assembly's efforts to challenge his decision. Browne was classified a pirate and hanged, but it was hardly a model for institutionalized coercive power of the consistent and orderly sort most effective as a deterrent. The outcome spoke more of bad luck for Browne and of Vaughan's vigilantism than of a bad institutional environment for pirates.

The fate of a third pirate sailing out of Jamaica during this period further underscores the chaotic character of state interpretation as it related to piracy. Joseph Bannister stole the ship *The Golden Fleece* in 1684. He was captured and returned to Jamaica, where he was to be tried for taking a foreign commission, an act that years before had been defined as treason. The evidence for this case fell apart, and Bannister was instead tried for unlawfully taking Spanish captives despite having no commission. The alleged captives, however, denied that they had been taken against their will, and this case, too, collapsed. While the authorities tried to find another way to charge him, Bannister managed to outfit his ship again and made a dramatic escape:

Captain Bannister one dark night sailed in a desperate manner passed the fort. He had, it is said, fifty men ready in the hold with plugs to stop shot-holes. But the sentries being careless, the night dark, and the wind fresh, he was abreast of the fort before Major Beckford, the commander, was warned, and had passed fourteen of the guns. Beckford did all that he could, but could only place three shot in him. He at once sent me word of the occurrence, which was a great surprise to me, for I thought that Bannister's want of credit would prevent him from ever getting the ship to sea again. . . . It was done so artfully that no one suspected it, or I should have found some pretext for securing him. Directly after he was gone Captain Stanley sailed after him, fired several shots to recall him, without effect, and finally sent a note on board to say that, unless he returned, he would be treated as a pirate. Bannister answered that he had no piratical intention, that he was sailing to Honduras for logwood, and that the reason for his leaving the port in that manner was that he was forced to fly from his creditors. Captain Stanley then returned, finding himself unable to do more against a ship of her strength and size.[24]

Bannister fled from Jamaica and joined up with a huge gathering of French privateers who were preparing for a raid on Campeche. He continued to wreak havoc in the Caribbean and posed a constant embarrassment to Jamaican efforts to control their privateers. In 1686 the governor sent out two naval vessels to hunt Bannister. They caught up with him and engaged in a fierce battle that destroyed his ship, though Bannister survived. But Molesworth, the lieutenant governor of Jamaica, wanted an example to be made of Bannister, and he thought the point would be best made extralegally. He ordered Captain Spragge of HMS *Drake* to hunt Bannister down on the Mosquito Coast, where he was in hiding.[25] Molesworth's order apparently went somewhat further. His report to the Board of Trade, a body charged with coordinating matters relating to trade and the colonies, describes a recourse often contemplated in legal discourses on piracy but rarely practiced among the English:

> On the 28th January, Captain Spragge returned to Port Royal, having succeeded in the task that I assigned to him, with Captain Banister and three of his consorts hanging at his yard-arm, a spectacle of great satisfaction to all good people and of terror to the favourers of pirates, the manner of his punishment being that which will most discourage others, which was the reason why I empowered Captain Spragge to inflict it. Banister seemed to have no small confidence in his friends. I find from letters that he wrote to some of them that he intended to plead that he had been forced into all that he had done by the French. How far this would have prevailed with a Port Royal jury I know not, but I am glad that the case did not come before one.[26]

It was a standard claim of piracy law that pirates had placed themselves beyond the law; and that if they refused to surrender it was within the right of their captor to engage in summary justice: string them up unceremoniously from the yardarm. But Bannister's case is one of the few where such summary shipboard judgment was actually carried out. Why Jamaican authorities did it was clear: they rightly concluded that they could not achieve Bannister's death through the legal process, and so they went around it.

This prompts the question of why summary justice of this sort was uncommon. Could it not have been a powerful technique for dealing with pirates? The problem is that among contemporaries, few seemed to share Molesworth's brutally pragmatic views. He was correct that a jury trial in Port Royal would be an uncertain business, as Bannister's earlier trial showed. And while spectacles and terror were indeed a principal mechanism in the fight against pirates, it was as a symbol of the rule of law that the display of executed pirates' corpses became an effective signifier of coercive power. Summary executions achieve exactly the opposite, turning an otherwise lawful shipboard environment governed by the strictures of naval discipline into a site of lawless violence. We can further ask why Molesworth felt compelled to order Bannister's summary execution. The immediate cause was the repeated failure to find a charge that the authorities could get to stick. Despite an elite consensus that Bannister was guilty, there was no straightforward way to make him guilty using the interpretive mechanisms available in colonial legal institutions. Thus, in an even more aggressively extralegal way than in the Browne case, state elites were forced to go outside the institutionalized powers of the English state to use ad hoc, situationally specific maneuvers to achieve their violent ends.

One final figure will complete this review of how the ambiguity of maritime violence remained largely unaffected even when state agents successfully lashed out at pirates: Captain William Kidd.[27] Kidd was involved in a number of lawfully commissioned raids on the French in the late 1680s and early 1690s. After having his ship stolen by a mutinous crew and replaced by another, he came to New York at the height of the political turmoil created by the Glorious Revolution and used his ship to support the royalist cause. He married a wealthy New York woman, Sarah Bradley Cox Oort, but soon devised a return to privateering. He sailed to London and after a complex negotiation was eventually issued what had become rare: a privateering commission. In fact, he had two: one against the French and the other authorizing him, ironically, to hunt for pirates. Upon reaching the Indian Ocean in 1697, Kidd and his crew began to hunt for rich prizes. They unsuccessfully battled an East Indiaman, one of the large, heavily armed ships of the East India Company, in an attempt to capture the Mocha trade fleet. They failed a number of other times to capture merchant ships, but then in January of 1698 seized the *Quedah Merchant*. They refitted their prize in Madagascar and then returned to the West Indies. Kidd was apparently oblivious that his piratical exploits had led the East India Company to begin vociferously demanding his capture back in London. He returned to New York more infamous and more dangerous to his former backers than he could have imagined. Upon his return, he was caught, imprisoned, returned to London, tried by a commission of oyer and terminer in Admiralty Sessions, convicted, and hanged in 1701.

Kidd's body hung in chains at Tilbury Point on the Thames for years afterward as a warning, but it was an ironic omen. He was the last of the West Indian pirates to be tried and executed under the legal system governing the matter through all the careers discussed in this chapter and actively fostering the ambiguity these men of violence relied on to consistently get away with their plunder. In the context of tremendous ambiguity, where other pirates who had done as badly or worse had been knighted, or escaped, or been pardoned, or been executed summarily, the lesson of Kidd's execution was simply another piece of bad luck. So even as the body count increased with cases like Browne, Bannister, and Kidd, ambiguity persisted, because each case involved highly contingent political circumstances and legal maneuvers. It was not the case that the interpretive infrastructure of English piracy institutions could not produce violence, but it was sporadic and rare. For every narrative of execution, several of riches absconded with existed to inspire hope in the hearts of those willing to take a chance on the ambiguity of the law for the lure of plunder. It was entirely plausible to read the message of Kidd's body and other symbols of state power against piracy during this period as an inducement as much as a deterrent.

THE END OF AMBIGUITY

Kidd's execution is also significant because it marked a turning point. In 1700 as a result of the disruptions caused by rampant piracy, state agents introduced legal changes upending the interpretive infrastructure that generated the ambiguous sociolegal environment in which these seventeenth-century pirates and privateers had thrived. During the later seventeenth century, English elites came round to the realization that without making changes to the restrictive interpretive infrastructure they had at their disposal to categorize this troublesome aspect of the social world, gallows posed little threat and cannons had no target. The production of coercive power against piracy in the English Empire was in important ways a classification problem.

Before turning to the process of institutional change in the next several chapters, it is useful to consider the ambiguity described in this chapter more analytically. In terms of the conceptual framework used in this book, this ambiguity has two sides. In the concrete circumstances where mariners, captains, governors, and other English state agents confronted private maritime violence, ambiguity can best be understood as a problem of social performance and coordination. It was impossible in many circumstances to define another as a pirate and to have that definition taken up by others to become the sort of collective, coordinated imposition of meaning that can powerfully shape situations and, by symbolically and materially linking situations together, the social world more broadly. This performative and coordination problem whereby piracy could not be consistently or consequentially classified was itself closely connected to an institutional interpretive infrastructure, embedded in the legal constitution of the English colonial state, that made authoritatively labeling pirates complicated, difficult, and rare.

To illustrate the performative dimension of this cultural ambiguity, it helps to begin with one more pirate story. On September 20, 1697, Sir John Houblon, lord commissioner of the admiralty, received a letter from Robert Snead, a Pennsylvania justice of the peace, complaining about the prevention of his efforts to detain men he accused of being members of Henry Every's crew by William Markham, lieutenant governor of Pennsylvania. Snead's tale is extraordinarily detailed but ordinary in the classification problems it catalogs. It is quite a yarn that captures the situated, personal, microsociological dynamics of classification failures and struggles from the stuff of which the broader ambiguity of piracy in this period was built, so I will quote it in full:

> Robert Snead to Sir John Houblon. I am sorry for the occasion that makes me write to you. On the 10th of August, 1696, a proclamation came to my hands and another to Mr. Penn's deputy, William Markham [Markham was lieutenant governor but is referred to as governor in this letter], who took no notice of it. I thought it my duty as a subject and a magistrate to prosecute the purport, which was to apprehend Henry Every *alias* Bridgman and the rest of the rogues who ran away with the ship Fancy and committed several piracies in the Rattan seas. I at once went to the Governor and told him that several of Every's men were here, well known to him and to all persons. He said he knew it not. I told him here was enough to prove it, and that if he did not apprehend them I did not know how he could answer it. He said he would venture that; why had not the Houblons, whose ship it was, sent to him about it? if people came here and brought money he was not obliged to ask them whence they came. I told him that those who had suffered losses by these rogues could do no more than they had done by procuring the proclamation of the Lords Justices, and therefore that in my opinion he needed no further direction. He refused to hear the proclamation when I offered to read it to him, but seemed very angry, so I left him. No sooner was I gone than he sent and acquainted the pirates with what had passed between us, and they by his encouragement impudently called me informer, though I saw Governor Markham trying to stifle it. We all knew he had a great present made to him and his family by them and others of the same crew though not in the same ship, which they sank or burned. I thought it my duty to apprehend them and called upon two of my fellow justices to join me, who knowing the

Governor's inclinations at first refused, but on my threatening to send to England if they did not, at last consented. Three of the pirates were brought before us and there was sufficient proof that they belonged to the Fancy. I ordered them to be sent to gaol, but one of my fellows went to the Governor, and he and the others were for bailing them, which they did, though I declared against it, and one pirate for another; but, some weeks later I heard from England that the factories, in which you and several others are concerned, were seized on and likely to be damaged by these rogues. I then seized them again, and enclose their examinations. My *mittimus* was to keep them close prisoners. The Governor was much displeased at me, called me before his Council and asked what I had against those pirates to hinder their discharge. I told him there was proof enough that they were Every's men, and had the proclamation read. The Governor would have had them join him in clearing them out of prison, but they told him that they should be sent to England, and offered to pay the expenses if he sent them. This he refused to do, and dismissed them. I then issued my warrant to apprehend the old pirates before mentioned, who I was told had brought here £1,000 each man and given £100 each to the Governor. I am but a stranger here, having moved my estate and family from Jamaica two years ago, but I am ashamed to see such rogues encouraged. They ran away from Jamaica with a ship, went to the Persian seas, and took and murdered many. A princess, who was given in marriage to a great man, was on her way to him by sea when they took the ship; they killed most of the men and threw her overboard. They brag of it publicly over their cups. When the Governor heard that I was going to apprehend them he sent for me, threatened to send me to gaol and dared me to do it, telling me I should not frighten people with my warrant, I had done too much already. He abused me very much, and caused my arms (which I wear for defence against these rogues) to be taken from me. He has lately given commissions to other such rogues. One Day came with a large ship full of sugar and indigo to Carolina, sold the cargo, laid the ship up, bought a vessel for piratical purposes and came here. The Governor gave him a commission, and they are gone on their errand, as they themselves own. On the 16th inst. I received from his Excellency a copy of a letter from the Council of Trade ordering the apprehension of all these pirates. I understand that the Governor had one directed to him and also the proclamation, to be published forthwith. But he did not do so until he had warned the pirates, who made their escape, those in gaol as well as those without, which shows pretty clearly that it was by consent. Next day the proclamation was published. Several people came to tell me where the pirates were hidden in the town, and I went to the Governor for a warrant for a special force to take them; but none was issued, so that all people see how Arabian gold works with some consciences. A gentleman at the same [time] arrived from England and told me that one of the Council of Trade was concerned. He desired the Governor that the pirates in prison might be better secured, and a guard set over them, and that Every's men might be sent home in one of the King's frigates then in Virginia. No guard was set on them, so that the same night two of them got away. He then asked to take the other man to the frigate, but was refused. The gentleman's name was Robeson, a man of pusillanimous spirit, who was frightened by the Governor. Several of these men have purchased estates here, and if you will procure me a commission and direct that, as the proclamation says, those that shall assist shall be paid out of the estates, I will undertake to seize them all and their estates. Please take care that the commission be so firm that the Governor cannot upset it, and I will do my part faithfully. When I first came here I wrote to some relations of mine to inform Sir Josiah Child about it, but have heard no more. Do not think that I propose it for my advantage, for I have a competent estate, but for the public good, and that these parts may no more be a receptacle for these rogues. If you wish to make use of me, address me at my Plantation near Philadelphia. *Signed*, Robt. Snead[28]

Jailbreaks, threats, obstructions, feigned confusion—Snead's efforts to classify men who were desperately wanted by metropolitan state agents for their disruptive piracy in the Indian Ocean were stymied at every turn by colonial state agents and others who refused to go along with his classificatory efforts. In Snead's frustration we can see the performative dimensions of the social ambiguity of piracy. Social performance, in this sense, is about the construction of sociocultural realities through action. When Snead declares that someone is a pirate, he is making a social claim with his action. Austin calls this sort of a performative speech act a "verdictive." He writes that "verdictives consist in the delivering of a finding, official or unofficial, upon evidence or reasons as to value or fact. . . . Verdictives have an effect, in the law, on ourselves and on others. The giving of a verdict or an estimate does, for example, commit us to certain future conduct" (Austin 1976, 154). Centrally important to the social operation of verdictives is Austin's point that they must affect ourselves and others. Specifically, the pragmatic success of a verdictive speech act—"He is a pirate!"—can only be judged in light of the patterns of conduct that the verdictive causes. Is it propagated through chains of social action that empower and realize it by orienting themselves toward its symbolic structuring of the social world? The one making the claim and others need to act in ways that ratify the initial performance and that propagate it through wider social networks. It is these networks of coordinated performances that ratify, at least in a general sense, a common core of meaning to the signifiers of state action that constitute state power. Verdictives are performative when they shape collective social behavior in ways that make them true.

The problem that state agents like Snead faced confronting piracy in the later seventeenth-century English maritime world was that their attempts at verdictive utterances were blocked and rejected at every turn. Those around Snead refused to ratify his accusations by adjusting their behavior in ways that treat them as authoritative social performances. The ambiguity of piracy afforded them a wide-enough range of action that they could ignore Snead and in so doing secure their own material interests in harboring the pirates without significant threat of repercussion. His accusations were not propagated and instead were rebuffed, rejected, and mocked. Verdictive performances that are refused ratification by other state agents or that fail to or only partially propagate through the network of actors, materials, and meanings comprising the state in turn weaken state power in the areas where they occur, for in a narrow but important sense state power is nothing other than a pattern of conduct that ratifies the state as a predominant context of meaning. Cases like Snead's are examples of the failure of interpretive power at the level of interaction, and it is this level of analysis that we should consider when we focus on the performative context of interpretation.

The sorts of performative failures that Snead's letter exemplifies were endemic to the English colonial maritime world at this time. Intertwined with performative failure, the interpretive problems facing English state agents were also the result of institutionalized interpretive infrastructure that made it very difficult to classify pirates in colonial waters. The system for classifying pirates at the transsituational, systemic level also had notable weaknesses encoded into it that made it an inept infrastructure for making piracy a signifier—a word, an accusation, a category, a type of person, a sort of crime—capable of mobilizing state collective action in the colonial maritime world (the story was different in European waters). The next chapter goes into this infrastructural problem in more detail, for it was the loose thread that ultimately led to the unraveling of the whole ambiguous, piratical cultural system; but basically, existing piracy law made it impossible to legally classify someone as a pirate outside a special trial in a court of oyer and terminer sitting in London. For an accused pirate to be worth transporting back to London, he needed to be extremely inconvenient politically, and even then the logistic hurdles for a conviction were formidable. This frustration is visible in Snead's letter as well. It is in part because he is never able to lay charges in a court with the actual authority to try and convict the men he accuses that his performative attempts never go anywhere. Ignoring a formal court verdict would be riskier, but such a verdict was inaccessible because of how the interpretive infrastructure of England's maritime law had been constructed.

Because the interpretive infrastructure for authoritatively classifying piracy as a crime was so inadequate for the job, verdictive performances attempting to use piracy as a way to mobilize and generate state power against certain types of private maritime violence routinely failed. And because such performances routinely failed, the matter of what counted as piracy, the meaning of piracy, remained essentially ambiguous.

THE CASE OF PRIVATEERING

Another important factor contributing to the ambiguity of piracy was the closely related category of privateering. Through its overlap with piracy, privateering provided a kind of semiotic safe harbor that practitioners of private maritime violence could use at times to provide a veneer of legality for their predation. This is because the border between privateering and piracy was for much of the seventeenth century poorly defined and because privateering itself had no clear boundaries. The transformation of the interpretive infrastructure related to privateering in the English Empire that also occurred at the end of the seventeenth century was thus substantively important to the regulation of piracy. In addition, it foreshadowed the extension of institutionalized state interpretive power that would later encompass piracy as well.

Privateering has become a generic way to refer to a more or less lawful form of private maritime violence. The term emerged in popular usage in the mid-seventeenth century but only in the later seventeenth century as a legal category with practical implications for the control of maritime violence (e.g., 4 William & Mary, c. 25). That this was not an ancient term but rather an emergent category of practice in the mid-seventeenth century is worth noting. Its emergence marks a new stage in an ongoing social struggle over the control of private maritime violence between its practitioners and the state agents increasingly concerned with the implications of untrammeled maritime lawlessness for their nascent political-economic visions of empire. Contrary to the primly tidy understanding of privateering as a clear social, political, and cultural category of "authorized private maritime violence," *privateering* denoted a social space of perpetual ambiguity and a site of struggle between state agents and assorted men of violence in the later seventeenth century.

To treat privateering as a clearly established modality of legal violence is to obscure its seamy ambiguity, a defining feature for contemporaries. As Alexander Justice writes in his treatise on admiralty law, "Our laws take not much notice of these privateers, because the manner of such warring is new, and not very honourable."[29] Privateering remained a suspicious endeavor to many and was at times of only very marginal legality (Rodger 1996, 160, 186). Contemporaries were keenly aware of how easy it was to cross the line from privateering into piracy—the author of the tract *Piracy Destroy'd*, for instance, explains the rise of piracy in the Indian Ocean at the end of the seventeenth century as the result of an influx of privateers from the West Indies accustomed to the culture of easy commissions and conniving governors.[30] Reflecting this essentially suspicious character, the term was routinely used in a way that insisted on its ambiguity. The title of James II's proclamation in January of 1688 captures this persistent suspicion nicely with its goal of "Reducing and Suppressing of Pirates and Privateers in America," lumping the two practices together in its analysis of the sources of violent disorder in the imperial maritime world. One of Justice's subheadings reflects the same ambiguity: "The Method to be observ'd by the Commanders of Her Majesties Men of War and Privateers, in Examining and Securing the Prisoners taken on Board Privateers and Pirates."[31] The men-of-war and the pirates had clear-enough positions with respect to the raids that Justice envisioned, but privateers occupied an uneasy middle and might fall on either side—or both.

As with piracy, achieving even a modicum of control over privateering[32] required an interpretive infrastructure that allowed state agents to authoritatively answer what counted as privateering. Those interpretations needed to flow through chains of propagation and ratification to achieve and reinforce the social reality of its classification through coordinated, collective, transsituational action. In the case of privateering, prize law played this role. As a general matter, prize law consists of nationally and historically specific solutions at the juncture of four dilemmas of maritime control: international maritime competition, reliance on maritime trade, essential supplementary paramilitary maritime resources, and acceptable levels of piracy. As the English Empire expanded, these problems were further complicated by geographical contexts that exacerbated the difficulties of controlling private men of violence. Developments in English prize law from the mid-seventeenth century comprised an important transformation of this system.

One part of this transformation involved letters of reprisal, essentially authorizations to merchants and seamen to plunder the shipping of other states as a form of redress for claimed losses. The use of these letters as a solution to the problem of controlling private maritime violence was on the decline in the English maritime world, displaced from the mid-seventeenth century on by privateering commissions. The difference between these forms of redress reflects the deeper transformation of maritime violence under way. Letters of reprisal allowed injured parties to pursue redress for their losses against foreign states on their own behalf. Privateering commissions, however, were issued by state agents to private actors, authorizing them to act in pursuit of state objectives without regard to previous loss. While the issuance of letters of reprisal was always subject to international political considerations, the shift toward issuing privateering commissions made states of war and peace a definitive aspect of the social meaning of private maritime violence. Though it ultimately reshaped the practices of English privateering in fundamental ways, the importance of states of war and states of peace to the regulation of privateers was at first complicated by unsettled questions of the relationship between the international relations of European states in European waters versus the relationship of those states in the seas of the colonial periphery (Mattingly 1963). As described in chapter 2, from the English invasion of Jamaica in 1655 through the 1670 Treaty of Madrid, administrators in the metropole seem to have had little interest in controlling colonial governors' issuance of privateering commissions. In the Jamaican case most notoriously, a series of governors issued commissions with abandon, intentionally cultivating a community of privateers who provided the island with some measure of maritime protection from a Spanish reconquest of the island as well as a crucial early source of capital (Crump 1931; Zahedieh 1990).

The periodization of the regulation of privateering roughly parallels that of the regulation of piracy. During the period between the conquest of Jamaica and the Treaty of Madrid, we can see two ultimately irreconcilable faces of privateering. On the one hand, privateering violence flourished. On the other, an impetus for greater control over privateers gradually stirred among English state agents and merchant capitalists. During the Commonwealth regime, Parliament passed a series of laws that attempted to control privateers by regulating letters of marque and reforming prize law (Marsden 1916, xi). This trend continued with the Restoration, as a series of acts and instructions sought to bring privateering and prize-taking practice in line with developing interpretations of the law of nations, particularly as written into many of the treaties England agreed to in the later seventeenth century (Deák and Jessup 1934a). The impetus to codify prize law continued through the Glorious Revolution: William III passed an important act in 1692 that formalized a number of matters of prize law previously left to custom, including rules on the division of prizes as well as forbidding the transport of prizes to neutral ports for adjudication, the abuse and torture of crews of ships taken as prize, and the use of foreign commissions.[33]

The clarification of admiralty courts as the sole jurisdiction for the adjudication of prizes during the early seventeenth century meant that those courts would become the institutional locus for the practical application of prize law and the central site for ensuing semiotic struggles over the sociolegal meaning of *prize* (Deák and Jessup 1934a, 679–80).[34] Following the Restoration, the key moment for the development of the institutional foundations for controlling privateering in distant waters was the Navigation Act of 1696. Before the creation of vice admiralty courts, colonial prize institutions were shambolic, politicized, pretextual, and impotent. The various colonial vice admiralty courts established after 1696 would ultimately make significant strides in reordering and regularizing this system. As Charles Andrews describes the watershed of 1696 in prize law, the colonial admiralty jurisdiction of the eighteenth-century empire "traces its origin only in the slightest degree to the conditions that existed before 1696–1697" (1936, 1).

This new system of legal institutions solved the geographical problem of legal authority in a global empire along the same lines as the solution to the geographical contradiction of the piracy jurisdiction described in the next chapter: creating many dispersed sites of institutionalized legal interpretation. The new vice admiralty courts were hardly settled and established institutions, but crucially, from the early eighteenth century they started to issue legal judgments based on a body of laws and legal practices that made their judgments more predictable and legally legitimate. As a result, they began to clarify the boundaries of the concept of prize in a manner practically important and ultimately influential in shaping the actions of would-be privateers. This institutional efflorescence in the later seventeenth century turned the semiotics of colonial prize jurisdiction from a plaything in the hands of the avaricious into a classification mechanism with a degree of autonomy from influence that individuals needed to navigate if they were to benefit from their past acts of purportedly lawful violence. Crucially, that navigation was impossible without some care as to the character and conduct of their violence, along with attention to its possible future intersection with the semiotics of *prize*.

At the heart of prize law are two distinct questions: which ships could be forcibly taken (including its corollary—which could not be) and who could take them. The new pressures put on these questions in the context of the later seventeenth-century English maritime world led to the development of a thicket of new signs and symbols characterizing these two aspects of prize. The question of whether a ship was liable to seizure remained contentious, but by the later seventeenth century various European treaties had coalesced on the position that this question is one that in all cases requires formal adjudication by an impartial court according to established legal practices (Deák and Jessup 1934a, 682).[35] This was to be the bedrock principle of English prize law throughout the eighteenth century.[36] What it entailed was an insistence that the semiotic question of good-prize or not good-prize was in principle to be determined legally, through institutionalized arrangements based on an interpretive infrastructure reflecting the precepts of prize law rather than on the basis of extralegal considerations such as violence, politics, or economic expediency. While previous approaches to prize taking required a complaint before any adjudication, by the later seventeenth century the practice was firmly in place that only a judicial condemnation would suffice for classifying a given ship as a good prize that could then be sold.[37] As Deák and Jessup write, "From at least the seventeenth century it was generally conceded that a prize judgment followed by a prize court sale gave good title against the world" (1934a, 684). By the beginning of the eighteenth century, the enshrinement of a formalized adjudication as the determinant of the basic classification question of prize law had established an all but inevitable future context of institutionalized interpretation that privateers would need to transit before realizing the benefits of their prize—whether in waters near England or far.

The central interpretive question on which prize court decisions turned by the later seventeenth century was whether either the captured ship or the captured goods on that ship belonged to the subjects of a state at war with England.[38] To answer that question, courts looked to the statements of officers and crew of the captured ship and to its various papers—charter party agreements, bills of lading, invoices, and passes were all considered as evidence[39]—in an effort to determine the ownership of the vessel and goods "out of her own mouth," as the practice was known by the eighteenth century (Deák and Jessup 1934a, 692). Prize courts also, however, used a set of presumptions as to the significance of various signs in determining whether a ship was a good or fair prize. For instance, the use of violence in resisting a lawful search was construed by prize courts as evidence that the ship in question was a good prize, as was the failure to make a claim for the return of the captured vessel, or any effort by officers or crew to destroy the ship's papers (1934b, 825–36). Prize courts gathered all this evidence in written form, as was the practice in admiralty law, to adjudicate it—a great, consequential shuffling of papers that became increasingly inevitable to determining the meaning of purportedly lawful private maritime violence, wherever it occurred. The judgments of prize courts were not, of course, universally above reproach, but they did significantly advance the notion, as a practical constraint of the early modern maritime system, that there were limits to the ships that could be legally taken. Moreover, those limits would be determined after the fact by individuals and institutions other than those who had done the taking and according to roughly consistent interpretive procedures that fit the particular circumstances to a more general and transposable system of relational signs.[40] The terrain of contestation for the lawful taking of ships at sea by the early eighteenth century had been significantly legalized, revolving less around the crude pantomime of legality that had at times defined prize as a practical matter in colonial waters. The future of any act of privateering ran through the institutionalized paper shuffle, and the resulting lawful and binding interpretation, of a prize court.

The question of who could act as a privateer was likewise clarified in the later seventeenth century. In the mid-seventeenth-century English colonial world, the commissioning of privateers often served to provide a pinch of legality to otherwise outright piracy, but the commission by the later seventeenth century was increasingly an instrument with practical implications for the control of maritime violence. In the 1690s, for instance, the long-standing practice of obtaining letters from foreign states as a way to circumvent the outbreak of peace so dreaded by privateers came under direct, sustained legal pressure, with the Prize Act of 1692, an act of council of 1694, and the Act for the More Effectual Suppression of Piracy of 1700 all equating the use of force under foreign commissions with piracy.

The privateering commission signified a relationship between colonial governors and privateers during the seventeenth century, but it was not a relationship of control in a system with multiple options for predation, disposition of loot, and commissions. But as the prize system and its capacity to define prize taking as a category of state meaning with important practical consequences spread through the English maritime system, the commission and the boundary it signified between lawless piracy and merely suspicious privateering became more powerful in shaping the social meaning of isolated maritime encounters. The state-issued commission became a powerful determinant of how a given captain and ship could interact with the entire prize system.[41]

The case of a prize taken off the coast of Guinea by a Captain John Broome in 1695 provides a good example of this change. Broome had no commission but seized a valuable French ship loaded with gold, silver, ivory, and some two hundred enslaved men and women. Under the terms of the general reprisals declared against France at the outbreak of war, this capture was not classified as piracy. But was it a prize that Broome could lawfully sell? Broome brought his "prize" to Jamaica and sold it. When the admiralty became aware of the encounter and subsequent sale, it initiated a case in the High Court of Admiralty, which promptly condemned the ship "to our said lord the king as enemy goods and lawful prize, and as perquisites of the Admiralty. . . . and that he, John Brome, willfully, wrongfully, and in fact disposed of the same at his will, without rendering or making, as of right he should have, any account or reckoning thereof to our said lord the king" (Marsden 1916, 175–76). The Broome case shows that the possibility for the illicit disposition of goods in colonial waters was still open, but that state agents, in prize law as in piracy law, were concertedly using their newly restructured and invigorated interpretive powers to close it, thereby forcing the future trajectories of such encounters through the state's interpretive infrastructure.

A 1694 proclamation on the flags privateers could fly provides a further example of this effort to make privateering a distinct semiotic category. The proclamation responds to the problem of private ships wearing jacks, pendants (or pennants, as they are more commonly known), and ensigns reserved for royal ships or alternatively adopting various flags so similar to the royal versions as to be indistinguishable. Merchant ships were permitted only to fly St. George's Cross for their flag and jack. Privateers bearing commissions were restricted to the same presentation, but the proclamation recognized their warlike character—or perhaps, better understood, their marginal status—by allowing them to fly a pendant. On August 8, 1708, Woodes Rogers, a commissioned privateer (and later the governor of the Bahamas, responsible for the knife's-edge execution of eight men for piracy detailed in chapter 5), reported that he encountered the queen's ship *Arundel*, which ordered Rogers and company to strike their pendant. "Which we immediately did," writes Rogers, "all privat commission ships being oblig'd by their instructions to pay that respect to all her Majesty's ships and fortifications."[42]

Exerting greater control over the privateers through innovations in the interpretive infrastructures of the empire had direct effects on piracy. It also marked out a similar trajectory and goal of reform. As the next chapter shows, though, the piracy case was more convoluted, because the existing systems of piracy law were rooted in different and more complicated parts of the legal structure of England's maritime empire.

CHAPTER FOUR
The Classification of Pirates

In 1664 Thomas Lynch, then commander in chief and judge of Jamaica, responded to demands from England that he act to restrain the maritime violence originating from the island by voiding privateering commissions. He expressed his doubts about this strategy:

> Calling in the privateers will be but a remote and hazardous expedient, and can never be effectually done without five or six men-of-war. If the Governor commands and promises a cessation and it be not entirely complied with, his and the English faith will be questioned and the design of trade further undone by it. Naked orders to restrain or call them in will teach them only to keep out of this port, and force them (it may be) to prey on us as well as the Spaniards. What compliance can be expected from men so desperate and numerous, that have no other element but the sea, nor trade but privateering.[1]

Lynch knew that rescinding the commissions of ostensible privateers sailing from Jamaica would not curtail their violent depredations because the reclassification of their violence from authorized privateering to unauthorized piracy was toothless. In order for conceptual distinctions to become potent, structuring social meanings, they must be connected to a social apparatus, including means of violence, that makes them real by facilitating their translation into the concrete settings and situations where meaningful action occurs. This is the key role of the interpretive infrastructures that translate institutionalized rules and relations into the lived realities of social life. What Lynch is telling us is that this apparatus, this interpretive infrastructure, for answering the question, What is a pirate? and making that answer matter in consistently realized ways did not exist. Hence his dilemma.

Lynch's lamentation, though, understates the full scope of the piracy problem that he and his contemporaries faced. While he suggests that only a dramatic increase of naval force would give the proposed semiotic maneuver any weight, the real dilemma went beyond the simple application of force. In this, Lynch was like his contemporaries among English state agents in the later seventeenth century attempting to rein in the pirates. The possibilities and limits of coordinated action encoded within any given institutional structure are often shrouded from those acting within that institution. The ways in which institutional realities, through the mechanisms of social performance, coordinated action, and distributional incentivizing, guide, limit, direct, and enable action are not transparently or wholly known in general, and even less so in specific and novel circumstances. How an institution relates to a given circumstance is only ever worked out through trial and error, efforts and failures, the people on the scene acting creatively within the institutionalized social reality of their situation as they understand it and seeing what happens (Joas 1996; Gross 2009).

Neither Lynch nor his contemporaries had a full understanding of the precise problems that piracy posed in the context of their existing institutions and state powers because they had not tested those institutions and powers against piracy. They quickly realized, however, that the coercive restraint of piracy was not a simple matter of state capacity to project naval force. It required a significant transformation of the legal constitution of the late seventeenth-century English colonial state and of the distribution and nature of authority within it. In the terms that I have used in this study, it involved the creation of a new interpretive infrastructure that allowed contemporaries to make the distinction between lawful and unlawful maritime violence a real, powerful, and collectively enacted social meaning capable of shaping circumstances of action across the colonial maritime world.

These innovations in the interpretive infrastructure involved in the classification and punishment of piracy came through the practical problem-solving efforts of state agents. State agents in different positions in the structure of the English Empire, experiencing different frustrations, setbacks, and failures, advanced a series of solutions to the problem of classifying and punishing pirates beginning in the 1670s. The answer to the question of how to more effectively prohibit piracy, however, was neither simple nor obvious. Nor was it merely a matter of the will and ingenuity of state agents, for their available lines of action were constrained by existing codes, procedures, and concepts of state meaning making just as surely as they were constrained by geography, organizational limitations, and naval force numbers. English state agents were not wrestling with simply practical, logistic questions. The interpretive powers in question in the creation of a new legal regime were powers over life, death, and property. The political struggles over piracy law reform, far from turning on mere juristic technicalities, were fundamental struggles over the foundations of political and social order.

The transformation of the interpretive infrastructure for dealing with piracy in the English Empire was therefore a contentious process that took the form of classification struggles (Bourdieu 1985) among actors within the state over who would have access to the apparatus of state meaning making and how those meanings would be made. Those struggles were waged by actors embedded in the existing piracy institutions' cultural, organizational, and institutional structures of state power. Thus, the existing piracy institutions contextualized and constrained the struggles over how they were to be transformed. This dynamic of state making through struggles waged under the constraints imposed by existing codes was at the heart of the series of failures marking the first thirty years of efforts to reform the interpretive infrastructure for dealing with piracy. Those institutional structures, forms, networks, and materialities "were what there was" to work with, the ground on which and through which their reforms would occur (Geertz 1981, 136). It was in this manner that contemporary state agents slowly felt their way toward changing the interpretive infrastructure of their piracy institutions.

"WHAT THERE WAS"

In the later seventeenth century, institutions tying together the far-flung outposts of the English Empire proliferated. State agents created various bodies to address the challenges of governance and administration that had become so salient to the meaning of empire, and both within and outside those bodies actors engaged in transimperial discourses in which they constructed problem spaces and domains of social meaning that raised expectations for state action. Piracy is one such area, and it was constructed as a domain of intersubjective and transoceanic meaning through the intersection of institutional formulations of what piracy meant.

Governors played a central role in this story, and so they are a fitting place to begin. The governors of the various colonies were appointed in different ways, depending on whether the colony was proprietary, corporate, or Crown. All governors, though, received instructions from their monarch that established priorities, policies, and restrictions. This was one of the most obvious tools that metropolitan state agents had available in their

The Classification of Pirates | 85

efforts to shape colonial social, political, and economic orders. In 1698, for example, the instructions to the governor of Bermuda read:

> Whereas we have been informed of great depredations . . . done by pirates . . . who have either sailed from or been too kindly received and harbored in some of our plantations in America . . . we do therefore strictly command and require you to take due care that no pirates or sea robbers be sheltered, entertained, or any manner or way favored or encouraged within our islands under your government; but that on the contrary you use your utmost endeavor to discover all such persons and their abettors, in order to their being brought to condign punishment.[2]

This was just one of the multiple appearances of piracy in the direct instructions from the Crown to the governors of its colonies. Governors themselves occupied a critical position in the fight against piracy and played an active role in creating an imperial antipiracy policy (or, in the breach, in undermining such a policy).

Thomas Lynch, quoted at the beginning of this chapter, provides one model for how governors attempted to make piracy a functional criminal category in the later seventeenth century. Lynch served two terms as governor of Jamaica, from 1671 to 1674 and from 1682 to 1684. He was, among other things, a factor for the Royal African Company, which had interests in the opening up of the Spanish Empire to the English slave trade, and he was part of the growing constituency opposed to the chaos of uncontrolled privateering. In his role in the empire's effort to placate Spanish anger over attacks by Jamaica-based English privateers, Lynch had a warrant to arrest his predecessor, Thomas Modyford. Shortly after sending Modyford back to London, he was ordered as well to arrest Henry Morgan and return him to London to potentially face charges over the sack of Panama in 1671. Privateers fled the islands, understanding that Lynch represented a new, less hospitable view of the legality of their maritime adventures. He was removed as governor when Henry Morgan came back into favor, but returned in 1682 to resume his harsh policies toward the restriction of privateering and the regulation of piracy.

As governors were increasingly instructed to enact the meanings of piracy more aggressively through the later seventeenth century, other state agents were also integrating piracy into the performative repertoires of a series of new as well as preexisting imperial institutions. The special Admiralty Sessions of oyer and terminer in London, for example, was the only court having the undisputed legal authority to hear cases of piracy until the 1700 legal reforms discussed below. Perhaps the most famous of all piracy trials, that of Captain William Kidd, took place in a London piracy tribunal and was followed with interest throughout the English maritime world. Likewise the trials of Captain Henry Avery's men, who had obtained great fame and notoriety for their piratical voyages against the Mughal emperor Aurangzib in the Indian Ocean. While governors were ex officio vice admirals, contemporaneous legal opinions held that the vice admiralty powers were insufficient to try capital cases. And despite significant confusion on this point, vice admiralty courts did not even exist in most colonies until 1696. Efforts to use these institutional forms as a basis for fighting piracy thus amounted to a series of failures and confusions. Colonial assemblies played a sporadic role, as they occasionally saw fit to pass antipiracy laws, attempting to structure local governmental regimes against pirates. The role of these assemblies was often also of the negative variety, though, as a coordinated effort to pass legislation against piracy in the 1680s foundered on the assemblies' refusal to pass the bills.

The Royal Navy was another contributor to the institutionalized response to piracy by agents of the English state. Naval vessels had long been commissioned to hunt pirates,[3] and the demand for a naval response to piracy in the West Indies increased through the later seventeenth century. The Board of Trade wrote to King William III in 1699 of the "mischiefs committed by Pirates . . . and of the great danger of the continued growth and spreading of that infection." It requested that a "sufficient force of well sailing [naval] ships as may be thought necessary and proper to clear those seas from the Pirates."[4] The navy further responded to the threat that pirates and foreign privateers posed to English commerce (especially during wartime) by organizing protective convoys.[5] These defensive and offensive efforts were limited, though, by the geographical scope of the seas they sought to patrol and just as much by the ambiguity produced by English piracy institutions and their inability to consistently classify pirates and give the navy a target.

Of all these developments, it was perhaps the creation of the Board of Trade in 1696 that was the most significant innovation in remaking the interpretive infrastructure of the English Empire as it related to piracy. The concept of a body charged with coordinating matters relating to trade and the colonies was not new. James I created the first iteration of this institution, the Lords of Trade, in 1621 as a committee of the Privy Council. These responsibilities were then passed through a shifting constellation of boards and authorities, most notably taken up by the Committee and Standing Council for Trade and Navigation of the Council of State during the Commonwealth regime. Then with the Restoration, the responsibilities were divided between a Privy Council committee and the Select Council of Trade and Plantations, the latter largely a result of merchants' lobbying efforts meant to include members with greater experience and interest in the intricate problems posed by trade and empire (Andrews 1908; Root 1917). This division collapsed in 1674 with the dismissal of the Select Council; several weeks later, in February 1675, the resumption of direct administrative duties by the Privy Council committee took place (Root 1917, 23). Displeasure with the quality of this administration, particularly on the part of politically connected merchants trading with the colonies, came to a head in 1695–96. The House of Commons decided on December 12, 1695, to address the continuing costs of what it and its merchant lobbyists perceived to be inadequate administration in issues relating to imperial commerce by creating a Council of Trade. The council would be given administrative powers by parliamentary legislation. The issue was thus also an intervention into the highly charged political question of the constitution of the English state after the Glorious Revolution of 1688: to what extent would executive power remain a prerogative of the Crown or be taken over by Parliament? The moment of the question was such that on the same day that the Commons reached its decision, William III "countered it by announcing his purpose to establish by royal authority a council composed of 'some of the Greatest Quality, and others of Lesser Rank, and acquainted with trade'" (40). The king issued the commission for the new Council of Trade and Foreign Plantations, known as the Board of Trade, under the Great Seal as an independent body in May of 1696 (41; Sainty 1974).

For several reasons, including administrative confusion, different priorities, and differences over the significance of piracy or its character as a problem, the coordinating efforts of these bodies when it came to piracy were inconclusive through the 1690s and in some respects into the 1700s. Yet from the outset, the Board of Trade approached the administration of empire more systematically and had the capacity to manage multiple issues over long periods of time. The board's incorporation of piracy as one of its ongoing concerns and as a regular subject of its efforts to collect data and administer imperial relations reflected the status of piracy as a recognized problem space for imperial governance; it also deepened the integration of antipiracy policy in the institutional structure of the state. By more effectively combining a whole range of problems of imperial administration among its concerns, the Board of Trade represented a more ambitious effort to govern the empire as an integrated system, with trade at its center; in this system, piracy was represented clearly and consistently as a threat. In its report to the king on December 23, 1697, the board makes the scope of its interests clear, writing that its commission "required us amongst other things, to enquire, examine, and take an account of the state and condition of the general trade of England, and also of the several particular Trades to all foreign parts, and how the same respectively are advanced or decayed, and the Courses and occasions whereof, and to enquire into and examine what trades are or may prove hurtfull, or are or may be made beneficial, and how advantageous trades may be improved and extended, and such as are hurtfull and prejudicial rectify'd."[6] Its report is analytical in its efforts to identify successful trade relations, damaging ones, and obstructions to trade such as piracy, smuggling, and war. The report also shows the board's systematic approach as it moves through all the important, geographically distinct nodes in the trade network of the empire. Its approach to issues of trade was also practically inclined, with effort devoted to ascertaining "in what manner, and by what proper methods, trade may be most effectually protected and secured in all the parts thereof."[7] In pursuit of this ambition, the board sought to use the tools provided by the late seventeenth-century English state, and it also sought to develop new powers of governance over the far-flung social environments where the trade relations it sought to order transpired.

It is in the context of its ambitious, systematic, and pragmatic approach to the administration of imperial trade relations that the Board of Trade's effort to transform the interpretive infrastructure of the English state relative to piracy in colonial waters became so significant. From the outset, the board took piracy to be a clear and urgent impediment to trade. It actively sought to analyze the piracy problem and to come to grips with it through a variety of measures. For instance, in a 1700 response to questions posed by the House of Commons about the general state of trade, the board sought to advance what proved to be an effective theory of the support for piracy in the empire and the legal remedy that might alleviate the situation:

> Being informed by many instances of the great countenance given to pirates in some of the plantations, and chiefly in the Proprieties and Charter Governments, by fitting out their ships from thence, and furnishing them with all sorts of provisions and ammunition, and receiving them with their plunder and booty at their return, and acquitting them upon feigned tryals, we did make severall representations thereupon, and proposed the enacting of laws there for the trial and punishment of pirates, in conformity to a law heretofore passed in Jamaica to that effect, which having been refused in the said proprieties and charter governments. We proposed as the only remedy for so great an evill the

offering a bill in Parliament for that purpose. . . . Such a bill has been prepared and is now lying before this honourable House.[8]

The legal reforms referenced in this passage resulted in part from the establishment of the Board of Trade as a new nexus for policy making in the empire. The board displayed new energy and analytical interest in discerning the sources of the piracy problem, and it actively sought to craft ways that state power could be brought to bear against pirates more effectively.

TRIALS AND ERRORS

From 1670 through the 1720s, many efforts were undertaken to reform piracy law in order to effectively coordinate coercion in the colonies, with the most consequential moment in this legal history coming in 1700 with the Act for the More Effectual Suppression of Piracy. These legal changes created the new coordinating structure that state-affiliated actors interpolated into the situations relating to private maritime violence they found themselves in. It was by doing so that they created and deployed interpretive power over piracy linked to a credible and consistent threat of violence. It was this configuration of power that they brought to bear with devastating effect during the war against the pirates of the 1710s and 1720s.

English admiralty law emerged from the conjuncture of a desire to create state-oriented legal order at sea and the meaning of the jury in the common law. During the medieval period, legal actors empowered jurors to determine verdicts on the basis of their likely familiarity with the case in question and connections to the community where the events at issue occurred. Jurors were understood to be local experts who could draw from their knowledge of the community to find out what was really going on in a given case. This theory of the jury suggested a real limit to the capacity of the common law to hear cases having to do with events that took place at sea, beyond the geographical and communal competence of any jury. The creation of a separate admiralty law with different procedural, evidentiary, and hermeneutic underpinnings resolved this contradiction. The basis for the earliest English admiralty law was the Rolls of Oleron, a document relating cases and judgments from the French island of Oleron, which had developed a reputation for legal competence in hearing cases related to trade and other maritime issues. The adoption of the rolls and the creation of English admiralty law were likely gradual processes, but we know that the rolls had "the status of law" by 1351 (Runyan 1975, 99). Admiralty law was based on civil law, which had descended from Roman law and transmuted over the centuries in different continental European states. In contrast to the common law, judges heard and determined civil law cases, judgments were made on the basis of legal principles rather than precedents, different trial procedures were used, and different definitions of evidence pertained. Admiralty law generally had two areas within its jurisdiction: prize and instance. Cases of prize had to do with whether enemy ships taken during wartime had been seized in accordance with law and were therefore lawful prize, or if they had been improperly seized and thus must be returned to their rightful owners. Instance jurisdiction had to do with suits relating to maritime affairs, with one of the most frequently occurring examples being cases brought by seamen against shipowners (Marsden 1909, 1910; Owen and Tolley 1995, 1–3).

In an earlier iteration of the theme of policing piracy to better control the seas, Henry VIII stripped jurisdiction over piracy from the admiralty in 1536 with the Act for Punishment of Pirates and Robbers of the Sea (28 Henry VIII, c. 15). He gave it instead to a special court commissioned under the Great Seal that would include the admiral as well as common law judges. The ostensible reason for the creation of this new court to try piracy was that, in the words of the statute,

> where traitours, pirotes, theves, robbers, murtherers, and confederatours upon the see, many tymes escape unpunysshed because the trial of their offences hath heretofore ben ordered, judged, and det[er]myned before the Admyrall or his Lyeutenante or Comissary, after the course of the civile laws, the nature whereof is that before any judgement of death canne be geven agenst the offendours, either they must plainly confesse their offences (which they will never doo without torture or paynes) or els their offences be so plainly and directly [proved] by witness indefferente [i.e., admiralty procedure excluded accomplice testimony], such as sawe their offences comytted, which cannot be gotten by chaunce at fewe tymes by cause such offendours comytt their offences upon the See, and at many tymes murder and kill suche persons being in the ship or bote where they comytt their offences which shulde wytnes agenst them in that behalf, and also suche as shulde bere witness be commonly maryners and shipmen, which by cause of their often viages and passages in the sees departe without long tarrying . . . to the great cost and charges as well of the Kynges Highness as suche as wolde pursue such offendours.[9]

Civil law procedural rules had, in the view of state agents in the 1530s, made it too difficult to police piracy because they required a confession or else the testimony of two uninvolved eyewitnesses, particularly unlikely in cases of piracy that occurred on the lonely high seas. The new court would hear piracy cases following common law procedure, which allowed for accomplice testimony, but it provided the accused with the protection afforded by a jury.

The fundamental changes to the legal structures surrounding piracy introduced in the 1536 Act for Punishment of Pirates and Robbers of the Sea became the foundation of judicial coercion against pirates for the next century and a half. The basic problem that eventually emerged was that the 1536 law predated England's colonial expansion and could not be easily extended. The law gave jurisdiction over piracy to a specially commissioned court of oyer and terminer that only existed in London. Only in the context of that court were the common law procedures that made obtaining convictions possible an authorized mode of jurisprudence. In the context of a global empire, this posed rarely surmountable logistic challenges, because it meant that piracy could only be tried in London. Pirates captured in the colonies needed to be shipped back to London for trial (along with any witnesses), which was costly. Piracy trials of this sort thus only occurred in the most egregious cases.

Yet, as described in the preceding chapters, piracy was not a significant problem for the English Empire throughout the early seventeenth century. To the contrary—the piratical exploits of English mariners were a significant problem for other nations, especially Spain, and perceived as beneficial to the colonies and ambitions of the English. As the meanings of empire and trade changed through the mid-seventeenth century, however, and state agents began to see piracy as a more disruptive force, contemporaries began to experience the limitations of the 1536 legal regime. This was especially so as the activities of the buccaneers in the murky legal environment of the mid-seventeenth-century West Indies reached their zenith. Jamaica in particular was at the center of multiple countervailing forces: many privateers used that island as a base of operations, significantly contributing to its economy and its viability as a colony; but the new emphasis on rule-based international relations that introduced peace "beyond the line" meant that Jamaica was also subject to significant metropolitan pressure to reform. These forces came to a head under the leadership of Lord Vaughan (governor, 1675–78), whose unlawful trials of John Deane and James Browne were described earlier.

In Vaughan's slapdash trials and executions in the late 1670s and the rebukes they earned him, we can see an important fault line in the sociopolitical struggle over how to classify pirates. Vaughan's approach was in a sense an eminently practical one to a problem that all parties agreed was serious. He took the most expedient way to execute (or credibly threaten to execute) men who all agreed had engaged in piracy. His approach was likewise highly portable, and it could have been used immediately by like-minded governors throughout the empire. The rebuke delivered to Vaughan by the admiralty judge Sir Charles Hedges, and the controversy over the legally tenuous execution of Browne, however, marked a fatal flaw in the simple and practical expediency of just letting governors get to the work of execution: this approach required a repudiation of the idea that the empire would be governed by the rule of law. According to the vision of an empire of law, it was only when officials' actions were properly embedded in a code of legal meanings that they were to be ratified as actual and authoritative exercises of state power that other state agents were compelled to ratify and reproduce in turn. For all its efficiency, Vaughan's approach clearly violated the law, and its expediency came only at the cost of directly undermining the principle of law as one of the fundamental mechanisms for coordinating action in the empire. Hedges's decisive opinion in the Deane case should be read as a broader indictment of the expedient but lawless interpretive infrastructure that Vaughan's approach to piracy entailed. In rebuking Vaughan, he reflected the controlling view that the classification of piracy could only be authoritatively and legitimately achieved through a binding legal interpretation by a properly constituted court, adjudicating established legal powers in a procedurally correct way and not through extralegal strongman vigilantism.

THE JAMAICA PIRACY ACT GAMBIT

But what could be done within the law? The next phase in the struggle to remake the English interpretive infrastructure for defining piracy in colonial waters again centered on Jamaica, and it took the form of the Act for Restraining and Punishing Privateers and Pirates, better known as the Jamaica Piracy Act, in 1681[10] (though the Privy Council had promoted and worked on drafting such an act from at least 1678).[11]

The act begins with a focus on the disruption to the management of international relations caused by pirates and unregulated privateers departing from Jamaica: "Whereas nothing can more contribute to his Sacred Majesty's honour, than that such Articles as are concluded and agreed on in all Treaties of Peace, should by all his Majesty's subjects, according to their duty, be most inviolably preserved." The act forbade privateers, under pain of death, from acting under foreign commissions against states with whom the English were in amity. Piracies were to be

> enquired, tried, heard, determined and judged within this Island in such like form as if such offence had been committed in and upon the

land, and, to that end and purpose, commissions shall be had under the King's Great Seal of this island, directed to the judge or judges of the Admiralty of this island . . . which said commissioners . . . shall have full power to do all things in and about the enquiry, hearing, determining, adjudging, and punishing . . . as any commissioners to be appointed by commission under the Great Seal of England, by virtue of [28 Henry VIII, c. 15].[12]

The Jamaica Piracy Act recreated the powers and procedures of the 1536 act that formed the basis of common law English judicial authority and procedure for trying pirates, but it vested its powers of interpretation in a special commission in Jamaica instead of in the special oyer and terminer piracy tribunal in London. This created, for the first time, an interpretive power over piracy in the colonies, with a clear location in the legal structure of the English colonial state and a legitimized claim to wield sovereign power to classify in the specified ways.

There were, however, at least two major problems with this mechanism for creating judicial power over piracy in overseas territories. First, the Jamaica Piracy Act followed 28 Henry VIII, c. 15, in relying on a jury to convict accused pirates. This was occasionally a problem even in London[13] and posed an even greater threat of failed trials in the colonies. Indeed, the colonies that provided the greatest support for pirates, and would presumably have been the most likely to provide pirate-friendly jurors, were the colonies where coercive legal authority was most needed. A second problem was that the act took an intrinsically piecemeal approach to an imperial problem. The legal authority the act created was a creation forged with the sovereign powers delegated by the king to the Jamaican Assembly. While those powers ultimately derived from the English state, the law they passed was a Jamaican law, and to use it as a framework for an imperial antipiracy policy would require a similar act to be passed by each other colony. In fact, this was exactly the approach to the piracy problem that English state agents adopted for the next decade. The king and his Privy Council ordered on February 27, 1684, that in light of the

great damage that does arise in His Majesty's service by harbouring and encouraging of pirates in Carolina and other governments and proprieties where there is no law to restrain them . . . that a draught of the law now in force at Jamaica against pirates and privateers be sent to all other governments and proprietys in America with His Majesty's directions that it be passed into a law in each place, and that all possible care be taken by the respective governors and proprietors that the same be put in execution as they will answer to the contrary . . . and did order that the Right Honourable Mr. Secretary Jenkins to transmit copies of the said law made at Jamaica . . . to all other . . . plantations in America.[14]

Copies of the Jamaica law were indeed disseminated, and some colonies even passed them,[15] but only a few, and most of those not until the end of the seventeenth century, when the legal reform process had already moved on. Many colonial assemblies, particularly in the colonies most closely associated with supporting piracy, had incentives to maintain the status quo. Others, such as intransigent Massachusetts, passed its own version of the Jamaica Piracy Act that the Privy Council subsequently rejected on review. The hope of passing "Jamaica Acts" in all the colonies to create a legal infrastructure for trying pirates was to remain merely that. The Jamaica Piracy Act partially succeeded in creating authoritative interpretive power over piracy. But by vesting interpretive authority in a jury likely to be sympathetic to the accused, this approach obstructed the classification powers it sought to create. And by embedding that authority in the sovereignty of the colony, and thus relying on other colonies to pass similar laws, it was politically awkward as the basis for a systematic response to piracy.

THE VICE ADMIRALTY QUANDARY

One of the more curious features of the piracy law reform process is that the foundations of a legal infrastructure for trying pirates would seem, to an outsider and to many insiders, to have been in place all along. While there were several early efforts to establish vice admiralty courts in America and the West Indies, these were sporadic and largely failed. With the Restoration and the intense interest in trade of the later Stuarts, as Owen and Tolley write, "efforts to extend the vice admiralty system to the American and West Indian colonies intensified" (1995, 27). From 1660 through the early eighteenth century, the vice admiralty system came to play an increasingly prominent role, particularly with the establishment of vice admiralty courts responsible for the enforcement of the Navigation Acts in 1696. From the early sixteenth century, the admiralty had played a central role in piracy trials. The vice admiralty courts, as institutional extensions of the admiralty jurisdiction overseas, thus would seem to have been a reasonable place to try pirates in the colonies. To many contemporaries, this indeed seemed to be the case, and the trial of John Deane turned on just such a misunderstanding of the vice admiralty's power. In light of the jurisprudential confusion over piracy in Jamaica during the late 1670s, the Lords of Trade asked the King's Counsel and Advocate General to clarify the powers of the vice admiralty courts in the plantations. Their answer in March of 1684 scotched the hopes of reformers, noting that the "vice admiralty power extends only to lesser offences, not capitall, committed within their several districts and not to offences committed upon the high sea out of their districts." Furthermore, an admiralty court established there could only try pirates according to the admiralty procedures that had been found ineffectual and replaced in 1536 with the Act for Punishment of Pirates and Robbers of the Sea. They found that the 1536 piracy law, 28 Henry VIII, c. 15, "doth not extend to the plantations and so no commission can be granted thither upon that law."[16] The issue here was not that the law had no bearing in colonial waters—it did, as piracy committed in the West Indies or America could be tried under the 1536 law by the special court it created in London. What this opinion found, though, is that the interpretive power created by that law could not itself be transferred by commission to colonial courts.

The hope for using the vice admiralty courts as the foundation for an antipiracy policy did not die, however. The 1690s saw a new, and newly global, surge of piratical activity. Crews based in the American colonies, often with commissions to provide them with legal cover, would voyage to the Indian Ocean and raid the rich and poorly protected shipping of Aurangzib, the Mughal emperor. These attacks posed serious threats to England's India trade, with the emperor holding the East India Company responsible for the actions of English pirates. The issue came to a crisis point in 1695 in an episode previously described: Henry Avery's sack of the *Gunj-i-suwaee*, a richly laden ship owned by Aurangzib and returning from a pilgrimage to Mecca. The rape, murder, and theft perpetrated by Avery, Thomas Tew, and their men drove Aurangzib to imprison East India Company factors and ban all further trade until the company agreed to provide convoy protection for Mughal shipping.

The continuing failure to create a satisfactory legal structure for producing coercive power against piracy once again loomed large in the consciousness of imperial state agents. Some hoped that the 1696 Navigation Act, the Act for Preventing Frauds, and Regulating Abuses in the Plantation Trade (7/8 William III, c. 22), would provide such a mechanism by empowering vice admiralty courts. This Navigation Act fundamentally reorganized the relations of governance between London and the colonies by granting clear, sweeping jurisdiction over the enforcement of the provisions of the Navigation Acts to colonial vice admiralty courts (Hall 1957, 502). In its operative seventh section, the act reads: "that all penalties and forfeitures . . . [are] to be recovered in any of His Majesty's courts at Westminster, or in the Kingdom of Ireland, or in the Court of Admiralty held in His Majesty's

Plantations."[17] Hall has shown that the House of Lords introduced this language in a deliberate attempt to fundamentally restructure the relations of authority, governance, and enforcement between the metropole and the colonies (1957, 504). One of the striking things about the act, however, is that no such system of Courts of Admiralty existed. While vice admiralty powers had been provided to governors, before 1696 only one properly constituted vice admiralty court, established in Maryland in 1694 (Owen and Tolley 1995, 31), existed in England's colonies. While some have suggested that this represents an error in the act (32), Hall persuasively argues that the House of Lords was privy to advice from Edward Randolph, surveyor general of the customs in America since 1691, a man intimately familiar with the political and legal structures of the colonies, and thus it was well aware that no such a system of courts existed. Rather, Hall argues, the curious grant of sweeping powers to courts that did not yet in fact exist reflects the classification of the Court of Admiralty as a prerogative court—that is, a court whose commission and powers are delegated by the royal prerogative, not from custom or parliamentary statute. The Navigation Act of 1696 thus took the form of an inducement to create these courts rather than acting to create them directly because the admiralty jurisdiction was inherently tied to royal sovereignty and prerogative (Hall 1957, 504). In any case, new courts were quickly created in the colonies to exercise the new powers.

With high hopes, on November 22, 1697, William Popple, secretary of the newly formed Board of Trade, wrote to Sir Charles Hedges, judge of admiralty, to inquire "by what law and in what manner the Courts of Admiralty erected in the Plantations by Commission of the Lords of the Admiralty, do or may try pirates, and whether they have power to inflict capital punishment upon those that are proved guilty."[18] On November 24, Hedges informed the board, one imagines to its great displeasure and confusion, that "the Admiralty Courts in the Colonies [created in the wake of the 1696 Navigation Act] have no power to try and punish pirates except under a local law, such as exists in Jamaica, though they have power to arrest pirates and send them home to be tried."[19] Hedges's opinion brought up short yet another mechanism for coordinating state interpretive and coercive power against piracy. While colonial vice admiralty courts now had sweeping new powers, those powers did not include jurisdiction over piracy.

The Board of Trade was left to propose again the enactment by individual colonies of the Jamaica Piracy Act of 1681, but it recognized that this piecemeal approach was hopeless. To the king, the board wrote,

> the most effectual remedy [to the piracy problem] would, we think, be
> a law enacted here to extend uniformly through all your Plantations by

which the methods of trying pirates might be directed, and the punishment of that crime made capital. Till such an Act shall be made we propose that you direct that copies of the Act of Jamaica, for restraining and punishing privateers and pirates, be sent to the Governors of all your Colonies, the Proprieties and Charter Governments included, with orders to each of them to use their utmost endeavours with their Assemblies to pass an Act to the same effect.[20]

The last years of the seventeenth century saw high levels of piracy in the Indian Ocean,[21] the American colonies,[22] and the West Indies.[23] Colonial support for piracy also ran rampant, with New York as the most prominent colonial backer of pirates. This drumbeat of piratical depredations and corruption throughout the English Empire created an urgent context for piracy law reform. On April 6, 1698, Hedges submitted a draft law to the Board of Trade that would create the new legal structure for trying pirates that many thought necessary.[24] The records of this period are filled with accounts of piracy throughout the empire. Alarmed state agents in the colonies complained of great disruptions to shipping and commerce. Pirates on the Madagascar trade swarmed the West Indies, the Atlantic coast, and the east and west coasts of Africa. Colonial state agents could do little but bemoan their lack of legal tools to use against the pirates.[25] At precisely the same time, the high-profile exploits, capture, trial, and execution of Captain Kidd provided a dramatic display of the piracy problem, pressuring Parliament to adopt the new law (Nutting 1978; Ritchie 1986).

On the crest of these events, a version of Hedges's model law passed Parliament in 1700 as An Act for the More Effectual Suppression of Piracy.[26] The new law with its new rules for the authoritative classification of pirates proved to be the key to unleashing coordinated state violence against piracy in the English maritime system. The law included a number of significant innovations, including a new procedure for piracy trials. Table 4.1 summarizes the major differences between the old and the new systems. While piracy trials under Henry VIII's law took place in a special court in England and were decided by a jury, under the new law specially commissioned courts throughout the empire would indict, hear evidence, and determine guilt. This meant that piracy could now be judged by a simple majority of state-appointed commissioners, making verdicts more predictable. Also under the new law, defendants were given access to defense counsel but only to assist with points of law. They were also give the opportunity to cross-examine prosecution witnesses, though through the president of the court rather than directly. Given the removal of both grand and petit juries, however, these protections were minimal, and the

TABLE 4.1. Major legal changes of 1700

28 Henry VIII, c. 15 (1536), Act for Punishment of Pirates and Robbers of the Sea	11&12 William III, c. 7 (1700), Act for the More Effectual Suppression of Piracy
Sentence for the guilty: execution	Sentence for the guilty: execution
Trials generally limited to England	Trials could take place in England as well as its colonies, ships, and other outposts
Grand jury indictment, petit jury verdict	Commission indictment and verdict
Locally selected juries, no special requirements (for versions of the law passed in the colonies, such as the Jamaica Pirate Act)	Commission members limited to state officials and merchants who had to swear that they had no financial stake in the trial
Applied only to robbery and murder at sea	Expanded the definition of piracy to include those who supported pirates and received their goods and mutiny for the purpose of taking a merchant ship
No positive or negative inducements for compliance	Provided for rewards to seamen who resisted mutinies and pirate attacks; threatened the revocation of the charters of colonies that did not implement the law

Note: The new law and the old operated concurrently, with trials in London continuing under the old system.

law created sweeping new powers. Because the only statutory punishment for piracy was execution, the new legal framework created an extraordinary formulation of interpretation and violence under English law: the execution of an English subject by a colonial court on the basis of a legal classification applied by an appointed commission without the benefit of a jury.[27]

The act brought into existence the basic legal structure used to persecute piracy over the following years, though efforts to modify and tinker with its provisions continued over the next two decades. The act expired within seven years. It was renewed for five more years by 5 Anne, c. 34, in 1706, and again in the second year of the reign of George I. Apparently by accident, An Act for the More Effectual Suppression of Piracy lapsed for a time around 1717, but a clarification of the law in 4 George I, c. 11, which gave the special piracy courts the option of using the legal procedures of 28 Henry VIII, c. 15, appears to have covered this legal gap; only one high-profile trial, that of Stede Bonnet, pursued this alternative procedure that

The Classification of Pirates | 99

required the use of a jury. Finally, 8 George I, c. 24, in 1721 extended the jurisdiction of piracy courts to encompass accomplices as well as principals, and it made permanent the legal structure introduced by the 1700 act.

LAW, CONSTITUTION, AND CULTURAL STRUCTURE

One of the more important factors shaping the English response to piracy is the nature of the legal obstacles English state agents encountered in their efforts to crack down on the problem: why and how those obstacles of legal meaning making were binding on their efforts, and why they ended up with the particular legal solution of the Act for the More Effectual Suppression of Piracy of 1700. In this section, I will argue that the answer to both these questions lies in the deep cultural structures within which English legal and constitutional questions were considered, contested, and made sense of.

The process of legal change described above occurred in a profoundly meaningful field of political relations known keenly by contemporaries as the question of constitution. The basic questions of constitution involve the existing state powers and their relation to one another. These constitutional questions were sites of strategic action where various constituencies sought to pursue their interests, as we saw with the role of the East India Company in lobbying for piracy law reform in the late 1690s, for example. But of equal and distinct analytical importance is that these questions were also negotiated in a structured field of historically contingent but strongly established meanings. In the case of piracy, attention to these meaning structures has important analytical benefits. We can better explain the twists and turns of piracy law reform, and the efforts of state agents to create the political-structural tools for imposing order on private maritime violence, if we analyze them as political struggles structured by the relations of meaning characterizing the constitutional principle of the rule of law (Reid 2004). Indeed, the classification struggles over piracy described above were not primarily between anti- and pro-piracy contingents but rather among members of the broad antipiracy/imperial consolidation constituency; they turned on how the new judicial powers could be reconciled with the rule of law as a deep principle of the emergent imperial constitution (Benton 2002, 253–65). Struggles over practical coercive power were of necessity struggles over semiotics.

The principle of the rule of law was a constant theme in the struggles over the English constitution and state power during the seventeenth century. These efforts peaked at the time of the Glorious Revolution, a constitutional struggle between, as Pincus argues, the rival political programs of Catholic, absolutist modernity championed by James II and the bureaucratic, participatory modernity of the revolutionaries (2009). Already by the time of the revolution, however, the legal field had developed as a significantly autonomous center of state interpretive power. While the king was nominally the "head of the judicial system," as Gray writes, "by firmly rooted usage he was foreclosed from sitting judicially in person" (2004, lxiii). But the revolution marked a conclusive victory for the restriction of the sort of absolute, prerogative, and personal sovereign power advocated throughout the century by the Stuart kings in favor of a legally mediated constitutional monarchy (Raffield 2004, 5). These questions of the place of law in the English constitution reverberated through the colonies and were themselves transformed by the colonial context, especially by the problems raised by geography and the high degree of variability in social orders and circumstances between the colonies and England as well as among the colonies themselves.

As government by license gave way to more direct relations of rule between metropole and colonies, one of the most important ways that actors resolved these questions of imperial constitution was through the legal concept of repugnancy (Bilder 2008). The idea of repugnancy took as its starting point that the common law, as a derivation of inherent, natural law, traveled with English subjects to the colonies. But statutes did not automatically do so. The colonies were possessions of the Crown, and thus it was the prerogative of the Crown to govern them. Parliamentary laws, unless otherwise specified, did not apply, though there were a number of mechanisms through which the main body of English law was imported in practice (Brown 1963). The general framework of the relationship made colonies responsible for creating their own laws to meet their diverse needs, so long as those laws were not repugnant to—that is to say, in contradiction of or in direct conflict with—the laws of England. The doctrine of repugnancy thus provided both a freedom for colonial bodies to legislate as well as a limit to what laws they could pass. Repugnancy was judged by various bodies, but the Privy Council played the central role in determining whether a colonial law violated the laws of England in some respect, for example through the arrogation of powers not included in their commissions. In conjunction with this constitutional framework, as Bilder argues, through the seventeenth century "transatlantic legal culture" (2008, 3) came to play a critical role in maintaining the coherence of imperial law, with significant movement of texts, legal literates, and judgments across the Atlantic instantiating a loose interpretive infrastructure itself, more general than the one involving piracy, that provided a common body of signs and legal meaning-making procedures which made questions of politics and constitution more commensurable throughout the empire.

Through the seventeenth century as the empire centralized, in a distinct but complementary movement it also legalized. The rule of law became embedded in the constitution of the empire as one of its fundamental meaning systems. What is meant by *rule of law* in this context is, "the belief that law ought to rule over governor and governed alike . . . the rule of law requires . . . recognition and enforcement of basic rights inhering to the individual in his relations with the state. It denies arbitrary power to the government by requiring that no person be made to suffer in body or goods unless by regular legal process. It requires equality of treatment, in the sense that every man is subject to the ordinary law of the land and to the jurisdiction of ordinary courts" (RHC 1960, 1001). In practice, political and legal power in the seventeenth- and eighteenth-century English Empire only approximated this ideal. Nonetheless, the rule of law was sufficiently entrenched as a constitutional principle that actors who sought new legal powers needed to embed those new formulations into the existing structure of legal meanings. The rule of law was a potent interpretive reality in struggles over the imperial constitution, if not always a judicial reality. Legal authority was an entirely constructed social power, but it was a power deeply embedded throughout the institutions of the state, in the moral intuitions of the populace, and in the state-society relations of the constitution. Even the king's power to create new courts, as Gray writes, was not infinite (2004, lvii). By the end of the seventeenth century and the struggles over Stuart absolutism, the law had become the pragmatic and symbolic center of legitimate, sovereign, interpretive power for matters involving the life, death, and property of rights-bearing Englishmen throughout the empire.

Another aspect of the rule of law that likewise shaped legal reforms was that the authority of the law relied on systematized approaches to legal hermeneutics (i.e., legal interpretation). Legal judgments exercised authoritative interpretive power only insofar as they were *legal* judgments, integrated into the existing system of legal meanings and legal performances through the interpretive acts of legal actors. Legal hermeneutics is essentially a demarcation of the translation point where people synthesize the codified, transsituational elements of the law with the details of the case or matter under consideration in a specific situational context of judgment. It involves, in other words, both codified classification rituals and the performance of those procedures in specific interpretive instances. In Peircean semiotic terms, it captures the process whereby actors associate legal signs with objects, people, relations, entities, or other aspects of the world and through that associative representation generate (or at least hope to generate) a pragmatic effect such as a fine or a jail sentence. Achieving this translation, doing it happily, as Austin (1976) puts it, putting forward "a version of the world that works" (Douglas 1986, 62) in law-related settings, often demands significant semiotic expertise. The authority of the law in seventeenth-century England, for instance, depended on the complex web of relations between traditions, jurisprudence, statutes, precedents, derivation, ceremonies, roles, records, procedures, parcellized powers, contending legal bodies and organizations, and aesthetics. Together these elements constituted the law as a cultural system and an institutionalized formulation of social power; legal hermeneutics involves the representation of the world in terms of these codified relations in a way that leads to some desired outcome.

For explaining the trajectory of piracy law reform, the most significant aspect of the structure of early modern legal hermeneutics was one of its primordial "principles of vision and division" (Bourdieu 1985, 726): jurisdiction. The English legal system, from which imperial legal structures emerged, was an inherently jurisdictional project. The system was structured as a "congeries of quite distinct courts" (Gray 2004, viii), and the principles of jurisdiction brought order to this complex assemblage of powers, procedures, and institutions. The many common law courts were at the center of the legal system, but multiple distinct ecclesiastical courts and courts of equity, as well as the admiralty courts, all had significant and active jurisdictions. In addition to these national jurisdictions, a multitude of local courts also existed, each with their own procedures. Within each of these broad areas were many finer jurisdictional divisions, resulting in a great number of distinct institutional manifestations of interpretive legal powers. This many courts meant great potential for conflict. The principles of jurisdiction sought to order this complexity, or at least to organize the field of battle for the partisans of different jurisdictions to fight out who would ultimately decide.

Jurisdiction is essentially a definition of the geographical and topical scope of legal powers (Cormack 2007, 1; Ford 1999). The renowned English jurist Edward Coke provided this definition in 1606: "Jurisdiction is the authority of adjudicating or stating the law between parties concerning actions of persons and matters, according as they are brought to judgment, by ordinary or delegated authority."[28] Jurisdiction, following Coke, is the authority to decide, the procedural and legal-semiotic forms of that authority, and its spatial and topical limits. Not merely a desiccated and technical legal discourse (though it is also that), the creation of jurisdiction involves the arrangement and demarcation of powerful politico-legal meanings (Benton 1999, 2001, 2010). Jurisdiction is a system of signification that constructs a meaningful boundary around a particular topic or place and constructively asserts certain interpretive powers and procedures within that boundary. A jurisdiction is thus a construction of meaning that asserts a limitation on a given power (Mukerji 2011, 227), but by the same token constitutes and legitimizes those powers within the boundary it defines. As a discourse, then (Ford 1999, 855), a well-defined jurisdiction creates a language for both claiming certain powers of coordination linked to a set of procedural parameters and contesting those powers through a definition of their limit. Coke's introduction to his 1606 volume on jurisdiction speaks to the dual constitutive and limiting nature of the principle of jurisdiction. He writes evocatively of what is at stake in matters of jurisdiction, and so I quote him at length:

> Of Jurisdictions some be ecclesiasticall, and some civill, or temporall; of both these some be primitive, or ordinary without commission, some derivative, or delegate by commission. Of all these, some be of record, and some not of record, some to enquire, hear, and determine, some to enquire only, some guided by one law, some by another, the bounds of all and every severall courts being most necessary to be known. For as the body of man is best ordered, when every particular member exerciseth his proper duty, so the body of the common wealth is best governed, when every severall court of justice executeth his proper jurisdiction. But if the eie, whose duty is to see, the hand, to work, the feet, to goe, shall usurp, and incroach one upon anothers work, as for example, the hands or feet, the office of the eie to see, and the like, these should assuredly produce disorder, and darknesse, and bring the whole body out of order, and in the end to distruction. So in the common wealth (justice being the main preserver thereof) if one court should usurp, or incroach upon another, it would introduce incertainty, subvert justice, and bring all things in the end to confusion.[29]

The language and logic of Coke's discussion of jurisdiction speak not only to its dual creation and restriction of interpretive authority but also of the complex English legal field it structured. A staggering number of distinct institutions made up the English judicial system, and the importance of questions of jurisdiction, as Coke suggests, derives from the constant threat of legal confusion.[30]

Another important feature of jurisdictional claims, following Ford (1999, 852–53), is that they order the territory to which they refer by constituting it as a legal abstraction, homogeneously conceived. At this purely symbolic level, then, jurisdictional claims can be perfectly systematic, with definite, conceptually ordered boundaries; and so long as the principles of abstraction constituting different jurisdictions—for instance the high seas, ecclesiastical matters, Massachusetts, matters where justice may be subverted if the law is exactly applied—are organized appropriately, they can coexist in perfectly bewildering complexity and perfectly orderly rationality simultaneously. In the practical exercise of these jurisdictions, such order is of course constantly in question. Thus, as a cultural structure governing real-world relations, with matters of life, death, and property at stake, jurisdictional questions can become preeminent locations where struggles over legal and state interpretive power occur. The sort of struggle over the structure of political authority that Benton identifies as "jurisdictional politics" (1999, 2001) could, in a more general sense, be understood as a situation of semiotic politics, where struggles over political authority take the form of struggles over the matrices of signification that determine the contours of interpretive infrastructures.

These questions of the actual exercise of authority within a legal jurisdiction bring us to the question of the procedures, traditions, doctrines, precedents, and other elements of legal hermeneutics that were so central to English law as an interpretive infrastructure. The powers that jurisdiction defines are not generic but specifically tied to particular interpretive procedures, practices, performances, and systems of meaning. They are grounded in and created through legal hermeneutics. Actions within the interpretive framework of a given jurisdiction are on the strongest footing in the attempt to wield the power of that jurisdiction, while actions that seek to wield jurisdictionally specific powers beyond the pale of the semiotic boundaries of that jurisdiction are most vulnerable to challenge.

John Deane's case proves instructive here. Consider again the admiralty judge Sir Richard Lloyd's opinion of the trial that Governor Vaughan had conducted in Jamaica. The Lords of Trade asked Lloyd's "opinion whether the trial and condemnation of John Deane for piracy by Lord Vaughan, as Vice-Admiral to his Royal Highness in Jamaica, can be justified by law, [and] also what has been the practise of the High Court of Admiralty here before the Statutes of 27 & 28 Hen. VIII. and since as to the trial of pirates." Lloyd's opinion was that "Lord Vaughan has not regularly proceeded in said trial and condemnation. . . . Pirates and sea rovers . . . are to be tried criminally according to the prescribed form and the practise in such cases."[31] The focus of this exchange is on the procedures that Vaughan used in relation to the jurisdictional power to try pirates, both before and after 28 Henry VIII, c. 15. The interpretive power that Vaughan claimed, according to Lloyd, was based on fundamentally flawed legal hermeneutics, given Vaughan's position in relation to the jurisdiction over piracy that existed in the legal structure of the English state. Vaughan had purported to exercise a power he did not have using a procedure that, untethered from legal codes and the jurisdictional structure of English law, did not work. Despite his claims to the contrary, he had not produced an authoritative legal interpretation, and its further propagation was stymied.

The challenge faced by state agents intent on creating a legal apparatus to classify and thus coerce pirates was not just a struggle to respond to the challenge of producing legal powers across vast geographical distances at a sufficient scale to create a credible threat of legal sanction. Those were real problems. But because the powers they sought to create were legal powers, the semiotic problems of jurisdiction and legal hermeneutics posed their own set of no less practical problems of meaning. The structured sign systems of jurisdiction, procedure, precedent, tradition, and law provided the structure of meanings within which legal actors understood themselves to wield authoritative and legitimate interpretive power. These limitations of legal power were also its source, and their structure shaped the legal reform process.[32]

The limitations of this sort experienced by English state agents in the later seventeenth century had their roots in the sixteenth century and earlier. The 1536 piracy law, Act for Punishment of Pirates and Robbers of the Sea, made jurisdiction over piracy the exclusive province of a court commissioned "under the Kinges greate Seale directed to the Admyrall . . . and to 3 or 4 other such substanciall persons."[33] This framework derived from the perception by state agents at the time of Henry VIII of their own dilemma of jurisdiction and procedure relating to piracy. The 1536 act stripped jurisdiction over piracy from the admiral acting in his capacity as admiral and instead gave it to the admiral as the head of a commissioned court appointed under the Great Seal because, as the preamble to the act explains, "pirotes [and those who commit other crimes] upon the see, many times escape unpunysshed because the trial of their offences has heretofore ben ordered, judged, and determined before the Admyrall . . . after the course of the civile laws." The problem the act sought to correct was that legal powers over piracy were within the traditional jurisdiction of the admiralty and thus constituted through the civil law procedures of that court. The mechanism utilized in the act to address this situation was to invest jurisdiction over piracy in the new, royally commissioned court and to specify that the court should proceed against pirates "in like

106 | CHAPTER FOUR

fourme and condicion as if any such offence or offences had ben comytted or done in or upon the lande"—that is to say, to try pirates according to the procedures of the common law.[34]

One of the effects of this act, unforeseen in a precolonial context, was to concentrate the more effective procedures for trying pirates that it introduced and the jurisdiction over piracy to a single court. And while the admiral presided over the court, it was not a Court of Admiralty, and thus the jurisdiction over piracy and the procedures it specified did not travel, as some contemporaries expected, with the admiralty powers. This confusion emerged in 1676 with the trial of Deane in the Jamaican vice admiralty court on the theory that the vice admiralty inherently had jurisdiction over piracy. The "solution" to the rejection of that theory by Lloyd was to issue commissions of oyer and terminer to colonial governors,[35] the commissions to form courts of the sort contemplated by 28 Henry VIII, c. 15. When the Lords of Trade solicited the opinion of the King's Counsel on the oyer and terminer maneuver in 1684, those powers were again rejected. The King's Counsel held that in the first place, the jurisdiction of the vice admirals, an office typically held by colonial governors, was exclusively over noncapital maritime cases, never to include capital crimes such as piracy. Such crimes were, in a general sense, only within the jurisdictional power of properly constituted admiralty courts. If properly constituted colonial admiralty courts wanted to try piracy, however, their only legal option was to use the civil law procedures that predated 28 Henry VIII, c. 15. According to the King's Counsel, "The statute of 28 Henry VIII for trial of [piracy] . . . doth not extend to the Plantations, and so no Commission can be granted thither upon that law."[36] The oyer and terminer option thus foundered on the precise legal semiotics of jurisdiction and procedure. It was apparently in ignorance of these developments of the 1670s and 1680s that some thought the 1696 Navigation Act that made properly established admiralty courts in the colonies necessary for enforcement of the laws of trade would provide a legal infrastructure for trying piracy. As in these other cases, however, this hope hung on the incorrect understanding of jurisdiction over piracy with common law procedure as part of the general jurisdiction of the admiral. But the legal changes that created this new formulation of jurisdiction and procedure took jurisdiction over piracy away from the admiralty, and so the new colonial admiralty courts had no such powers.[37]

The two successful legal remedies, the 1681 Jamaica Piracy Act (successful in the sense of creating an acceptable formulation of jurisdiction, procedure, and thus legal authority—but a failure as the foundation for an imperial antipiracy policy for the reasons described above) and the

1700 Act for the More Effectual Suppression of Piracy, also turned on the same issues of the cultural structure of law. Jamaica itself had a certain sovereign legal power in the seventeenth-century imperial constitution. It could make laws, including criminal laws, and apply penalties, up to and including execution, insofar as such efforts were not repugnant to the laws of England. The Jamaica Piracy Act of 1681, as well as the similar acts passed in several other colonies, avoided the pitfalls of jurisdiction and procedure by creating a locally authorized jurisdiction over piracy that was to proceed, as the 1684 Connecticut Act put it, "as if such offence had been committed . . . upon the land." In addition, the governor could call a special Court of Assistants that "shall have full power to doe all things in and about the inquiry, heareing, determining, adjudging and punishing of any of the crimes and offences afoarsayd, as any commissioners to be appointed under the great seale of England by vertue of [28 Henry VIII, c. 15] are impowered to doe."[38] In effect, these laws constituted local courts whose powers were defined as those of the specially commissioned courts of oyer and terminer that heard piracy trials in England. But whereas 28 Henry VIII, c. 15, was considered not to extend to the colonies, preventing the establishment there of piracy tribunals under this law, the creation of a local version, with a local jurisdiction over piracy linked to the precise procedures of the English courts, was a perfectly acceptable formulation of sovereignty, jurisdiction, and legal hermeneutics. Balky colonies and pirate-sympathizing juries remained fatal flaws for this strategy, though.

The 1700 Act for the More Effectual Suppression of Piracy also achieved a formulation of sovereignty, jurisdiction, and hermeneutics that legal actors saw as successfully embedded in and consistent with English legal structure. It did so, however, in a more radical way: through a fundamental transformation of both the structure of piracy jurisdiction and the procedures associated with that jurisdiction. The 1700 law emerges from the conclusion by contemporaries that the basic structure of piracy jurisdiction and procedure posed insurmountable obstacles to their efforts to craft a legal mechanism for policing piracy in a global empire. It was on these codified shoals of jurisdiction and procedure, performed as real constraints of the legal system by elites strongly invested in that system and deeply interested in both the distributional and coordinating consequences of changes to legal codes, that the many reform schemes of the later seventeenth century had foundered. Only by convincing Parliament to specifically take up the structure of piracy law were contemporaries able to revisit the foundational principles of jurisdiction and procedure. What emerged was a new arrangement of jurisdiction and hermeneutics within the broader interpretive horizon demarcated as the rule of law.

While the 1700 act fundamentally reorganized jurisdiction over piracy, it is important to note that even this radical approach itself took place in a legal field structured by a plethora of legal powers, each with their own institutions, practices, and constituencies. The new jurisdiction over piracy was not written onto a blank slate. The scope of the act is defined first by the crime it seeks to regulate, and here the new jurisdiction is consonant with the geographical scope of the admiralty jurisdiction in general and with the jurisdiction specified by 28 Henry VIII, c. 15. The powers of the 1700 act cover "all piracies, felonies, and robberies committed in or upon the sea, or in any haven, river, creeke, or place where the Admirall or Admiralls have power, authority, or jurisdiction."[39] But then the 1700 act introduces this jurisdictional innovation: "[the aforesaid crimes] may be examined, inquired of, tried, heard and determined, and adjudged according to the directions of this Act in any place at sea or upon the land in any of his Majesties islands, plantations, colonies, dominions, forts, or factories to be appointed for that purpose by the King's Commission." This language was central to the success of the act, because it "parcellized" (Adams 2007, 67) the power to authoritatively interpret piracy—that is, made it a form of power that could be exercised with at least some autonomy by state agents on the periphery rather than reserving it to actors and entities more central to the system of power. In doing so, the act created the foundation for an interpretive infrastructure that could be constituted in all parts of the empire with a clear, statute-mediated connection to ancient, sovereign, and authoritative state powers. A court with the jurisdictional power to hear piracy cases could now exist anywhere in the empire that the king and his advisers wanted one to exist. The new act represented a fully imperial understanding of legal power, in opposition, for example, to the piecemeal approach to piracy law of ineffectually demanding that each colony pass and enforce similar legal provisions for trying pirates. Another radical point of the act, and another point where it departed from both the piecemeal Jamaica Act strategy and the strategy of Henry VIII based on the common law, is that it gave the ultimate interpretive power in the new jurisdiction to seven-person commissions, appointed by the king and his agents.

The achievement of the new law was not the recruitment of more sailors, the arming of more ships, or the building of more gallows. It created new powers by finally solving the semiotic knot made of jurisdiction, the different sources and procedural requirements of different legal powers, and the geography of interpretive power. Notably, this knot was entirely of English state agents' (and their predecessors') own making. In a purely behavioral sense, there was nothing to prevent them from collectively abandoning the constructed fictions that bound them. As a sociological matter, though, what bound them and what constituted and coordinated them were of a piece, and could not so blithely be discarded. Finally, though, with the Act for the More Effectual Suppression of Piracy they had finessed the knot and created a parcellized and distributed power to classify pirates that had the reach and scale to match the threat while remaining grounded, as contemporary legal and political elites saw it, in the legitimating scope of the law.

CHAPTER FIVE
Guns, Gallows, and Interpretive Infrastructures

The interpretive infrastructure constructed to combat piracy involved more than just a new law. The interpretive powers created by this newly codified legal structure only mattered when they were translated into social situations in a way that remade dynamics of power. This chapter conceptualizes the translation of semiotic structures and codes, such as those supplied by the new legal framework, into situations as social performances. Through social performances, actors make claims about the meaning of the situation that they are in. They define situations and explicitly or implicitly assert meaningful relationships within each situation and between the situation and other contexts of action and significance. They do so not in the abstract but through situated action, flesh and blood, voice and breath. It is only ever through such situated, meaning-oriented interactions—be they in Boston, Westminster, or an encounter between ships in lonely reaches of water far from any immediate involvement of outsiders—that institutional models become concrete social realities. Different social performances will have different conditions of success or failure. In the case of piracy, the most significant way to assess the success or failure of interpretive legal performances is by looking at their effects on the actions of others. Creating coordinated social power, including coordinated powers of force and violence, requires that a performance causes a chain of ratifying, enforcing, and propagating social performances by other actors (guards, for instance, who actually guard an accused pirate rather than facilitate a jailbreak). The question this chapter examines is how these chains binding the text of law to guns and gallows on the colonial periphery were activated to make legal powers of classification real.

THE THEATER STATE IN THE EARLY EIGHTEENTH-CENTURY ENGLISH MARITIME WORLD

To follow the dynamics and drama involved in bringing this new interpretive infrastructure into being, it is important to remember that English state agents were acting in situations shaped by constraints and affordances, and that those patterns of possibility were structured by heterogeneous forces, from travel times and naval deployments to semiotic structures and the limits of social performance. To conceptualize the significance of these heterogeneous affordances and constraints as sociocultural realities with a sociological density and inertia, a realism embedded in beliefs, patterns of action, records, rituals, and supporting institutions, it is useful to recall Geertz's analysis of Negara, "the theater state in nineteenth century Bali," noted in chapter 1. Geertz writes:

> That Balinese politics, like everyone else's, including ours, was symbolic action does not imply, therefore, that it was all in the mind or consisted entirely of dances and incense. The aspects of that politics here reviewed—exemplary ceremonial, model-and-copy hierarchy, expressive competition, and iconic kingship; organizational pluralism, particulate loyalty, dispersive authority, and confederate rule—configurated a reality as dense and immediate as the island itself. . . . [The people] who made their way through this reality—building palaces, drafting treaties, collecting rents, leasing trade, making marriages, dispatching rivals, investing temples, erecting pyres, hosting feasts, and imaging gods—were pursuing the ends they could conceive through the means they had. The dramas of the theatre state, mimetic of themselves, were, in the end, neither illusions nor lies, neither sleight of hand nor make-believe. They were what there was. (1981, 136)

In considering this pomp and aesthetic display, Geertz enjoins the reader to think of these elements not as decorative overlays atop the real instantiations of state power. Rather, he argues, they were the form of power that existed, and their power was inseparable from their decorative manifestation. It was not power that came into the world in some fanciful way; the manifestation *constituted* the power because its aesthetic form, its semiotic significance, provided the framework of coordination that social power always depends on. The elaborate rituals and adornments of Negara were how that power worked there. "They were what there was," and anyone seeking to actuate, change, or otherwise interact with state power could only work with and through what existed. The cultural forms of state power have an autonomous reality that must be negotiated to be made manifest or to be remade.

To be sure, not all of Geertz's argument is generalizable. In his account, the particularity of the nineteenth-century Balinese theater state is that Balinese state agents elevated the theatricality of pomp above their other interests and made aesthetics the point of state power. "The stupendous cremations, tooth filings, temple dedications, pilgrimages, and blood sacrifices, mobilizing hundreds and even thousands of people and great quantities of wealth, were not means to political ends: they were the ends themselves, they were what the state was for. Court ceremonialism was the driving force of court politics; and mass ritual was not a device to shore up the state, but rather the state, even in its final gasp, was a device for the enactment of mass ritual. Power served pomp, not pomp power" (Geertz 1981, 13). This accentuation of the spectacular makes Negara good for theorizing. But to generalize its model, we do not need to ascribe the ascent of the aesthetic over other interests to all systems of state power. Rather, the general point to be drawn from the spectacular particularity of the *negara* is that state power—indeed, social power generally—always has a form, and the aesthetic and cultural forms that power takes in a given time and place, austere or intricate, baroque or bureaucratic, are what power there is and how it works. And that the forms power takes have consequences that need focused attention.

PIRATES AND PROCEDURES

One way to think of measures like the 1700 Act for the More Effectual Suppression of Piracy is that it attempted to increase the success rate of attempts by authorized state agents to classify people as pirates and to punish them. It did so by creating a formalized set of conditions for what Austin (1976) calls a "happy" performance, a performance that succeeds. To use Alexander's term for this, an important part of the power of the law lay in its facilitation of "fusion" between codified semiotic relations and specific situated circumstances, reshaping the situation in line with the signs. It is through this fusion that social performances become "convincing and effective—more ritual-like" (Alexander 2004, 529). So long as the specified procedures were followed in the specified way by the specified people at the specified places and times with the specified speech and action occurring, the law's guiding expectation demanded, the classification asserted was an authoritative legal interpretation that should be ratified and propagated by other state agents. Or so the procedure promised, in any case.

At the most fundamental level, the efficacy of the new piracy law as a means of actuating chains of propagating social performances depended on the emergence and widespread acceptance of an understanding of law as constituting a legitimate interpretive power. Shapiro argues that the courtroom in early modern England became a central site of "knowledge making" where "juries, judges, witnesses, and counsel participated in a process that was designed to produce 'morally certain' verdicts. . . . By following certain procedures, using written documents of specified types, listening to witness testimony produced by certain kinds of persons and under certain conditions, and considering 'circumstances,' 'judges of the fact' were able to produce just and true knowledge" (Shapiro 2003, 30). Courts, in this sense, operated as epistemic authorities able to authoritatively wield classifications. Importantly, this understanding of the law as a site of true knowledge making spread throughout the empire (Benton 2002, 31–79) as a foundational aspect of a "transatlantic legal culture" (Bilder 2008, 3).

The emergence of the overarching cultural significance of legal procedure as a way to create true knowledge and to assert classifications that were real in their consequences provided the ground on which the 1700 Act for the More Effectual Suppression of Piracy operated. The main thing that the law did was to establish a radical new procedure for colonial courts authorized to exercise jurisdiction over piracy. Procedure, as discussed in the previous chapter, plays an important role in legal institutions as a key part of the interpretive infrastructure that they create. It supplies a model of the semiotically consequential things differently situated actors can do within a particular legal setting (demarcated by jurisdiction). Maneuvers like writs, pleadings, legal fictions, witness questioning, and oaths, all parts of a broader framework of procedure, can be helpfully understood as moves that obtain meaning with reference to a codified horizon of law. It is also good to keep in mind that such maneuvers purport to do something within a specified legal process: giving a right, making a claim, establishing a parameter for decision-making, eliciting speech that counts as evidence, ascertaining truth, or doing some other significant thing. Viewed more broadly, procedure specifies a possibility space for legal performative action within a particular legal setting by mapping pathways for activating and associating the legal categories constituting that setting's "imaginative universe" (Geertz 1977b, 13). Procedure supplies codified answers to the question, paraphrasing Alexander, of what paths can be taken and what meanings can be projected in a constructed legal universe (Alexander 2004, 550). However arcane or arbitrary they may appear, it is useful to remember that the adornments of the theater state are not merely decorative. Their specificity is how power is constituted.

The procedures supplied by the 1700 piracy act created a framework for specified state agents to use to enact social performances that intervened into the meaning structure of the social world. The procedures created by the law fused practice and meaning in order to claim epistemic authority. They had the potential, in a wide range of situations, to directly link certain actors, classifications, and claims to the legitimizing force of the law and to the practical powers associated with efficacious coordination. In this sense, procedure introduced both the moral power of the law (legitimization) and its practical power (coordination) as salient matrices of meaning; procedure provided actors with a language to performatively assert that a given situation was a piracy situation, thus a situation where interpretations of social meaning were fused with other state and social powers such as powers of arrest, the issuance of warrants, command over militias, and the power to execute. To note again the guiding perspective of this argument, it is important to think about procedures like this not just as bureaucratic instructions, or just as classification rituals imbued with significance, but as models for performing a significant classification ritual that because of its location in a web of institutional meanings becomes the linchpin for coordinated action chains and the coordinated production of a specific, directed, and brutal violence.

The new procedures marked a radical break from the procedures of the Act for Punishment of Pirates and Robbers of the Sea of 1536 as well as from those specified by the Jamaica Act of 1681 and its imitators. The 1700 piracy act, 11&12 William III, c. 7, begins with perhaps its most important innovation, the expansion of jurisdiction over piracy to special courts in the plantations: "all piracies . . . may be examined, inquired of, tried, heard and determined, and adjudged . . . in any place . . . to be appointed for that purpose by the King's commission . . . under the Great Seal of England."[1] Those commissions were to be issued to vice admirals, admirals, officers, and governors throughout the British Empire. They asserted the power of commissioners to issue warrants for taking pirates into custody and to assemble a Court of Admiralty as required to try pirates. The courts were to have a minimum of seven commissioners. If a sufficient number commissioned under the Great Seal could not be assembled, then three duly appointed commissioners would "have full power and authority, by virtue of this Act, to call and assemble any other persons on ship-board, or upon the land, to make up the number of seven." Those so assembled could not, however, be just anyone. The law specifies that only "merchants, factors, planters . . . captains, lieutenants . . . masters, mates" and other such worthies would do.

The core powers of the law are contained in section 4. It is through

Guns, Gallows, and Interpretive Infrastructures | 115

this paragraph that the act asserts the performative powers of the body it contemplates. Through the authority of the king and Parliament, the act gives duly constituted commissions

> full power and authority, according to the course of the admiralty, to issue warrants for bringing any persons accused of piracy or robbery, before them to be tried, heard, and judged; and to summon witnesses, and to take informations and examinations of witnesses upon their oath; and to do all things necessary for the hearing and final determination of any case of piracy . . . and to give sentence and judgment of death . . . according to the civil law, and the methods and rules of the admiralty.

The act goes on to elaborate the procedures for the exercise of these new powers in greater detail than was provided under the 1536 piracy act.

At the outset of a trial, the new law required that the king's commission be read aloud[2] and that all members of the commission were to swear an oath, the precise text of which is included in the act, to honestly and impartially execute the king's commission. They would then issue a warrant to have the accused "formally brought before them" so that the Register of the Court (one of three court offices specified by the law) could read the indictment. The indictment, specifying "the particular fact or facts of piracy . . . with the time and place when and where, and in what manner it was committed," was of particular importance, because it at least nominally ensured that the prosecution would need to provide evidence for specific criminal actions, potentially limiting the use of circumstantial evidence or the introduction of evidence for additional crimes during the trial. The accused were then required by the act to plead guilty or not guilty, with a refusal to plead amounting to a confession.[3] If the accused entered a not guilty plea, then the Register of the Court would produce the witnesses, who would be sworn and questioned in open court by the prosecution, with only oral testimony permissible.[4] The restriction of the written testimony that was standard in noncriminal admiralty proceedings was necessary to ensure that the accused had the opportunity, provided by the act, to cross-examine witnesses. During the cross-examination the witness remained under oath, a critical concession. In this period of early modern English law, cross-examination was becoming increasingly important as a means for challenging the reliability of testimony, but oaths were the more ancient way of ensuring that witnesses were properly motivated to tell the truth (Hill 1968; Langbein 1983). Only the testimony of a sworn witness counted as evidence, and so the defendant's right to cross-examine a sworn witness was important.[5] The cross-examination was not direct, however, and instead the accused would pose their questions to the President of the Court (a second of the three specified court officers), who would ask it of the witness. After the witnesses had been examined, the accused had the opportunity to offer a closing statement, though as they were not under oath they were not technically able to provide evidence on their own behalf, only arguments.

The court would then debate the charges in private, and then the President of the Court would "collect all the votes of the persons who do sit and have voices in the said court, beginning at the junior first, and ending with himself." If a majority of commissioners voted in favor of the judgment, it would be publicly announced. The only penalty the statute contemplates for piracy is death. "The person or persons attainted shall be executed and put to death, at such time, in such manner, and in such place upon the sea, or within the ebbing or flowing thereof, as the President or major part of the court, by warrant directed to a Provost Marshal [the third of the court officers] (which the President or said major part shall have power to constitute) shall appoint."[6] The act then goes on to specify the president's power to appoint the Register of the Court if the commissioned register is unavailable, as well as the latter's record-keeping duties, including the responsibility to keep the minutes of trials and to regularly send information on trials to the High Court of Admiralty in London.

The second half of the Act for the More Effectual Suppression of Piracy sets about expanding the category of piracy to include English subjects who served under foreign commissions, those who engaged in mutiny or violence against ships' captains, and those who aided pirates.[7] Section 14 of the act speaks directly to the expectation that classifications made in this way would be propagated by state agents, requiring "that all and every Governor and Governors, person and persons in authority in the said colonies and plantations . . . shall assist the Commissioners . . . in doing their duty, and also in the execution of such warrants and otherwise, and shall deliver up . . . any pirates . . . and their confederates and accessories." Given the widespread belief that charter and proprietary colonies in particular provided support for piracy, section 15 follows up on the demands of section 14 that the powers asserted by the act be treated as real by threatening to revoke the charters of colonies that fail to comply.

SCRIPTS AND TRANSLATIONS

In this view, procedure is a classification ritual—a routinized model for activating the signs, sign-relations, and chains of propagation that define meaning making in particular legal domains. The procedures just described define those processes at a level of general legal abstraction. They define things like who could do what, when they could do it, what categories of meaning mattered to the course of the trial, and what kind of evidence could be heard. The generality of the model that procedure provides leaves a further gap to bridge between piracy as a codified semiotic-legal category—the procedure for classifying pirates established in a general sense—and what people on the spot in the concrete situations and circumstances where those procedures needed to be performed should actually do.

This was a particularly important gap in the case of the creation of a new interpretive infrastructure for defining and punishing pirates. By design, the new law of 1700 enabled people to conduct these trials who had little experience with piracy law, civil law, admiralty law, or sometimes even the law in general. One of the main innovations of the act was the parcellization of state powers of interpretation over piracy, which meant that people in far-flung reaches of the empire would be using these powers to interpret authoritatively. Because of their location in the colonial periphery, they would not be immersed in a dense, high-volume metropolitan legal culture to pick up the implicit performative elements associated with legal-procedural moves, and they could not easily request help or guidance on what to do. It was to bridge this gap that English state agents developed a script for those authorized to try pirates under the 1700 Act for the More Effectual Suppression of Piracy. The script told them what to say and do to enact the classificatory procedures established by the law. It laid out the main path through the universe of procedural possibilities established by the act's legal framework for achieving the legal classification of pirates.

One of the first things that the Board of Trade did after the passage of the law was to send George Larkin, "he being a person well versed in the civill law & proceedings of the Court of Admiralty," to the colonies so that he "might instruct the other Commissioners in the most proper methods and accordingly settle the former for the holding of these courts."[8] The board instructed Larkin to travel to Newfoundland and then to Massachusetts, New York, Maryland, Virginia, the Leeward Islands, Barbados, and Jamaica; in each place, he was to leave duplicates of the commissions for these piracy courts. Larkin also "settled the forms of tryals for pirates and left such directions relating to those tryals in the hand of the proper officer there, that there could be no error in the proceedings and such pirates as may be taken in those parts."[9] The document that Larkin left with the various commissioners in the colonies whom he instructed on the proper forms of the new trials is a literal script (Alexander 2004, 550). It specifies the forms of oaths that commissioners and witnesses were to take, the form of the various written warrants that might be needed for a trial, the precise order in which actions must occur (reading commissions, then the oath, then the warrant for the witness, and so on, as specified in the 1700 law and described above). It also specifies the form that the indictment should take, the form of the cross-examination, the legal standards for evaluating evidence (i.e., witness testimony), and even details of the performance, such as this statement to be read by the Marshal of the Court before the public reading of the king's commission: "The court for trying of pyrates do strictly charge and command all manner of persons to keep silence whilst the commission is reading upon pain of imprisonment. All persons to stand up, uncovered whilst the Commission is reading."[10] That this script was a document meant to be used, in many cases verbatim, is suggested by the fact that blanks are left in it for case-specific details, such as names or specifics of the indictment.

Larkin's voyage and the script for the legal performance of piracy trials that he distributed had the intended purpose of ensuring that colonial governors and other commissioners knew what to do so that they would do it and could be held accountable if they did not. It was an effort to build the chain of propagation out to the key state agents in the colonial world who would be responsible for extending it yet further, into the situations where piracy could be confronted directly. This objective is clearest in the instructions that the Privy Council gave to Larkin "for the better execution of a late act of Parliament concerning pirates."[11] One of the problems the council apparently saw with the execution of the law was procedural, and Larkin was well positioned to help meet this need. Among the documents the council provided Larkin was a letter to the commissioners of the new court for the Bahamas and Jamaica, where they indicate that one of the purposes of Larkin's visit is to settle, with the other commissioners, "the rules and forms of proceedings in the courts for the trying of pirates as ought to be observed, pursuant to the powers and authoritys given by our said commission."[12] The question of procedure here, as suggested above, is more than simply a question of the proper rules for a trial. Rather, it reflects the idea that the proper rules and procedures are what makes a particular set of actions a performative exercise of legal powers. As in the Privy Council's instructions, there is a close connection between rules and forms of proceedings as well as powers and authorities given by a commission. Procedure is the visible, staged performance of legal authority and state power. In the newly decentralized jurisdictional scheme for trying pirates—especially given its radically novel formulation of interpretive power that asserted the power of a majority of an appointed commission to condemn accused persons to death—the consistent, ritualized performance of a legal script was an essential bulwark in maintaining the assertion of the connection of such proceedings to the rule of law and distinguishing it from the arbitrary exercise of state power.

The trial of Captain John Quelch in Massachusetts, for example, precisely implemented the procedures contemplated by the law and elaborated during Larkin's visit.[13] Quelch's trial began with the proclamation, described above, for silence. Then, 11&12 William III, c. 7, was read, the commission was read, and the Register of the Court was appointed and sworn. Next, the register administered the oath to the President of the Court, and the president administered it to the other commissioners, "in open court, pursuant to the Act aforesaid."[14] The linkage between the precise proceedings under way and the sovereign power of state and Crown was then reaffirmed through a public reading of instructions from the new queen to the governor that the 1700 act was to govern the trial of pirates. A warrant was issued to the keeper of the prison to produce Quelch, the court adjourned until three o'clock, and upon its return it read the "articles" (i.e., indictment) specifying the crimes of which the prisoner was accused. The legal details of the case are interesting and will be discussed later in this chapter, but the point here is how closely the actual trial conformed to the legal script provided by the law and by Larkin's subsequent elaboration.[15]

PIRACY UNSCRIPTED

These new performances of the legal classification of piracy were not without their problems and particularities, of course, and such particulars were not something that could be answered formulaically by a script. The people translating the codified semiotic relations and procedures of the law into actual social performances also needed to engage in on-the-spot legal hermeneutics to adaptively translate the particulars of a given case and the happenings of the eventful unfolding of the specific trial situation into the symbolic universe of the law. The legal script just discussed created a form and procedure with which piracy could be authoritatively interpreted, but it did not by itself secure the performative achievement of legal meanings; the actors on the scene had to bring the classification home while remaining at least roughly within the universe of semiotic relations and procedural possibilities imagined and established by the new legal regime.

Quelch's trial provides a good example of this in a debate that emerged between the Queen's Advocate, Thomas Newtown, and the defense counsel appointed to Quelch, James Meinzies.[16] One of the problems that the

1536 piracy law, Act for Punishment of Pirates and Robbers of the Sea, sought to remedy was that under the civil law, a conviction for piracy required either a confession or the testimony of "witnesses indifferente,"[17] thus ruling out accomplice testimony and the strategy of allowing the least guilty of the accessories to become a Crown witness in return for leniency (Langbein 1983, 84–105). The common law procedures for trying pirates had no such restriction on accomplice testimony, relying instead on the jury to assess how much weight it deserved. However, the 1700 Act for the More Effectual Suppression of Piracy explicitly reintroduced civil law procedure for the new trials. Though civil law admiralty jurisprudence in matters related to piracy had been moribund for over 160 years, the wording of the new law raised the question of whether the old exclusion of accomplice testimony was again in place. Quelch's trial, the first under the new law, was the circumstance where this consequential question was raised and answered.

Meinzies, Quelch's defense counsel, reminds the court that the text of the 1700 act requires that trials proceed "according to the civil law" and that "by the civil law . . . no accomplice can be a Witness, being equally guilty with those he accuses."[18] Newtown, the Queen's Advocate vacuously responds that the 1536 act rejected the civil law standard and made it possible to "bring criminals to their just punishment . . . by singling out some of their company, that may be the least guilty, and make use of them to convict the rest."[19] This answer ineptly avoids the tricky procedural question, but the defense counsel continued to clarify the point, acknowledging that under the common law procedures of the 1536 law, accomplice testimony was perfectly valid, but the meaning of that testimony was different given the insistence of the 1700 act that civil law procedure be used. Meinzies goes on to characterize this as a basic question of fairness, noting that "those that are tried for piracy in the plantations, being deprived of the benefit of a jury, the statute seems to design an equivalent to a jury, by directing the commissioners of such courts to proceed according to the civil law."[20] Newtown responds that the use of the common law to try pirates in Admiralty Sessions of oyer and terminer since 1536 was "a term long enough to make a method of any court," suggesting that accomplice testimony was now to be understood to be a customary part of civil law piracy jurisprudence. Furthermore, Newtown argues, the reference of the statute to the civil law refers only to the "summary way of proceeding by the commissioners, and depriving the prisoner of a jury." He justifies this view by noting that the point of the new law was to *strengthen* the Act of Henry VIII. Since that act rejected the bar to accomplice testimony as unworkable in piracy trials, it was odd to think that the new strengthened law would reintroduce that notorious weakness of pre-1536 civil law piracy jurisprudence.[21]

This argument proved decisive, and accomplice testimony played a pivotal role in many of the major piracy trials of the early eighteenth century. At stake in this debate between Meinzies and Newtown were fundamental questions of legal hermeneutics. What could be said by whom? And what would the meaning of that saying be in terms of its effects? Could accomplices speak? Would their speech be construed as evidence? The power of the new courts to reclassify some accomplices as witnesses in conjunction with the theories of evidence described above became one of the fundamental ways that the classification of pirates proceeded. While the practical and political context of the trials demanded this capacity, as Newtown suggests, the precise question of accomplice testimony and its resolution only makes sense in the context of the conjunction of the new field of legal semiotics created by the new law with the more ancient but evolving fields of piracy jurisprudence from 1536 and of a civil law tradition rich in its own hermeneutic customs, rules, and procedures.

In thinking about the departures of piracy trials from scripted, procedural expectations, it is also important to note that the trials regularly fell short of these standards. Baer argues convincingly that legal laxity of various sorts was endemic in piracy trials, even in those cases where the new legal procedures were rigorously followed. Indictments, for instance, were often written very broadly. This made the case for the prosecution easier, and it was only possible because the legal structure of 1700 eliminated the common law practice of indictment through a grand jury. The commission that would hear and judge the case was the same commission that would indict. In such a system, overindictment is an unsurprising consequence, but it did undermine one of the few protections remaining to the accused under the new legal system. As Baer writes of the trial of John Rackam and his crew, "If the court was exemplary as regards form, it repeatedly over-indicted and based its lethal verdicts on weak evidence" (2007, 3:2). A lack of expertise also led to a certain degree of legal laxity, despite the specificity of the script for piracy trials. In the trial of 169 crew members of Bartholomew Roberts in 1722 on the west coast of Africa, legal expertise was in short supply (3:69–70). As a result, the proceedings followed the procedural script associated with the new legal structure, but they introduced invented evidentiary standards under the argument that "such Evidence, tho' it might want a form, still carried the reason of the law with it."[22] Sympathetic collaborators can do as much for assembling effective chains of propagating and ratifying action as procedure can in the right circumstances, albeit contingently.

NOVELTY AND LEGITIMACY

The use of procedures, scripts, and hermeneutic performances oriented toward the law were all part of an interpretive mechanism designed to secure epistemic authority for the classification of pirates. The procedure and script in particular were intended to formalize and routinize as much as possible these performances of meaning, leaving as little to idiosyncratic dynamics of interpretation and performance as possible. In this sense, they were an effort to achieve performative fusion (Alexander 2004, 529), which in this context meant the instigation of chains of propagating and enforcing social performances by other state agents and members of the broader public that ratified the authority of the initial classification. While the broader epistemic authority of the law was more or less established by the early eighteenth century in most parts of the English Empire (Benton 2002, 31–79; Shapiro 2003, 30), the radical nature of the new commissions and the popularity of piracy in many colonies raised questions about the legal legitimacy of these new tribunals.

The civil law was a puzzling novelty for many commissioners, leading to a constantly recurring trope in piracy trials of the prosecutor explaining to the commissioners why it is acceptable to do a certain thing that might not be possible under the common law. The King's Advocate in the trial of Samuel Bellamy's crew, for example, notes that while crimes that occur solely in the mind "cannot fall under the censure of any humane judicature," under the civil law when "inward notions come to discover themselves by undoubted tokens, and break out in some open act, tho that proceeds no farther, than an endeavor or bare attempt . . . the guilt and punishment are the same as if the intended mischief had been fully executed. . . . It is otherwise at Common Law."[23] We see the same proactive defensiveness about the legal character of these new piracy trials in Quelch's case, when the Queen's Advocate exhorts the commissioners that "it may be thought by some a pretty severe thing to put an Englishman to death without a jury, yet it must be remembred, that the wisdom and justice of our nation, for very sufficient and excellent reasons, have so ordered it in the case of piracy, a crime, which as before I observ'd, scarce deserves any law at all."[24] Such questions were critical, because the success of these legal performances in transmuting the accused into the guilty depended on their legitimacy, and legitimacy was nothing more or less than ratifying through confirming word and deed the meanings made in the trial situation.

NOT GUILTY

Another dimension of the performance of meaning in piracy trials touching on procedure, hermeneutics, and legitimacy was the obverse of the classification of pirates: the exoneration of those caught up in piracy but not culpable for it. The new piracy tribunals quickly found themselves facing this knotty problem endemic to the legal handling of piracy. They were compelled to decide, on the basis of often ambiguous evidence, whether members of pirate crews were willing participants or had been forced to join.

An act of piracy is itself a complex social encounter, and on the side of the pirates this involved very different levels of complicity. The epistemological problems posed by having the classification of a given actor depend on that person's intent led the prosecution in some trials to adopt "the flawed practice . . . of equating presence on a pirate ship with proof of adherence to the pirates" (Baer 2007, 3:2). This practice ran roughshod over moral distinctions that were clear to contemporaries familiar with the circumstances facing men at sea who encountered and joined with pirates. Some aboard pirate vessels were willing participants who had freely joined, others were forced to join when their ships were taken, and yet others were positioned ambiguously between. Forced men themselves varied. Some would be directly involved in boarding other ships, firing on them, robbery, and torture, while others would only minimally participate in non-violent shipboard duties under constant threat from the pirates who had taken them. As contemporaries understood it, the crime of piracy required *animo furandi*, an intent to steal. In the context of piracy trials, distinguishing intent was thus important; but intent could only be determined through the interpretation of available signs in light of codified meanings, in the context of which they became signifiers of innocence or guilt.

What were the elements of this code of innocence? There were four main ways that piracy classifications could be ameliorated. Acquittals, pardons, and general amnesties all provided ways for those accused of piracy, convicted of it, or admittedly guilty but allegedly repentant to escape the piracy classification. One other possibility that occurs in the records with regularity is the commutation of sentences, usually to imprisonment or some form of indentured servitude. In practice, all these outcomes occurred with some regularity, and trials usually involved a mix of different verdicts, suggesting that these options were used with some care. In Quelch's trial, for instance, 25 men were indicted, 2 were acquitted, 3 became Crown witnesses and were pardoned, 6 were executed, and 14 had their sentences commuted, probably to naval service (Baer 2007, 2:259).

The mass trial of pirates at Cape Coast Castle on the Gold Coast of West Africa provides another convenient reference point where all possibilities were used. The court convicted and executed 52, commuted the sentences of 20 to indentured servitude with the Royal African Company, commuted the sentences of 17 more to imprisonment at Marshalsea in London, referred 2 to the king for potential pardon, and acquitted 74.[25]

The universe of legal meaning within which questions of acquittal, commutation, and pardon were deliberated included a wide range of elements. Some were very specific. In the case of Mary Read and Anne Bonny, captured with John Rackam in 1720, both women were found guilty of piracy, but "after judgement was pronounced . . . both the prisoners inform'd the Court, that they were both quick with child, and prayed that the execution of the sentence might be stayed." The court ordered that an "inspection should be made," and apparently the results confirmed Read and Bonny's claims, for the court commuted their sentences.[26] The special protection offered by the legal meaning of pregnancy was not a reason available to most, of course.

Another example of a specific basis for acquittal was age, at stake in the trial of the Mi'kmaq and French pirates in Boston in 1726. Defense counsel raises a point of law on behalf of one of the accused, John Baptist Junior, that his case was distinguished from his codefendants "on account of his tender years; being (as his father informs me) not fourteen years of age; an age which renders a person incapable in the law, of committing any crime so as to be punished with death, he being set upon the same foot with a mad-man."[27] The prosecutor rejects this argument, noting that the weight of jurisprudential authority on this subject suggested that

> an infant within the age of discretion, kills a man, no felony . . . but if by circumstances it appeareth he could distinguish between good and evil, it is felony; as if he hide the dead, make excuses, & c. That the pirates looked upon this John Baptist Junior as a person capable of distinguishing, is evident by committing the greatest trust and charge unto him . . . [by which] and by many more incident matters of fact that turned out in the evidence, it clearly appears he was a free agent, and capable of making legal distinctions . . . as your honour values the preservation of the laws of the land, the lives and properties of his majesty's subjects, and would studiously avoid any fatal consequence that may attend an illegal acquittal; I hope there will be as little distinction in respect to their sentence, but that your honour will justly pronounce them equally guilty.[28]

Guns, Gallows, and Interpretive Infrastructures | 125

In this case the court obliged, but as even the prosecutor acknowledges, youth could indeed be the basis for acquittal.

During the trial of Stede Bonnet's men in Charlestown, South Carolina, three of the accused offered different versions of the argument that they had been forced, with instructively different outcomes. Alexander Anand gives the most half-hearted version of this argument, telling the court that he had only signed on after Major Bonnet had told him that "he design'd to go to St. Thomas's for a commission . . . so I suspected nothing till we were out at sea, and then I could not help it." "Why did you not declare against it then, and so not join with them?" one of the judges asks in response, to which Anand offers the plaintive but legally irrelevant observation that "I was but one man, and a stranger, and I was afraid I should have lost my life." George Ross offered a somewhat more compelling story, telling the court that he was a crewman on one of the sloops taken by Bonnet and his men. "Next day," he says, "two of the men told me I must go with them. I answr'd them, No; I did not design to leave the sloop; but they told me I must; and they told me, if I would but consent I should have any thing." Ross, though his initial decision to join the pirates had allegedly been forced, soon began to evince contradictory signs. "You had your share of Manwareing's goods?" one of the judges asks with reference to a subsequent piratical attack. "Yes," replies Ross, thus making his position in relation to the semiotics of piracy clear—in receiving goods he ceased to be forced and became complicit. This interpretation of his change of heart is explicit in the trial record: "So, tho you were unwilling at first, you was willing afterward, and also fought Col. Rhett when he came out against you," notes one of the judges. Both Ross's and Anand's arguments about their position in relation to the semiotic boundaries of piracy failed; the court found them guilty.

Another member of Bonnet's crew, however, had an argument better suited to the semiotics of innocence that developed in the new piracy jurisprudence. Thomas Nichols benefited from a number of witnesses who agreed that his case was different and who testified to a number of signs contemporaries accepted as evidence of this difference. One witness noted that Nichols, "after he came to sea, was very much discontented; but Maj. Bonnet said he would force him to go. However, he would not join with the rest of the men, but always separated himself from the company." The captain of one of the vessels that Nichols was accused of taking likewise testified in his favor, "that Nichols when he was aboard his sloop, said he did hope it would be over with him in a little time, for he hoped to get clear of them, and looked very melancholy, and never joined with the rest in their cabals when they were drinking." In addition to his disposition separating him from the pirates, two pieces of specific evidence were central to the outcome of Nichols's case. As another crew member testified, "When [Nichols] came on board, he told me, he would give the whole world if he had it, to be free from them; and when he was on board, and Maj. Bonnet sent for him, he refused to go on board the Revenge, till he sent to fetch him by force, and then he told me he would not fight if he did lose his life for it; and he was not with them when they shared; and he told them he hoped he should not be long with them; and he never was at their cabals, as the rest were." In refusing to fight and declining to share in the loot, Nichols set himself apart from the pirates; as one of his judges noted, "He seems to be under a constraint indeed," and the court exonerated him.[29]

Nichols's argument drew from one of the most common tropes used by mariners to mount a case for acquittal in a piracy trial. The "forced man" was at the heart of many of the deliberations and legal arguments for acquittal in the records of piracy trials. Advocate General Robert Auchmuty's complaint at trial reveals how central that trope had become to legal defense strategies, objecting to "that hackney defence made by every pirate upon trial, namely, that he was a forced man."[30] It was rightly seen by many accused of piracy to be their last best hope for achieving a not guilty verdict. In one dramatic case, eleven forced men rose up in rebellion against Captain William Fly in 1726, captured him and the true pirates on the crew, and turned themselves in. While the eleven had been part of a pirate crew and could therefore have been tried in the usual way, the purpose of this trial, presided over by twenty-five commissioners instead of the minimum of seven, seems to have been the obverse of the usual performance of guilt: a performance of innocence and celebration of the bravery of the men who rose up against Fly. No evidence was presented against these rebels, and they were all acquitted.[31]

We can see the impact of these new semiotic/institutional realities on seamen in phenomena that emerged in colonial newspapers of this time: notices of being forced. In these notices, crewmates of an allegedly forced mariner would post a notice in a newspaper such as the *Boston News-Letter* or *New England Courant* claiming that the mariner had been forced against his will to join the pirates. John Smith and Charles Messon published a characteristic notice in 1722, declaring

> that the said brigantine in her voyage from St. Christophers to Boston . . . was taken by a pirat sloop, commanded by one Lowder [Lowther], having near one hundred men, and eight guns mounted. . . . And the

declarants further say, that Joseph Sweetser . . . Richard Rich and Robert Willis . . . all three belonging to the above said brigantine, were forced and compelled against their wills to go with the said pirates.[32]

Similar declarations occasionally appeared in colonial papers at this time, showing the new awareness of the importance of signs of being forced as one of the only ways to surmount the presumption of guilt on the basis of one's presence among pirates. In Robert Willis's case, the signs of being forced proved crucial: Lowther's ship was captured later in 1722, and Willis was one of three men acquitted at a vice admiralty piracy tribunal held on Saint Kitts in the West Indies.[33]

In another, more minor but touching case, Thomas Davis was tried in 1717, and he claimed to have been forced because he was a carpenter. In a petition to the governor, his father wrote that Davis was a "dutiful and obedient son, and his life and deprtm't has been always regular and becoming as well as peaceable."[34] A number of crew members and even the Boston jail keeper also testified to his good character, how he had been forced, his continuing displeasure at being made a pirate, and his attempts to escape from the pirates. The prosecutor, in his closing argument, posed a common objection to the "forced man" defense: "if a man, for instance, is in danger of being kill'd or rob'd, he may lawfully in his own defence kill the aggressor . . . but if to ward off the danger he should kill or rob a third person, whom he knows to be innocent, he is without doubt punishable as a murderer or robber." The commissioners disagreed, however, and "were of opinion that there was good proof of the prisoners being forced on board the pirate ship *Whido* . . . which excused his being with the pirates; and that there was no evidence to prove that he was accessory with them, but on the contrary that he was forced to stay with them against his will." On the basis of this argument, the court acquitted him.[35] Whether one joined a crew of pirates willingly or had been forced, whether one engaged in violence, whether one accepted a share of the proceeds or refused, are all examples of the sort of signs and signifiers that state agents in the newly institutionalized piracy courts looked for in determining whether an individual was a pirate.

More expedient situational reasons for acquittal, leniency, or pardon also emerged. In the midst of a ferocious battle in 1700, Governor Nicholson of Virginia, who had joined in the fray, and Captain Passenger of HMS *Shoreham* discovered that the pirates aboard *La Paix* had "laid a train to thirty barrels of powder"[36] and planned to blow up the ship along with forty or fifty hostages.[37] The governor promised to request the king's mercy if the pirates surrendered. They did, and Nicholson kept his word, referring

128 | CHAPTER FIVE

111 men for trial in England with his recommendation for mercy. Three who attempted to escape and refused to surrender were tried under a Virginian version of the Jamaica Piracy Act and hanged.[38]

For most trials, the semiotics of innocence exhibited greater regularity. While many prosecutors and commissioners were willing to accept the presumption that one's presence aboard a vessel involved in piracy made one a pirate, the widely recognized violence of the pirates and their willingness to force unwilling mariners to join their ranks made others uneasy to apply this presumption universally. In many cases, commissioners attempted to discover whether those on trial were willing participants. Baer has covered this ground in a typically careful and thorough fashion in his introduction to a collection of printed reports of piracy trials. He notes that signs taken by jurors or commissioners to be evidence of piratical intent included "having voluntarily signed pirate articles, equipped themselves with arms, acted vigorously in fights at sea or on shore, gone aboard captured ships, treated prisoners badly, spoken well of the pirate life, taken a share of the plunder, and declined to leave the pirates when occasion presented." On the other hand were "proofs of innocence where the accused having done none of the above, but resisted going with the pirates, lamented their fate (preferably in tears), conspired to rise up against their captors, and sent their stories to English or American newspapers. Another usually reliable reason to acquit was that the accused were slaves or were indentured to mariners who had turned pirate and therefore had no choice but to obey their masters" (Baer 2007, 2:xvi).

Amnesties were a final way to "unmake" pirates that played an important role in post-1700 piracy law. These had been issued irregularly during the seventeenth century as a way to lure pirates onto the right side of the law in hopes they would stay there and were often used as compensation for insufficient coercive powers and resources. In the wake of the spike in piracy of the 1710s, amnesties for piracy were offered in 1717 and 1718 by royal proclamation. In the 1717 amnesty, King George I proclaimed,

> We do hereby promise, and declare, that in case any of the said pyrates, shall on, or before, the 5th of September, in the Year of our Lord 1718, surrender him or themselves, to one of our principal secretaries of state . . . or to any Governor or Deputy Governor of any of our plantations beyond the seas; every such pyrate and pyrates so surrendering him, or themselves, as aforesaid, shall have our gracious pardon, of and for such, his or their piracy, or pyracies, by him or them committed before the fifth of January next ensuing.[39]

The proclamation then went on to threaten those who did not accept the amnesty. In the case of Woodes Rogers after being appointed governor of the Bahamas, the classification loophole provided by the amnesty offered important leverage. One of the most famous pirates, Benjamin Hornigold, took advantage of the king's act of grace and became a fierce pirate hunter; indeed, most of the pirates who remained in the Bahamas after Rogers's arrival took the pardon as well. One major problem with such pardons, of course, was that they offered no institutional or legal support for ensuring that pardoned pirates would become law-abiding mariners. Many took the pardon and then immediately returned to pirating, as was the case with the pirates captured by Hornigold in 1718; they mutinied and took over a ship on their first voyage after obtaining the king's pardon.[40]

RATIFICATION, PROPAGATION, COORDINATION

The significance of legal performance of the sort that this chapter has focused on for understanding the creation of the power to punish piracy is ultimately a matter of coordination. One of the keys to coordinated, collective power is that when I lawfully, felicitously classify someone as a pirate, you and others act in ways that give that classification and its further meanings more weight and significance than just my say-so would afford. This basic microsociological observation was key to the production of systematized coercive power against piracy. Either state agents operate together to assert the pragmatic force of their interpretations, or those chains of coordination break, from the inside or outside, and reveal asserted powers of interpretation to be less than claimed—classification without consequence. Chains of ratification and propagation play a key role in the translation of meanings established through legal performances, further embedding them into the fabric of social situations. This translation matters at the trial and in the further rendering of the classifications made there into subsequent situations, driving them forward in their consequences.

The operation of these chains of ratifying signification—as well as the ever-present threat of the opposite, blocked signification and the imposition of alternative meanings—was on vivid display in one of the more touch-and-go executions from the history of piracy: Woodes Rogers's December 1718 execution of eight men on the island of Providence in the Bahamas. Over the course of the first two decades of the eighteenth century, the Bahamas had become preeminent among British possessions in its notoriety as a pirates' nest. Governors and other state agents continuously complained about the danger, disorder, and awful precedent set by allowing the islands to be overrun by marauders. By the later 1710s, the place had become ungovernable, at least by agents of the British state. As one colonial official wrote to the Council of Trade and Plantations, "A nest of pirates are endeavouring to establish themselves at Providence and by the addition they expect of loose disorderly people from the Bay of Campeachy, Jamaica and other parts, may prove dangerous to British commerce, if not timely suppressed. . . . It highly concerns [His Majesty's] service that some Government should speedily be established there and the place made defencible against sudden attempts by pirates or the Spaniards."[41]

In the summer of 1717, Woodes Rogers, a former privateer whose exploits in that career are related in more detail in chapter 7, petitioned the Council of Trade and Plantations to be made governor of the Bahama islands to reestablish British control, rid the islands of the pirates, and fortify them against Spanish incursions. In September, the council and the king agreed and drew up Rogers's commission.[42] The situation in the Bahamas had in part arisen, or so contemporaries thought, because it was held as a proprietary colony, and as part of the effort to reestablish control the Crown resumed direct control. This process, involving the surrender, extinguishment, or forfeiture of proprietary claims based on the original charter of the colony,[43] continued through early 1818 as Rogers waited with ships fitted out with various supplies, ammunition, provisions, and troops to garrison Providence.[44]

Rogers arrived at the city of Nassau on July 26, 1818, to find a ship ablaze in the harbor and a pirate sloop flying the black flag and firing "guns of defiance" as it made good its escape. The pirates numbered around ninety men and were led by Captain Charles Vane. They set the fire as a distraction to evade capture by Rogers's forces, and though Rogers sent two ships in chase, Vane and his company got away. Upon his arrival on the island, Rogers found its main fortifications long abandoned to ruin, a few hundred settlers who professed their "joy for the re-introduction of Governmt," and hundreds of pirates. To make matters worse, soon Rogers, his troops, and the other newcomers to the Bahamas were wracked by an epidemic that killed many and disabled many more. Several of the ships and the soldiers sent there to support his arrival were redeployed to fight piracy elsewhere, and renewed hostilities with the Spanish sent a fear through British New World colonies, including the Bahamas, that the Spanish would soon attack.[45]

Rogers's situation was by any measure isolated and dire. The character of his plight, though, focuses attention on the question of propagation. Rogers could certainly have come into port and started accusing dozens

Guns, Gallows, and Interpretive Infrastructures | 131

or hundreds of inhabitants of piracy with good reason. But those classificatory acts could not be supported—they would not be propagated. In the first place, they would not have been done in a legal way until a piracy tribunal had been established. But even once that was in place, the tribunal's ability to channel state power into its classifications depends on the ratification and propagation of the meanings it assigned. Calling some men pirates only has an effect if sufficient forces can be brought to bear to carry forward that definition, and in the Bahamas in 1718 that was no sure thing. As Rogers put the point, "Some . . . that committed acts of piracy . . . seem to be reform'd, this has been one great reason why I . . . [have not] exerted my power as Vice Admiral to seize many things that I might have laid my hands on because I would not quarrel at the time of my mens great sickness when they [the former pirates] might have sent us all back again [i.e., back to England]." In addition to the power to try pirates, Rogers had another element of the British interpretive infrastructure relating to piracy at his disposal. As part of the renewed effort by the British Empire to control piracy, the king had issued a pardon for all former pirates who surrendered and swore an oath to engage in piracy no more. This vital hinge of classification gave Rogers an inducement that he could use to persuade many of the men he found on the Bahamas to leave piracy behind, or at least bide their return long enough to allow him to get further aspects of government working again. This offer, though, was only as valuable as the danger of being classified as a pirate made it. Given the recent impunity pirates had enjoyed on the islands as well as the relative weakness of Rogers's forces and the many threats he was facing, it is not surprising that some like Vane vigorously refused the pardon, and others who initially accepted it returned to pirating.[46]

It was in this parlous situation that the trial of ten men for piracy in Nassau came about. The trial played a symbolically important role in Rogers's efforts to reestablish the Bahamas as a colony both unequivocally governed by British agents and British law and unequivocally hostile to pirates as a clear and despised category of criminal. The trial made the category of piracy and the interpretive powers that controlled it real. It could only do so, however, as an effect of coordinated chains of propagation, capable of translating into action a common system of state meaning. The start of that chain was the king's pardon, which all those ultimately tried and executed had accepted. The pardon placed them unambiguously in the category of noncriminal mariners, blotting out their past piracy. Tiring of this resumption of the lawful version of their trade, the accused, led by a Phineas Bunch, mutinied, took the *Mary*, the *Batchelor's Adventure*, and the *Lancaster*, and marooned the other passengers and crew on the desolate

Green Key. Captains John Cockram and Benjamin Hornigold, themselves reformed pirates, recipients of the king's pardon, and commissioned by Rogers to hunt pirates, caught up with the pirates by the Exuma Cays. Hornigold and Cockram killed three of the again-pirates in the fight, including Bunch, returning the rest to Nassau.

There Rogers faced a dilemma, for so many recently pardoned pirates inhabited the place that he feared a breakdown in what I have described as chains of meaning propagation: less theoretically, a jailbreak, which is nothing if not the interpolation of an alternative framework of meaning in place of the legally authorized one. As one Bahamian official described the situation, "As the necessary Soldiers and Seamen, who equally guarded the Fort and Ship; and as many as could be spar'd, daily work'd on the Fortifications, and did the Duty of Centinels at Night, thereby harassing our small Numbers of Men, and hindering the publick Work . . . and there being suspected Persons still remaining in these Islands, who may give frequent Intelligence of our Condition; should any Fear be shewn on our Part, it might animate several now here, to invite the Pyrates without, to attempt the Rescue of these in Custody."[47] The classification of the prisoners as accused felons to be held awaiting trial as opposed to there-but-for-the-grace-of-God-go-I brethren to be freed depended on the reproduction of the former meaning among a group who held their only edge through coordination. These chains of ratifying signification that started with the extension of the king's pardon to Cockram and Hornigold continued with their commission to hunt down the pirates by Rogers, and then circulated to the guards and crew of the *Delicia*, who propagated the accusation by holding the men prisoner and preventing a jailbreak. That propagation now returned to Rogers, who after some initial negotiation of his authority to do so,[48] established a piracy tribunal. Writing to William Fairfax, Esq., Captain Robert Beauchamps, Thomas Walker, Esq., Captain Wingate Gale, Nathaniel Taylor, Esq., Captain Josias Burgess, and Captain Peter Courant and asserting the "Power and Authority to authorize and empower, constitute and commisionate, proper Judges and Commissioners, for the trying, determining, adjudging, and condemning, of all or any Pyrate or Pyrates taken, apprehended, and brought into this Government," Rogers declared, "I do by Virtue of these Presents, authorize, commissionate, and appoint you Deputy, Judges, and Commissioners of the said Especial Court."[49]

Thus constituted, the court began trying the accused pirates using the procedure established by the 1700 Act for the More Effectual Suppression of Piracy. The Register of the Court read the governor's commission and cited the 1700 act to establish the legal character and authority of the proceedings before reading the accusation: "Being instigated and deluded by the Devil, to return to your former unlawful evil Courses, of Robbery and Pyracy . . . and that you . . . did on the 6th Day of October . . . plot and combine together, at a desolate Island, called *Green Key*, within the Jurisdiction of this Vice-Admiralty, to mutiny and feloniously and piratically steal, take, and carry away . . . the afore-named Vessels . . . and Cargoes, Tackle, Apparel, and Furniture . . . and by Force cause to be put ashore on the said desolate Island [those aboard the vessels]."[50] After hearing arguments and evidence against the ten, the court issued its judgment in nine of the cases (it delayed the judgment of John Hipps): "The Court having duly considered of the Evidence which hath been given both for and against you . . . it is adjudged that you . . . are guilty of the Mutiny, Felony, and Pyracy wherewith you and every one of you stand accused. And the Court doth accordingly pass Sentence, that you . . . be carry'd to Prison from whence you came, and from thence to the Place of Execution, where you are to be hanged by the Neck till you shall be dead, dead, dead; and God have Mercy on your Souls."[51] The convicted pirates then petitioned the court to delay the imposition of their sentence, but reflecting the tenuous character of the chain of propagation that put the court in the position of rendering authoritative judgment—in this case a hanging—Rogers denied the request.

> The Governor told them . . . that the securing them hitherto, and the Favour that the Court had allowed them in making as long a Defence as they could, wholly took up that Time, which the Affairs of the Settlement required in working at the Fortifications [against the feared Spanish attack]; besides the Fatigue thereby occaison'd to the whole Garrison in the necessary Guards, set over them by the Want of a Gaol, and the Garrison having been very much lessened by Death and Sickness since his Arrival; also that he was obliged to employ all his People to assist in mounting the great Guns, and in finishing the present Works, with all possible Dispatch, because of the expected War with *Spain*; and there being many more Pyrates amongst these Islands, and this Place left destitute of all Relief from any Man of War or Station Ship, much wanted, join'd to other Reasons he had . . . he thought himself indispensably obliged, for the Welfare of the Settlement, to give them no longer Time.[52]

He then ordered the guards to return the prisoners to the fort.

Two days later, on Friday the twelfth of December 1718, the prisoners were given to the custody of the Provost Marshal, another link in the chain propagating and enforcing their classification as pirates, who had them bound and proceeded to the ramparts of the fort for the execution. The spot was "well guarded by the Governor's Soldiers and People, to the Number of about 100"—a necessary precaution, as the spectators "got as near to the Foot of the Gallows as the Marshal's Guard would suffer them." This was an especially fraught moment, as one observer noted, since "there were but few (beside the Governor's Adherents) among the Spectators, who had not deserved the same Fate, but pardon'd by his Majesty's Act of Grace." The convicted pirates were well aware of the taut question posed by their execution in front of a pressing crowd of their uneasily pacified friends and fellow marauders against a garrison and group of supporters of Rogers stretched thin and pressed on many sides. The specter of a rescue attempt, which would be both a devastating practical and semiotic coup against the new regime and its antipiratical designs, occupied the imaginations of all sides. One of the condemned, Dennis Macarty, defiantly bedecked with "long blue Ribbons at his Neck, Wrists, Knees, and Cap," demanded as much from the crowd, saying that "he knew the Time when there were many brave Fellows on the Island, who would not have suffered him to die like a Dog." He then kicked his shoes "over the Parapet of the Fort, saying, he had promis'd not to die with his Shoes on." His former mates did not attempt a rescue, declining by their deeds, or lack thereof, to ratify Macarty's demand for countersignification: "however willing, they saw too much Power over their Heads to attempt any Thing in his Favour."[53]

Despite this group of just-pardoned pirates pressing in on the execution and the other pressures on the chains of authority and representation that Rogers commanded, he and his adherents managed to carry off the ultimate realization of their classification. The prisoners were brought across several ladders to a gallows with a black flag hoisted above it; beneath the gallows, three quarters of an hour was spent on public prayer and exhortation. Just at the point of execution, Rogers ordered a reprieve for George Rounsivil, whom the guards returned to the jail. (In later correspondence, the governor requests direction on how to proceed, as Rounsivil "is the son of loyall and good parents in Dorsetshire."[54]) As for the rest, the executioner pulled on the ropes attached to the supports under the gallows, "upon which, the Stage fell, and the Prisoners were suspended."[55]

This execution hardly settled the tense drama of Rogers's attempt to reestablish British control over the pirates in the Bahamas, but it was a clear and telling symbolic victory—or perhaps more precisely, a victory for the symbols he wielded. As the focus of this study suggests, a symbolic victory should not be understood as *merely* symbolic. Rather, much of its power came from its reinforcement of the practical social meaning of the category of piracy, the consequences for being so classified, and the power of Rogers and other state agents to constitute and command chains of propagation in support of their interpretive power. Their ability to do so was a key part of what I have been calling the interpretive infrastructure of British piracy institutions, and likewise drew from other parts of that infrastructure. The 1700 act provided the forms of authority Rogers drew from; the governor's commission allowed him to authorize pirate hunters; admiralty law and the scripts provided for piracy trials provided the forms that agents could use to coordinate their actions and to assert the meaning of their killing of eight men on a Friday morning in Nassau as an act of justice that was the opposite of the killings perpetrated by many pirates. Chains of propagation realize the interpretive infrastructure, and the interpretive infrastructure provides the meanings that allow propagation to happen, operating as the most relevant and pressing context of symbolically oriented action. Both the social performances of the people involved and the interpretive infrastructure that supplied the forms and significance of their performances explain how in this case of barely there state power, with extreme pressure from multiple directions and no hope of backup, the chains of propagation held and the pirates hanged.

PRINCIPALS EMPOWERED, AGENTS CONSTRAINED

It is also useful to consider the performative ratification of state classifications, of chains of propagation, in a more structural sense. From this perspective, the question of ratification and propagation can be treated as a matter of principal-agent dynamics (Adams 1996; Erikson and Bearman 2006; Kiser 1994; Kiser and Cai 2003; Kiser and Linton 2001; Norton 2015; Reed 2020). The legal semiotics introduced by the 1700 piracy act were effective in producing coercive power against piracy because they created a sophisticated symbolic, hermeneutic, and institutional framework for classifying pirates, but also because the law created a grid of meanings that gave principals far more control over their agents. In no position throughout the structure of the colonial state was this change more evident than with colonial governors. Their position was central throughout the field of colonial relations of governance. While transport links between England and the colonies improved dramatically in terms of speed, reliability, and regularity of traffic during the later seventeenth and early eighteenth centuries (Steele 1986), the distance nonetheless remained great, and the executive demands of colonial civil governance ensured that governors played an essential role. The entanglement of many colonial governors with piracy was but one case where the problem of governing an independently powerful colonial agent came to light. Complicity with piracy, as described above, was endemic in many colonies. One of the most flagrant cases was that of Benjamin Fletcher, governor of New York from 1692 to 1697. In November of 1698, after Fletcher had been replaced and recalled to England, the Board of Trade requested his response to a list of accusations that were the culmination of years of suspicious reports on his conduct of the government of New York. The first twelve of the board's charges all relate to piracy:

(1) That he accepted £700 to permit the ship Jacob, returning from a piratical voyage, to come up to New York, and to grant the crew protection. (2) That he prevailed with the Council to consent thereto under colour of allowing the said pirates the benefit of an Act of New York, to which they were not entitled. (3) That in consequence thereof the ship came up to New York and was accepted by him as a present and sold by him for £800. (4) That he granted protections to other pirates for money. (5) That there is no mention of securities given in the said protections, and that none of the persons so protected appear to have been prosecuted for piracy. (6) That in 1696 he released a chest of money which had been seized from one Rayner, a pirate. (7) That Edward Coates, the pirate, asserted that it cost him £1,300 to obtain Colonel Fletcher's protection. (8) That he granted commissions as privateers to Tew, Hore and Glover, though they had no ship at New York, and spoke openly of making piratical voyages. (9) That he was intimate with the pirate Tew, and received money for the aforesaid commissions. (10) That he granted a like commission to Thomas Moston of the ship Fortune, though intended only for illegal trade. (11) That the bonds which he took from the said pirates on giving them commissions were inadequate, and that one of them was tampered with by his Secretary. (12) That he connived at illegal trade, whereby the revenue of New York has been diminished though the trade has increased.[56]

Fletcher's responses to these various charges all play on the ambiguity of piracy. According to him, the captains to whom he gave commissions were privateers who already carried commissions from other governors (many of whom were also suspected of dealing with pirates). As for the money that changed hands, Fletcher was "very apt to believe that for such instruments so granted the parties concerned might pay fees to my servants or to such as drew their despatches, but whether they gave 100 dollars or other gratuity never fell within my cognisance nor to my profit." As for the charge that he was paid for protection, the owners of a ship allegedly involved in piracy had "publicly and openly offered her to [Fletcher] as a present."[57] The dogged pursuit of the charges against Fletcher by his successor as governor of New York, Richard Coote, Earl of Bellomont, has left a fuller record of accusations against Fletcher than against other governors of the time, but these sorts of breakdowns in principal-agent governance over complicity with piracy were endemic. Accusations along similar lines were leveled against the governors of Massachusetts, Pennsylvania, Rhode Island, the Carolinas, and the Bahamas, among others.[58]

In addition to giving governors new semiotic tools for fighting piracy through the mechanism of the piracy courts, the 1700 Act for the More Effectual Suppression of Piracy also created two mechanisms for solving the principal-agent dilemmas posed by the potentially lucrative alliance between governors and piracy. In conjunction with other changes to state structure such as increasing bureaucratization and faster, more regular flows of information between metropole and colonies, these measures played a critical role in turning the governors from a node of ambiguity in the network of state agents confronting piracy into the center of the judicial and police response to the problem. The first measure, discussed above and of the most bluntly dis-incentivizing sort, was the threat in section 15 of the statute to revoke the charters of charter and proprietary colonies that failed to implement the law. Since this measure was never enforced, and I have found little direct discussion of it by contemporaries, it is hard to know what contemporaries made of this threat. It seems to have been intended as an exercise in saber rattling to signal the seriousness with which metropolitan state agents were now focused on the piracy problem.

More subtly but no less importantly, the new law embedded the actions of colonial agents in a new semiotic structure that made their action and inaction on piracy more visible and legible to metropolitan principals as well as to one another. The new system, with its parcellized and distributed powers of classification, created a new visibility to both malfeasance and compliance by colonial state agents (Erikson and Bearman 2006; Norton 2015). It gave governors the power to try pirates under a commission for the piracy tribunal, and it created a clear expectation that governors would use that power when they encountered pirates. It gave governors immediate powers to call piracy tribunals and demanded that these powers be used to initiate immediate and decisive legal action rather than an indefinite use of jails and transport back to London. These measures had the effect of making the actions of governors and other colonial state agents more easily interpretable. They clarified the significance of action and inaction, in opposition to the ambiguity fostered by the earlier legal confusion and disempowerment of colonial officials. The new legal system also dispersed the power to authoritatively interpret piracy cases among many commissioners, making the interpretive performance a higher-profile public event, not the private arrangements with uncertain terms favored by Fletcher and his cohort of governors. By forcing coordination among the commissioners and providing only the one authorized script for how that coordination was meant to proceed, the law attempted to tie agents' actions and interests to the institutional scheme it envisioned. In any case, to engage in malfeasance would now require significant collusion, with multiple ways for other agents to defect and inform their metropolitan principals about any irregularities.

In this new model, with its more elaborate and immediate syntax of meaning making, agents' powers are constrained by both the demand that they be performatively ratified by other agents and by the matrix of meaningful symbols, including such elements as hierarchies, classifications, scripts, documents, and commissions. This denser thicket of institutionalized relationships and significations is very different from a system where principals are reliant on individual accounts from their agents, whose control over information provides them greater scope for malfeasance and defection (fig. 5.1). By encoding their interests into the coordinating cultural structures of colonial governance through the 1700 law and subsequent legal, political, and organizational changes, metropolitan principals bound

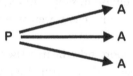

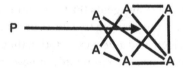

FIGURE 5.1. Two schemata of principal-agent relations. In the first, relations focus on efforts to directly regulate agents' behavior. In the second, the principals' interests are encoded in the system of relations between them and their agents. Powers delegated to any given agent are dependent on ratifying and propagating actions by other agents and are interpreted through a system of collective meanings. This interactive character makes action and inaction more visible. In this system, agents are constrained both by other agents, who performatively ratify one another's roles and thus constitute their powers, and by the system of signs, against which their actions are interpreted.

their agents in a thicket of signs where their every move became more legible and constrained in ways that structurally favored the principals' ends.

PIRACY, STATES, AND THEATER

What we see in the account given by this chapter of the creation of new, coordinated powers of classification by English state agents regarding piracy is people who are living in and working through their own version of the *negara*, the theater state in nineteenth-century Bali described by Geertz (related at the beginning of this chapter). To do things together, and thus to achieve effects of power, always and everywhere requires that power have a form, and form has density, inertia, meaning, and consequence. Aesthetics is nothing if not signification, and signification plays a constitutive role in the achievement of all forms of collective power, including the most bluntly material. Aesthetic formulations, along with other aspects of social performances, are a necessary dimension of meaningful state action, and when they are effective they lock action tightly to particular formulations of state semiotic structure, reduce the scope of interpretive ambiguity, and create the conditions for the coordinated orientation of situations toward the matrix of state meanings.

All the figuring that this chapter documents about what form the power to classify pirates should take, what procedures and scripts to use, and what to say to actuate the necessary signs and chains of propagation is revealed in the available light of Geertz's arguments as also an effort to constitute coordinated social power, find a form that would work, and in doing so map its limits and possibilities. That effort was a group of people, some only loosely affiliated, exploring new forms of symbolization and interpretation and tying those forms to chains of reifying action. Confronted by new possibilities for collective performance and new possibilities for interpretive power, what they were figuring, collectively, was how the new interpretive infrastructure could be realized and how it could not.

CHAPTER SIX

"Hung Up in Irons, to Be a Spectacle, and So a Warning to Others"

The title of this chapter is a quotation from the *Boston Gazette* newspaper on June 8, 1724, relating the aftermath of the execution of William White and John Rose Archer for piracy. As the paper reports, "On Tuesday . . . were executed here, for piracy, John Rose Archer, Quarter Master, aged about 27 years, and William White, aged about 22 years. After their death they were conveyed in boats down to an island where White was buried, and the Quarter Master was hung up in irons, to be a spectacle, and so a warning to others."[1] Making a spectacle of Archer seems to have worked. Jeremiah Bumstead records in his diary an outing to see the body a few days after the execution: "My wife and Jery and Betty [a boy of 16 and a girl of 17], David Cunningham and his wife, and 6 more, went to the castle to Governors Island, and to see the piratte in Gibbits att Bird Island."[2]

The creation of an interpretive infrastructure that allowed for coordination among state agents was a crucial part of creating the state capacity to classify and execute men like White and Archer for piracy, as the previous chapter argued. However, the performance of codified and institutionalized meanings as situational realities by state actors was not the only way that the social performance of meaning mattered. It is also useful to think about social performances like the great bloodletting against pirates in the 1710s and 1720s—as hundreds of pirates died at the hands of state agents from Boston to Cape Coast to London—in a more expressive, theatrical, didactic, and spectacular sense. Social performances are also communicative tableaux, scenes that realize meanings and by doing so project those meanings as vivid and visible public displays (Garland 1991; Reed 2019, 2020; Smith 2008). In this sense, social performances stage, dramatize, and assert state meanings and powers for a broader audience and can proclaim the existence of new sociopolitical orders. The possibility of such displays was the focus of previous chapters, but in this chapter we turn to the dramaturgy of these events as well as to the ways that the newly polluted category of piracy was taken up by nonstate actors as a naturalized part (Bourdieu 1999a, 2015) of the moral fabric of their world. The propagation of piracy meanings did not stop at the edges of state institutions. Rather, clarifying piracy as a legal category made it more readily available for incorporation by members of the public into moral discourses focused on the opposition between civilization and savagery. Classification translated into spectacle and from spectacle into a moral signifier circulating beyond state institutions, representing a defined and despised evil held in check by state power.

CLASSIFICATION SPECTACLES

Piracy trials of the later seventeenth century, as described in previous chapters, lacked crucial elements necessary for them to be effective in the symbolic and practical articulation of a coercive threat. They were inconclusive, rare, random, time consuming, expensive, and geographically limited to London. It was obvious that only the most high-profile cases would be tried, so even the spectacular trials that did happen, such as those of Henry Every's men and of Captain William Kidd, which garnered popular interest, were exceptional. Consequently, they were not a good basis for creating a routinized coercive threat against small-time mariners contemplating mutiny. The new trials, on the other hand, inverted all these characteristics. In place of the earlier ambiguity, the new legal structures and coordinating scripts made the new trials consistent displays of a terrifyingly clear and real interpretive power.

With the new legal and performative structures in place, hundreds of pirates were executed between 1704 and 1730, in places where they could not previously have been tried. Large trials of pirates that were publicized and followed throughout the British imperial world took place in 1704, 1717, 1718, 1719, 1720, 1721, 1722, 1723, 1724, 1725, and 1726, with multiple trials occurring in some of these years (Cordingly 2006, 245–47). After 1726, piracy trials became rarer, because the point had more or less been made and piracy was in steep decline. The level of public interest varied between trials, depending on the notoriety of the pirates involved, the numbers, the location, or some other element of novelty in the case. But the effects of this constant stream of trials cannot be properly understood simply as a matter of crime and punishment. First of all, legal actors in the early eighteenth century constantly went to some rhetorical lengths to refute the notion that piracy was just another crime. As the prosecutor in the trial of Samuel Bellamy's crew in Boston stated in a trope ubiquitous in these trials, "The laws of all nations that have settled into regular governments, define & declare a pirate to be *an enemy of mankind.*" The pirate, therefore, "can claim the protection of no prince, the privilege of no country, the benefit of no law . . . nor is he to be otherwise dealt with than a wild and savage beast, which every man may lawfully destroy." The prosecutor then turned to another trope that runs throughout the prosecutors' cases in piracy trials, that piracy "is in itself a complication of treason, oppression, murder, assassination, robbery and theft, so it denotes the crime to be perpetrated on the high seas, or some part thereof, whereby it becomes more atrocious."[3] What these representations of piracy do, and what they suggest as a general framework for understanding what was at stake in piracy trials, is to establish piracy as a uniquely terrible and consequential offense. Piracy in these trials then becomes an iconic crime having deep associations with the lawless horrors of a bestial, pregovernment past. Based on this understanding of the crime, piracy trials were more than just efforts to provide justice in given cases. In trying pirates—whose crimes occurred in a maritime wild, far from what contemporaries recognized as civilization—state agents staged intense, dramatic confrontations between the forces of state order and criminal chaos. The crime of piracy was committed against individuals, but it was tried as a crime against the peace of the sovereign, and thus it was an advocate for the king or queen who tried the case. In symbolic terms, these trials were struggles not between victims and perpetrators but between perpetrators and the state.[4] One of the most striking rhetorical moves here is the definition of piracy as occurring beyond the reach of justice at the same moment that justice is being performed against a pirate. Piracy trials staged and dramatized the expansion of justice, law, commerce,[5] and political order over the wild spaces of social life.

At times this theme was very specifically mobilized. For example, state agents could be deliberate in their efforts to use a piracy trial to expand their claims of the reach of imperial sociolegal order. On August 25, 1726, a case noted in the previous chapter, a group of Mi'kmaq and French sailors captured a New England fishing vessel in Nova Scotia.[6] The crew eventually took their ship back and captured five of their assailants. The captives were sent to Boston for trial where, despite significant problems of law and jurisdiction, a piracy court found them guilty.[7] All five were executed in Boston on November 2, 1726.[8] As with many significant piracy cases, the trial report was printed. In 1727, as Plank writes, the report was "read aloud to the Acadian inhabitants of the eastern village of Beaubassin. No English-style institutions of governance had yet been established in Beaubassin, and the records were read to the villagers in an effort to inform them about what to expect after regular courts were established" (2001, 83). The trial as a performance of state interpretive power became a symbolic resource for officials engaged in the project of bringing Nova Scotia into the British empire of law. Their project dovetailed perfectly with the order-disorder binary system at the heart of the dramaturgy of piracy trials.

EXECUTIONS

"Then the court ordered the prisoner back again to the bar, who was told by the President that the court, had unanimously found him Guilty of the charge laid against him . . . the President proceeded to pronounce the usual sentence; that he should go to the place from whence he came [the jail], and from thence, to the place of execution, where he was to be hanged by the neck, 'till he was dead, and the Lord have mercy upon his soul." Thus ran the verdict in March of 1720 concluding the trial of Charles Vane, the pirate who set alight a French prize and made good his escape upon Woodes Rogers's arrival in the Bahamas as its governor.[9] This verdict typified the death sentences that concluded many piracy trials and set the scene for the final, dramatic act of the legal performance. Executions (fig. 6.1) played a critical role in the success of the new legal regime in creating a credible coercive threat against pirates but not merely because they were violent. Violent they were, and the material violence in which executions culminated was central to the meaning of the event, but this just underscores the fact that executions were social rituals deeply textured by a system of meanings (Smith 2003).

One of the most notable features of pirate executions emerged from the jurisdictional structure of the legal authority to try pirates. Piracy fell under the jurisdiction of special piracy tribunals. But the jurisdiction of these courts was tied to the definition of piracy as a crime occurring at sea. The courts presided over, in the words of the statute, "all piracies . . . committed in or upon the sea, or in any haven, river, creek, or place, where the admiral or admirals have power, authority, or jurisdiction."[10] Just as these legal powers were limited by the scope of the admiral's jurisdiction, so executions under the 1700 Act for the More Effectual Suppression of Piracy were limited in this sense. The language of the statute gives the courts power to sentence convicted pirates to death, with the executions occurring "upon the sea, or within the ebbing or flowing thereof."[11] This otherwise odd requirement reflects the settled jurisdictional boundary between the common law courts and the admiralty. As a general matter, this division was made at the water's edge, though there were significant questions relating to rivers, bays, and other such locations (Prichard and Yale 1993, clxxi–clxxxv). The executions of pirates reflected this jurisdic-

FIGURE 6.1. The execution of Major Stede Bonnet in Charlestown, South Carolina, 1718. From the Dutch version of Charles Johnson's *General History of the Pyrates. Majoor Stede Bonnet Gehangen*. 1725. From *Historie der engelsche zeeroovers... door Capiteyn Charles Johnson* (Amsterdam: Hermanus Uytwerf). Courtesy of the John Carter Brown Library, Brown University.

tional divide, and usually occurred just within the limits of the admiralty jurisdiction, between the low- and high-tide marks. For instance, in the mass execution following the trials of Bartholomew Roberts's captured crew in West Africa, fifty-two men were hanged "without the gate of Cape-Corso-Castle, within the Flood-Marks."[12] The trial report for the execution of members of Bellamy's crew in 1718 similarly takes care to note that the sentence was carried out "within flux and reflux of the sea."[13]

A pamphlet titled *An Account of the Behaviour and last Dying Speeches of the Six Pirates, that were executed on Charles River, Boston Side* provides a detailed account of the atmosphere and the aesthetics of execution day for John Quelch and his crew. In accordance with the warrant from the court to execute Quelch and five others,

> the aforesaid pirates were guarded from the prison in Boston, by forty musketeers, constables of the town, the Provost Marshall and his officers &c. with two ministers who took great pains to prepare them for the last article of their lives. Being allowed to walk on foot through the town, to scarletts wharf, where the Silver Oar[14] being carried before them, they went by water to the place of execution, being crowded and thronged on all sides with multitudes of spectators . . . when [the pirates] were gone up upon the stage, and silence was commanded, one of the ministers prayed as followeth . . . (as near as it could be taken in writing in the great croud) . . . [The pirates] then severally spoke.[15]

The impression given by this account is of a spectacle with clear symbolic portents and commanding wide public interest. The reality of the coordinated capacity of state agents in Boston to interpret the legal meaning of a sequence of actions, and to propagate that interpretation through a network of state agents—jailers, musketeers, hangmen—and into the public— spectators, clergymen—was literally paraded through the town, displayed for all. The great number of spectators for the execution is captured in the diary of Chief Justice Samuel Sewall, who had been a commissioner for the trial:

> After Diner, about 3.p.m. I went to see the Execution. Many were the people that saw upon Broughton's Hill. But when I came to see how the river was cover'd with people I was amazed: some say there were 100 boats. 150 boats and canoes . . . when the scaffold was hoisted to a due height, the seven malefactors went up . . . ropes were all fasten'd to the Gallows. . . . When the scaffold was let to sink, there was such a screech of the women that my wife heard it sitting in our entry next the orchard, and was much surprised at it; yet the wind was sou-west. Our house is a full mile from the place.[16]

The crowds reported by Sewall, the shriek heard by his wife, and the trial report all speak to the great drama of the execution and the far reach that the spectacle had as a didactic moment (Garland 1991).

Quelch himself seems to have gotten right that the execution in which he was so unwilling a participant had significance beyond the immediate events and actions, calling out during the dying speeches that the "spectators . . . should also take care how they brought money into New-England to be hanged."[17] State agents indeed meant the execution as a message to spectators in Boston and beyond; its warning was not, though, that Boston had become uniquely deadly for pirates, but that a form of state power deadly for pirates now existed throughout the empire. Piracy trials, in this sense, staged the endemic symbolic problem of state formation—the entrenchment of a particular regime of political order over "disorderly" social and geographical space—and turned it into an acute drama that commanded the fascinated attention of colonial and metropolitan populations.

This interpretation of the meaning of the trial is supported by a dispatch about it from Governor Dudley of Massachusetts to the Board of Trade. In it, Dudley apologizes to the board for printing and disseminating the report of the Quelch trial before sending it to London. He writes, "My Lords, I should not have directed the printing of [the trial] here, but to satisfy and save the clamour of a rude people, who were greatly surprised that any body should be put to death that brought in gold into the Province, and did at the time speak rudely of the proceeding against them, and assisted to hide and cover those ill persons."[18] The surprise Dudley refers to over the ill-treatment of the pirates, a surprise echoing Quelch's complaint about what happens to people who bring gold to New England, was precisely the normalized meaning of piracy that the new legal regime needed to upend. Bostonians were not shocked that Quelch was a pirate, they were shocked that a pirate was actually hanged. Their surprise reflects their dawning awareness that the legal and symbolic ground had dramatically shifted, transforming pirates from ambiguous friends bearing gold into enemies of humanity.

The culmination of the execution ritual was also an explicit opportunity to create iconic displays of this new symbolic reality. After their execution, the bodies of pirates were sometimes hung in chains for public display. As the new piracy tribunals began hanging pirates in spectacular executions throughout the English Empire, the pirates' bodies, usually tarred to preserve them, were hung in gibbets throughout colonial ports. While trials and executions took but hours, tarred bodies could hang for years as reminders to passing mariners of the new powers that the agents of the empire could command against them, should they turn pirate. In the case of the most egregious violators among the fifty-two pirates convicted at Cape Coast Castle, the court incorporated the display of their bodies into their sentences. The pirates were to go to the "place of execution, and there within the flood-marks to be hanged by neck 'till ye are dead, dead, dead. And the Lord have mercy upon your souls. After this, you . . . shall be taken down, and your bodies hung in chains."[19]

FROM SPECTACLE OF PUNISHMENT TO MORAL MESSAGE: PROPAGATION IN THE PRESS AND THE PULPIT

Such displays extended chains of propagation beyond the state and its new interpretive infrastructure, carrying signs of the new legal order composed with the bodies of the condemned to spectators as well as through the dissemination of trial accounts: pamphlets, newspaper reports, and word of mouth around town and through networks of maritime trade and travel, eventually throughout the whole British colonial world. Social order was—as it still is—one of the most compelling moral questions that contemporaries faced. It is no surprise, then, that the moral drama of the confrontation between the new powers of the state over maritime violence and piratical depravity circulated widely, propagating the new legal meanings of piracy into far-flung and varied contexts where they were taken up, told, retold, and sometimes transformed.

Pirate stories were in favor before the early eighteenth century. Francis Drake's *World Encompassed*, focusing on his circumnavigation and pillage of Spanish America, as well as Henry Mainwaring's discourse on piracy drawn from his time as a pirate in North Africa were popular early accounts of the life. During the later seventeenth century, *The Buccaneers of America*, written by Alexander Exquemelin, was a publishing phenomenon, and it was hardly alone. Basil Ringrose's *Buccaneers Atlas*, multiple works focusing on the exploits of buccaneers such as Henry Morgan; Philip Ayres's *The Voyages and Adventures of Captain Bartholomew Sharp*; and Lionel Wafer's and William Dampier's accounts of their adventures all cover similar ground from different vantage points. Captain Charles Johnson's *General History of the Pyrates*, published in 1724, stands out as the most famous, detailed, and complex of these contemporaneous piracy volumes. From the early eighteenth century, regular newspapers began to appear in the colonies, and piracy was a consistent theme in their coverage. The first colonial weekly, the *Boston News-Letter*, included some 230 piracy-related items between 1704 and 1730, though during the war years piracy all but disappeared, with 215 items appearing from 1715 to 1730. While some of these articles deal with moral questions about law and empire, the vast majority are short and informational, providing matter-of-fact accounts of attacks, rumors, trials, and executions.

While all these works and genres introduce their own elements into the collective representation of piracy, for the purposes of understanding the production of coercive power over piracy, the significance of this extensive literature is that it turned piracy into a generalized sign of chaos and criminality as well as a symbolic challenge to state power and social order, even for those unlikely ever to encounter pirates directly. By the same token, it also made the eventual destruction of the pirates—under way in the late 1710s and clear to contemporaries by the mid-1720s—even more far-reaching as a symbol of state power and control over a maritime empire than the practical consequences of destroying pirates alone. It was partly because pirates were such pervasive and potent symbols of disorder and untamed alternatives to civilized society that their destruction was truly a powerful narrative of the triumph of state power. Yet in order to influence social life, performative scripts of justice, spectacles of state power and repentance, and dramas of social order require an audience. Though great crowds would gather for trials and especially for executions, these groups were necessarily local. With the explosion of print culture in the later seventeenth century, accelerating through the early eighteenth century, the press played an important role in multiplying manyfold the audience for tales of piracy, tales of trials, and tales of the bad ends to which the wicked would come.

Convicted pirates were also often the objects of significant attention by divines, who played a parallel but distinct role in the propagation of pirate dramas. The emergence of piracy as a recurring theme in religious discourse provides a useful vantage point for looking at the simultaneous propagation and transformation of the meanings of piracy as it circulated beyond state institutions. Clergymen saw the drama of crime and punishment surrounding pirates as an excellent opportunity to make allegorical points and teach moral lessons. Cotton Mather, the famed and influential New England Puritan minister, took the piracy trials that began to occur in New England after the 1700 piracy act as excellent opportunities to minister to the pirates and deliver sermons to the public, often just before an execution. Many of his sermons reflect fairly standard religious tropes of the time. A sermon of Mather's from 1704, for example, turns on the theme "evil pursues the sinner" and focuses on wickedness versus righteousness, good versus evil, hell, and, of course, lots of sin. Piracy executions brought multiple episodes and forms of violence into a single event, which seems to have given him and other preachers some license to explore the darker aspects of divine power. In these sermons, the reader is told of the "dreadful wrath of the holy and jealous God."[20] In the violent imagery employed by Benjamin Colman, a contemporary and a competitor of Mather's, this is a God that smites, wounds, rends, and punishes; his sermon preached at a piracy trial in 1726 celebrates the "power and force of [His] vindictive wrath!"[21] The God of these sermons is God the avenger, God of the gallows.

Yet ministers as well as state agents considered the conviction and execution of pirates as more than just another opportunity to deliver a sermon. Piracy trials were one of the premier social occasions in the early modern English Empire for state and religious actors alike to stage compelling dramas of moral order, both allegorical and real. To return to the theme introduced earlier in this chapter, these trials were also opportunities to create moral spectacles that might, it was hoped, command the attention of wayward publics. This notion of both the trial and the sermon as a moment for creating moral spectacles was explicit in how preachers as much as judges understood the opportunity represented by captured pirates. In another of his 1726 sermons, for instance, Mather warms to the theme that in order to escape from dying unrepentant, and thus to escape from the eternal torments of hell, sinners needed to hear the thoughts of condemned men. And lo and behold, the opportunity was at hand for just such timely instruction, for "the great God has ordered it, that a number of dying men appear among us, in some tragical and peculiar circumstances. Another company of pirates under sentence of death appear among us, and are within a few hours to be executed . . . it will be the wisdom of us all . . . to learn from these dying men."[22] In Mather's view, God intended the spectacular character of the mass execution to be used as an opportunity for mass repentance: "The glorious God expects that we do the best we can, to make this a profitable & a serviceable spectacle; and that our foolhardy sinners, knowing the terror of the Lord, may be dissuaded from going on still in their trespasses . . . if one went unto them from the dead, they will repent."[23]

The nature of the crime of piracy also had certain risks as a sermon theme that Mather and other clergymen were careful to manage. While "displayes of His vengeance"[24] might indeed terrify, piracy was such an extreme example of immoral and illegal action that audiences might easily regard the sermon's lessons as not applicable to them. Preachers were happy to refute this interpretation. Condemned pirates had moral lessons that all could benefit from. In a 1723 sermon of Mather's, for instance, he enjoins his audience to "mark the way that wicked men have trodden."[25] Men did not, of an instant, change from God-fearing folk into vicious criminals. According to Mather, there were six clear steps by which men became pirates. They scorned their parents,[26] profaned the Sabbath, gave themselves up to vice, engaged in the abomination of unchastity, cursed, kept evil company, and failed to live a Godly life and practice religion.[27]

One of the condemned pirates captures more succinctly the same moral message of piracy executions for sinners of the more quotidian sort, warning the audience to "keep clear from those paths of destruction that had brought them so far into ruine."[28] His path metaphor captures a common theme throughout these sermons, that pirates were once like anyone else. Then, through a series of small transgressions that grew larger, they were led to the gallows, where they faced not only the vengeance of the state but the very real prospect of, as Mather warns, being "thrown into a place of torment, and be chained up in blackness of darkness, forever, where the devils . . . will insult you, will torture you, will be very uneasy companions to you."[29] By making the path to hell a journey of small steps, the moral lessons of piracy became lessons for all.

There was one audience in particular, however, for which ministers and other moral agents had special fears and concerns. Mariners were often construed as a particularly vulnerable group because of the nature of their profession and the childlike character that contemporaries attributed to them. Their life was filled with peculiar temptations and hazards, according to the moralizers,[30] because their work carried them so far from the redoubts of civilization. The dense institutional framework supporting civil and moral law in the metropole, and to a lesser extent in the colonies, was of the greatest delicacy on a ship, weeks or months from home. This helped explain the unique grip that vices and lusts had over "men of the sea,"[31] but the seamen themselves were also notably weak. The *Seaman's Monitor*, a volume bearing a subtitle promising that it will provide "advice to sea-faring men, with reference to their behavior before, in, and after their voyage, with prayers for their use . . . with a caution to prophane swearers . . . to which is now added a seasonable admonition against mutiny and piracy,"[32] combines all these fears in a text sufficiently popular to go through many editions. It expresses the concern that ships at sea could all too easily become godless places, so it recommends that officers implement a program of religious instruction as well as ensure that systems of government were in place to control the conduct of seamen. As for the common mariners, it includes pages of recommendations, as promised in the title, of the sort that they remain sober, devout, and so on. Piracy, and especially the capture, trial, and execution of pirates, bore an especially important warning for these "sea-faring peoples." In a letter penned just before his execution and bundled with a 1726 sermon of Mather's, a pirate begs mariners in particular to avoid the "criminal pleasures" of swearing, blasphemous language, stealing liquor, drinking, dancing, whoring, "and the rest." For "happy is he, who corrects his faults by the faults of others. And now, happy would our sea-faring people particularly be, if the crimes and the ends of some whom they have seen drowned in perdition, might effectually cause them to beware of the faults, with which they may any of them charge themselves."[33] Mather, too, thought mariners were especially prone to drunkenness and swearing, and he believed that these behaviors were precursors to piracy,[34] but he also thought that one of the greatest moral failings leading down the path from common seaman to pirate was a haste to be rich.[35] In this he was simply channeling what Baer describes as the "conventional and widespread belief that pirates were motivated by 'aspiring thoughts,' a lust for wealth and power well above that of ordinary thieves" (Baer 2007, 3:194).

The living conditions of seamen were also the basis for a minor but important theme running through the moral discourse surrounding piracy as regards social justice issues. While most of the moralizers saw the problem of piracy as one of sin and weakness, others saw piracy as a problem that emerged from miserable, even abusive working conditions on merchant ships.[36] As William Fly, a convicted pirate, puts the case in discussion with Cotton Mather, "I can't charge myself, I shan't own myself guilty of any murder, our captain and his mate used us barbarously. We poor men can't have justice done us. There is nothing said to our commanders, let them never so much abuse us, and use us like dogs. But the poor sailors . . ."[37] Fly returns to the theme in his final speech on the gallows stage, saying "that he would advise the masters of vessels to carry it well to their men, lest they should be put upon doing as he had done."[38] This view was not confined to convicted pirates. It finds further expression in section 18 of 11&12 William III, c. 7, forbidding captains from willfully abandoning crew members far from home as a way to cut costs—one of the practices most hated by mariners. It was also the subject of an extended treatment in the anonymous treatise *Piracy Destroy'd*.[39] While the author bemoans "the general depravation of sea-men's manners" as the "grand cause of piracy,"[40] this is not in fact the focus of the work. Rather, *Piracy Destroy'd* is a volume of social analysis couched as an exploration of the reasons given by pirates "in order to excuse their horrid trade of piracy."[41] The main factors identified in the text include beatings, bad food, not being paid or only being paid at the end of a string of voyages that might last many years (causing particular difficulties for these men's families), and falling into mutinous company. A series of suggestions for fixing these problems follows the analysis.

But the social justice explanation for piracy never displaced the focus on the moral character and behavior of the seamen themselves. The dominant view saw the problems of working conditions as, properly understood, a problem of obedience. In a letter published with Mather's 1723 sermon, for example, a condemned pirate beseeches "all that are servants, to keep with, and be faithful to their masters, for if I had been dutiful to mine, 'tis likely, I had not been brought to the untimely end, which I am now come to."[42] The *Seaman's Monitor* gives a more extended account of the same argument. It maintains that in order to avoid mutiny, mariners should "submit yourselves readily and cheerfully to the commands of your superiours, tho' they should sometimes happen to prove untoward and imperious; to perform with diligence and care what you are engaged your selves to by voluntary agreement, for the better advancement of your mutual happiness in your several stations."[43] According to this tract, mariners must "demean [themselves] respectfully and submissively towards . . . superiours," not just to avoid mutinies, but because the fifth commandment, in a common contemporaneous interpretation, requires not just obedience to one's parents but "also the King, and all that are put in authority under him." The class aspects of this claim are explicit and seen as divinely inspired. Mariners needed to order themselves "lowly and reverential" to their betters, because God had placed "most of [them] in the station of common sailor." If any more evidence was needed, the author reminds readers that Saint Peter, in 1 Peter 2:18, commands that "servants be subject to your masters with all fear."[44]

The theme of obedience among mariners should be understood in the context of another moral formulation that represented piracy not just as a crime, or even a particularly pernicious and vicious crime, but as an eruption of wildness that threatened the civilized moral order. In various legal and moral documents, pirates collect a wide range of epithets, and the theme of wildness links many of them. Contemporaries described pirates as barbarians, predaceous animals, monsters and merciless monsters, cockatrices, madmen, unmerciful creatures, sea monsters, leviathans, savages, barbarians, wild and savage beasts, beasts of prey, and ravenous beasts. They are possessed of evil hearts, insatiable thirsts, and hateful characters, and they engage in barbarous murder and sail under the captaincy of Satan.[45] Pirates were not just wild by nature in the contemporaneous moral imaginary but had "declared themselves to live in opposition to the rules of equity and reason."[46] Thus, they were worthy of what was perhaps the most common of the epithets against pirates, used by judges, prosecutors, kings, and clergy alike: enemies of mankind, *hostis humani generis*.[47] In a sense, though, pirates were not even enemies, for agents of enemy states at war could lawfully attack one another, and the actions of such proper enemies were interpreted differently because of that status. But pirates, as the prosecutor of the crew of Edward Low points out, "are engag'd in a perpetual war with every individual, with every state, Christian or infidel; they have no country, but by the nature of their guilt, separate themselves, renouncing the benefit of all lawful society, to commit these heinous offences."[48]

In this context of a binary opposition between pirates and civilization, it is unsurprising that references to Rome, a well-known trope in early modern discourses of civilization, are common throughout the corpus of pirate texts. "The Romans therefore justly stil'd 'em *hostes humani generis*,"[49] noted the prosecutor of Low's crew in 1723; "A pyrate was justly called by the *Romans, hostis humani generis*," said John Quelch's prosecutor in 1704.[50] In describing the task of the court, the prosecutor of Samuel Bellamy's crew in 1717 extolled the great victory achieved by Pompeii over the pirates.[51] Mather, predictably, thought the specter of destruction a better motivator than victory, and related as a parable the first half of the same story, focusing on the surge of piracy after the destruction of Carthage and Corinth: "All commerce was interrupted; the city that was the empress of the world was well nigh starved; some of its magistrates as well as the other principal citizens, fell into the hands of the robbers. . . . The robbers with their vessels, entered the very *Tiber*, as if *Rome* it self were designed for a prey unto them."[52] The same fear of infiltration was on the lips of the prosecutor in Bellamy's case as he thanked God for the storm that had destroyed Bellamy's ships and drowned most of his crew, for otherwise the pirates would have "entered our harbours, and . . . might have been now giving laws to those, from whom they expect to receive their doom."[53] In this context, obedience as a cardinal virtue made excellent sense, as it was its opposite, rebellion, that turned mariners into the enemies of civilized order. The roots of piratical wickedness, thought Mather, were in a rebellion against God[54] that led to a "revolution aboard the ship."[55] Through such rebellion, pirates would place themselves permanently beyond the boundaries of civil life, in a "wilderness of savage beasts" where they would be "continually exposed to the great dangers of the winds and waves, and be like wicked Cain."[56] Through flowery descriptions, extended metaphors, and fantasies of destruction, actors oriented toward the new binary semiotics of piracy that could now be produced by state agents saw piracy as a spectacular staging ground between order (the state, merchant capitalism, godliness) and disorder, waged on the edges of empire.

The wildness of pirates was thus characterized as in a direct struggle with both God and the state, chaos versus order. But yet another connection needs to be made in this system, for many contemporaries saw strong ties between God and the state. In the piracy trials, this relationship appears sporadically, with occasional references to the Ten Commandments, divine law, and other religious concepts.[57] In Cotton Mather's writings, however, this theme has a powerful, central expression. In his piracy sermons, Mather routinely uses the semiotic apparatus of the civil legal process to describe the power of God. He says to one group of condemned pirates, "You have trampled on [God's] authority, and shaken off the government of your maker. You have defied his infinite power. . . . The law of God is arm'd with a penalty. The horrible thing you have done in breaking the law, deserves all that is in the penalty. Now, what have you to plead, why the penalty of the broken law, should not be executed on you?"[58] Elsewhere he speaks, in the same terms that the king was to use in his act of grace, of God issuing proclamations and pardons.[59] Even the question of procedure finds its way into Mather's theology. He is impressed by the new and "severe procedure of justice"[60] that the government of New England undertook in the Quelch trial of 1704, the first to use the new legal powers of 1700; and he extolls God's role as judge of the world whom we must all someday come before, just as the pirates came before their earthly judges.[61] For Mather, the punishment of pirates was a direct providential stroke, either when undertaken by storms and shoals, as with the destruction of Bellamy and his crew in 1717,[62] or through the exercise of state power. In 1724 he notes the massive destruction of pirates that had taken place since the late 1710s, and thanks God that through the combined forces of prayer and state action, the pirate threat was in abeyance. "A generation of pirates, have of late years, been an uncommon terror of them that haunt the sea. . . . ," he writes, "but a strange blast of heaven has followed that generation of sea-monsters. We know of several thousands, that in a little time have perished wonderfully! And no where more wonderfully than on the coast of New-England, where the prayers against them, have distinguishing ardours."[63] That strange blast from heaven, of course, was the powerful new apparatus of state classificatory legal power against the pirates.

To return to the notion of moral spectacles introduced at the beginning of this section, one final part of the moral semiotics of piracy should be discussed, and that is the trope of the pirate repentant. While pirates could be executed immediately after a trial, often some time was given in order to afford ministers a chance to bring them to a proper demonstration of contrition. These repentance accounts filled an important gap in the struggle between piracy as wildness and the state and God as order. While the execution represented a narrow, corporal triumph in this struggle, the aesthetic structure of the conflict meant that for a true victory, wildness needed to be not just destroyed but tamed. Public repentances became important dramas of subjugation that, when successful, represented a breaking of what was wild—though the risk, always, was that the best that could be done was destruction. Yet in many cases, either in the pamphlets of ministers or in the dying speeches of pirates, repentance dramas were successful. In this context, success meant a humiliated supination before the glory of God, the justice of the state, the wickedness of the crimes committed, and the wickedness of the path of sin that led to the gallows. One of Mather's condemned interlocutors gives a suitably miserable example of the genre. When Mather asks how he finds his heart disposed, the man answers, "Oh! I am in a dreadful condition! Lord Jesus, dear Jesus, look upon me!" "You are sensible that you have been a very great sinner?" Mather asks. "Oh! Yes, I am! And is it possible that such a sinner should ever find mercy with God! O God, wilt thou pardon such a sinner!"[64] And elsewhere, Mather is explicit that repentance can only be laid on a foundation of humiliation.[65] These personal, private semiotics of repentance would not do, however, for repentance in these cases was meant to be an instructive moral drama, and here the speeches and behavior of the condemned men at the time of execution were critical. In 1717, for instance, two of the condemned recited a psalm in Dutch on the execution stage before they were hanged, and in 1724 two convicted pirates, John Rose Archer and William White, "dyed with such expressions of repentance, as were greatly to the satisfaction of the spectators."[66] Even so, spectacles of repentance were always a matter of interpretation: the ultimate disposition of one's soul was a matter for God to decide.

Nonetheless, some signs were taken as clear indications of a pirate's successful conversion, while others were clear indications of an incorrigible character who could but be killed. William Fly, executed in Boston in 1726, was just such a "hardened wretch."[67] Fly was enraged that a conspiracy among men he had forced into piracy led to his being captured and turned over to the authorities. He refused, even under Mather's harsh gaze, to repent and acknowledge the justice of his fate. Mather bewailed Fly's obduracy in contrast to the supine compliance of his mates,[68] but he continued in his efforts to obtain the requisite signs of a true repentance, a true victory of order over chaos. Fly, though, gave no such signs, thus earning this comment in the account of the execution accompanying Mather's text: "as for Fly, he had been all along, a most uncommon and amazing instance of impenitency and stupidity, and what spectacles of obduration the wicked will be." Fly seemed intent on playing the part, arriving to the place of execution with a nosegay in his hand. He chatted with the crowd, leapt up on the scaffold, and then reproached the hangman for a sloppy knot before fixing it himself. In his final speech, related above, he warned ship masters who treated seamen badly to expect violence—no good sign of repentance there—and he refused all final efforts to get him to forgive those who had turned him over to the authorities. Fly's symbolic game was one of resistance to the end. In contrast, the other two pirates to be executed "had much greater signs of repentance," praying as well as enjoining spectators to take them as a warning. "They also justified the court, as well as acknowledged the justice of the glorious God, in the punishment they were now brought unto."[69] Their mortal end was the same, though: all three hanged.

But that was not that. Fly's performance, and his consistency in refusing repentance to the end, seems not to have struck the right chord for inclusion with a sermon encouraging the opposite. In the account of Fly's execution, Mather finds hidden signs to make up for the failed conversion drama and for Fly's continued insouciance: "But it was observed and is affirm'd, by some spectators, that in the midst of all his affected bravery, a very sensible trembling attended him; his hands and his knees were plainly seen to tremble."[70] Even that final, wishful sign was not enough. As with so many others, the final disposition of Fly's body was as a sign signifying the position of pirates in the moral order of the British Empire: "Fly's carcase hanged in chains, on an island, at the entrance into Boston-Harbour."[71]

PIRATES AND PERFORMANCES

The definition of social performance that I have used here focuses on the orientation of situational action to transsituational systems of meaning. These sorts of performances were critical in coordinating the actions of state agents in ways that brought piracy into an imperial system of law, and they allowed for the consistent use of violence against captured pirates throughout the empire. While state power over piracy is what I want to explain, that power was not just produced among state agents. The legal performances of the meaning of piracy—including the whole array of semiotic-performative expressions described above, from the formal ritual of the trials and their procedures, to the spectacular staging of state violence at public executions between the tide lines, to bodies tarred and displayed as eloquent signifiers—produced a framework for moral transformation. The vitriolic moralism of the preachers was likely not a fair gauge of average public sentiment, but public sentiment did shift, and the ambiguous integration of pirates into British colonial society and economy quickly unraveled in the 1710s and 1720s. Pirates could no longer expect a welcome for them or their coin in colonial ports; ambiguity ceded to danger.

The remaking of state classification rituals and the transformation of public moralism were not separate developments. By tearing apart the ambiguity that pirates of the previous century had enjoyed and turning it into a binary classification, publicly achieved and pronounced, the interpretive infrastructural developments in British piracy institutions created the conditions for a categorical moralism organized around polluting the category of piracy. It likewise made dealing with pirates a clear choice to consort with hated criminals. The ambiguity of the past was gone for all.

The ultimate locus of the destruction of piracy in the British Empire was not the gallows, the naval encounter, or colonial ports and pulpits. The key circumstance to breaking the back of the pirate threat often occurred far from these sites, on board the ships that plied the seas in ever-greater numbers in the early eighteenth century. With the curtailment of privateering and the easy access to ambiguous private violence it supplied, shipboard mutiny became the main point of entry to piracy. The dream of many mutineers turned pirate was that they could find an escape from the often abusive economic and political order in which they toiled. With the new powers of classification that state agents exhibited following the 1700 law and especially in the late 1710s, the dream of finding an outside to the semiotic, institutional, and material assemblages of state and commercial power dimmed and became desperate. As the bodies hanging in chains, the slavering sermons, the bloody-minded trial and execution tales displayed to all, even the fearsome and famous would ultimately be caught up in that infrastructure of power and usually before too long. What turning pirate meant had become all too clear.

CHAPTER SEVEN
Ambiguity Lost
Temporality and Fatalism on the Edge of Empire

The effects of the innovations in interpretive infrastructure that this book has detailed went beyond state agents and beyond pamphlets, ministers, merchants, and onlookers to impact the pirates themselves. These effects, like others already described, were not simply material, nor were they simply semiotic. Instead, they reflected elements of both qualities. Just as it spurred the transformation of pirates from rogues like Francis Drake and Henry Morgan to evil beasts in the cultural imaginary of the far-flung empire, the new interpretive infrastructure also remade the social world of the pirates and other men of violence on the empire's maritime periphery. This remaking led to the radicalization of piracy and eventually to its dissolution from one of the powerful forces of disorder facing the British maritime empire to a marginal if persistent nuisance.

An important driver of that change was the fact that the new interpretive infrastructure could deliver swift, certain, and severe punishment (Kleiman and Kilmer 2009; Schelling 1960). This rational and instrumental mechanism for changing the behavior of seamen who might turn pirate, however, depended on the interpretive and semiotic effects of the interpretive infrastructure now assembled to confront piracy. Rational choices in a world "perfused with signs" (Peirce 1978, 448) are necessarily oriented to the semiotic specifics of their circumstance. In particular, the new threat of punishment depended on the capacity of this new interpretive infrastructure to remake the *temporality* of violent encounters at sea, rendering encounters that were isolated, violent, and in the past symbolically present and accessible in contexts of power such as trials, where state interpretive categories could be imposed on them with blood.

It was through this mechanism, and the patterns of punishment that flowed from it, that the situations where in earlier eras pirates drew their strength, pillaged the weak, and sought legal ambiguity were remade in an inhospitable light. By attacking the impunity afforded by spatial isolation in each of these areas through their new semiotic, institutional, and temporal powers, the British elites' desire to purge piracy from the empire finally began to gather force. In other words, the state was unable to control the isolated spatial areas in which piracy took place—the open seas—but it could control the eventuality of punishment: at some point in time, the state would forcibly create the opportunity to adjudicate piratical actions, and it would have both the authority and the ability to redefine those events on its own terms. The British state made sure that time was on its side, even if space was not.[1]

It was in this remade maritime world that early-modern European pirate culture simultaneously reached its apotheosis and began its rapid descent.

TRIAL TIME

On Thursday, October 30, 1718, at Admiralty Sessions in Charlestown, South Carolina, Attorney General Richard Allein provided a scarcely necessary recounting of a recent communal trauma. He asked, "What a grievous Dilemma were we our selves reduced to in the Month of May last?, when Thatch the Pirate [Edward Teach, a.k.a. Blackbeard] came and lay off this Harbour with a ship of forty guns mounted, and one hundred and forty men, and as well fitted . . . as any fifth-rate ship in the Navy, with three or four pirate sloops under his command." The pirate fleet at the mouth of Charlestown Harbor snatched up five prizes, some fifteen hundred pounds sterling, and a number of prominent hostages. They then, in Allein's words, "had the most unheard-of impudence to . . . demand a chest of medicines of the value of three or four hundred pounds . . . or otherwise they would send in the heads" of all the prisoners they had seized, including one member of the province's council. Further deepening the humiliation, three or four "of the pirates, walked upon the Bay, and in our publick streets, to an fro in the face of all the people, waiting for the Governor's answer." The governor yielded and sent the medicines; the pirates freed the hostages and departed.[2]

But the trial under way in October 1718 was not intended to adjudicate any of these alleged crimes from the previous May. Rather, men from the crew of Major Stede Bonnet, one of Teach's lieutenants at the time of the attack on Charlestown, were on trial for a separate act of piracy more minor and remote. How Allein eventually brings his discourse around to the indictment actually at hand is instructive. After recounting a series of other depredations allegedly perpetrated by Teach (who, to be clear, was not on trial), the attorney general says,

> Gentlemen, most of the said Bonnet's crew . . . are old offenders, and were with Thatch [Teach, a.k.a. Blackbeard] and Bonnet at the taking of all, or most of these vessels I have mentioned, and were with Thatch and Bonnet when they lay off our bar in May last, and sent up that insulting message [demanding the medicine chest], and were in the Engagement against Col. Rhett [where they were captured], so that there is hardly any room left for the least pity or compassion: who can think of it, when you see your fellow-townsmen, some dead, others daily bleeding and dying before your eyes? But the particular fact or act of piracy for which the prisoners at the bar are now to be tried is set forth in the indictment . . . we shall prove, that all the prisoners at the bar were at the taking of [Captain] Manwareing's sloop, [and] that they all bore arms.[3]

In this speech, Allein fuses both the past of Charlestown's humiliation and the past plunder of Captain Henry Mainwaring's ship into the temporality of the trial. The new interpretive infrastructure and its procedures for enacting consequential, state-oriented representations of piracy enable him to make the past part of the present, poised for judgment.

Using the institutionalized interpretive authority of Admiralty Sessions, the aggrieved of Charlestown could revisit a humiliating episode from their past and reinterpret it in accordance with an alternative system of social meaning based on concepts of law, right, and sovereignty, which at the time of the trial—in stark contrast to the time of the attack—they could forcefully assert. The attack on Charlestown was not even formally at issue in this trial, but contemporaries were insistent on making that past trauma present. They built the temporality of this later moment in the life of the community around the representation of the past moment of powerlessness and humiliation in order to enforce an alternative interpretation—a more righteous one, as they saw it, in which the pirates submitted to *their* categories of rightness and hanged by the harbor. This linkage of the new interpretive infrastructures and the institutionalized powers of violence that they produced to a new temporality of piracy is the central mechanism through which the legal and other institutional and semiotic changes described above remade the maritime world and remade piracy (Abbott 2001a; Zerubavel 1987).

It did so by opening a new angle of attack on one of the main advantages exploited by pirates and other men of violence in the early modern maritime world: isolation.

ISOLATION

Achieving even a modicum of control over the maritime world poses a problem for terrestrial organizations (Benton 2010; Mancke 1999; Rodger 2005). The nub of that problem is isolation. The technical complexity and expense of being at sea for long periods of time combined with the vastness of the oceans make isolation and isolated encounters between ships a persistent structural feature of the maritime world. This was particularly so after European mariners gained the requisite skills and equipment to shift from coastal to deep-sea sailing beginning in the fifteenth century. But spatial isolation was not (and still is not) in itself a resolvable problem in the control of violence. State power cannot be everywhere, always, with sufficient intensity to assert sovereign dominance.

To understand the efficacy of the new piracy institutions, it is helpful to think about the lawlessness of the seventeenth-century maritime world as a problem of both spatial and temporal isolation. Piracy and other acts of maritime violence occurred far from the power centers of the state. In these isolated, violent encounters, the "sovereign" was the one with the most guns and men, and that individual's interpretive authority ruled. An institutional interpretive infrastructure that was patchy when it existed at all and was generally staffed by state agents both venal and feckless furthermore ensured that these spatially isolated violent encounters would also be temporally isolated, unlikely to be revisited symbolically in a future context of greater state power. Isolation both spatial and temporal was central to structuring the ambiguity within which private, lawless, maritime violence thrived in the later seventeenth century.

That isolation was at the heart of the problem of control over maritime violence was clear to contemporaries. As one participant in an early eighteenth-century piracy trial described the purposes of the newly stringent legal powers state agents possessed over piracy, "Piracy is in its self . . . more atrocious . . . because it is done in remote and solitary places, where the weak and defenceless can expect no assistance nor relief; and where these ravenous beasts of prey may ravage undisturb'd, hardened in their wickedness with hopes of impunity, and of being concealed for ever from the eyes and hands of avenging justice."[4] The occurrence of piracy in "remote and solitary places," where its victims were at their most helpless, was seen by contemporaries as a key characteristic of piracy as both a uniquely vicious crime and a uniquely difficult crime to control. The solution to this problem of controlling violence in remote reaches of the sea in the early modern English Empire was to transmute the problem of spatial isolation into a more manageable if still complicated temporal problem. State agents achieved this transformation through the creation of a sociocultural capacity to return to the scene of violence and adjudicate it using the institutional, semiotic, and legal changes described in preceding chapters. These new interpretive institutional infrastructures created defined, focused, and durable social settings for staging consequential reinterpretations of past moments of isolated violence as performative exercises in state power. Categories mattered, because they provided the semantic structure underpinning these moral-legal distinctions and their assertions of state meanings that could be made relatively coherent across a global maritime empire (Bowen, Mancke, and Reid 2012, 2). New judicial institutions and categories enhanced the state's capacity to create perceived and practical temporal linkages between its interpretive institutions and isolated sites of violence.

For the pirates, the new powers of classification enacted by state agents meant that their isolated, violent encounters at sea could now be revisited by vengeful state agents at a future time and place where they had the upper hand. The isolation of the high seas and the remote coast was no longer a guarantee of impunity. Through the retrospective of a trial, state agents symbolically overcame spatial isolation to render judgment and assert the practical reality of state categories of meaning. A typical passage from a piracy trial: "The prisoners at the bar stand arraigned for sundry acts of piracy, robbery and felony by them committed at the time and place and in manner set forth in the articles of their indictment."[5] The language of the trial, the classification ritual that manufactures guilt itself, is clear and insistent that the premise of its judgment is the symbolic return to a precise time and place in order to adjudicate the unlawful violence defining that crime in the present time and place of the trial. In substituting state interpretive categories for the individualized powers of violence that so often dominated these isolated encounters in the early modern period, the state made the maritime world more amenable to its political-economic worldviews and stratagems (Mancke 1999; Pincus 2009, 305–99; Zahedieh 1998). Over time, this technique of state power altered the temporality of isolated encounters by creating a contextualizing maritime legal order that forcefully interpolated a *future* encounter with state agents into otherwise isolated interactions dominated by the powers of men, guns, and boats.

There is another important way that the manipulation of temporality under the auspices of the institutional and semiotic changes culminating in 1700 attacked the problem of isolation. While state agents symbolically transcended spatial isolation at the time of trials, inspections, requirements for documentation, and other assertions of interpretive power, these mechanisms also had the effect of directly ameliorating the spatial isolation of maritime encounters as they insinuated themselves into the *mentalities* of pirates, privateers, and other mariners. That is to say, they changed how these actors thought about the significance of the use of violence in their isolated encounters while they were engaged in those encounters. By staging trials where they could symbolically return to the past, state agents induced mariners at moments of potential or actual violence to look to the future and in doing so make state interpretive categories actual circumstances of the otherwise isolated encounter. As the capacity of state agents and institutions to eventually have the final say over the use of violence at sea was enhanced, seamen increasingly saw what they were doing in light of state-centric interpretive categories (Mische 2009; Wagner-Pacifici 2010). By giving distant, violent maritime encounters a more predictable future, the new structures of English/British state power emerging in the later seventeenth and early eighteenth centuries altered the expectations and interpretive frameworks that participants brought to these situations, ultimately changing the meaning of unlawful maritime violence for those tempted to commit it. To be influential, state agents did not need to be present or act in every isolated maritime encounter if the mariners who were there increasingly brought "the state" with them as a symbolic reality and an expected future context of account.

WHICH SIDE ARE YOU ON, BOYS?

Even as the British acted to remake the temporal horizons of piracy, the time horizons of other, related forms of maritime violence were also under revision, simultaneously subjected to a growing thicket of institutionalized social control as state agents sought to regulate such violence using their new interpretive power to achieve the temporal amelioration of spatial isolation. These developments had direct impacts on piracy. In particular, as discussed in chapter 3, privateering had long shared a porous border with outright piracy, and it was crucial to the ambiguity sheltering private maritime violence during the seventeenth century. The new semiotic regime of the early eighteenth century sought to sharpen that boundary into a binary lawful/unlawful proposition, patrolled by an enhanced institutional-semiotic capacity to transform the spatial problem of isolation by creating the capacity to authoritatively interpret past, remote episodes of "privateering" in light of state categories of meaning—the same mechanism at play in the regulation of piracy itself.

The contrast between the practice of privateering in the later seventeenth century and in the early eighteenth century is indicative of this transformation and the influence state agents gained during this period over this form of private maritime violence. On the one hand, consider the privateering exploits described by William Dampier. His account begins with Captain Bartholomew Sharpe leading a small armada of privateers who from 1680 to 1681 plundered at will from Portobelo in the Caribbean to the Juan Fernández Islands in the Southern Pacific. The privateers voted Sharpe out as captain for a time until his replacement died, at which point they reelected Sharpe. A faction displeased with Sharpe's leadership, including Dampier himself, broke off to trace their own path of plunder across Panama and back to the Caribbean. One of the striking features of these accounts is the fractious freedom of the buccaneers. As Dampier writes, "Privateers are not obliged to any ship, but free to go ashore where they please, or to go into any other ship that will entertain them, only paying for their provision."[6] These men felt an enormous sense of freedom not just in determining their constitution as purveyors of violence and in determining the targets of that violence—in one notable scene recounted by Dampier, some eight privateering vessels with some four hundred men lay off the San Blas Islands of Panama for seven or eight days deliberating on which Spanish target they should attack—but also in having minimal contact with state agents and only desultory concern for the legality of their actions. In one of the rare instances of concern, Dampier explains that a Captain Yanky decided to consort, "because Captain Yanky had no commission, and was afraid the French would take away his bark."[7] The future encounter with state agents that Yanky feared was but an inconvenience to be negotiated, particularly in a social world of such rapid fluctuation of crews and boats, not a practical impediment to predation.

In contrast, Woodes Rogers's 1708–11 privateering cruise was starkly different from the exploits of the fractious roving crews of Dampier's "privateering," reflecting the newly tightened semiotic realities governing private maritime violence.[8] Each of his two ships received a commission from the Lord High Admiral. His crew had a sharply hierarchical character—a council that included Rogers, Stephen Courtney as commander of the second ship on the voyage, and Thomas Dover, a financial backer of the voyage, made all major decisions. Indeed, the voyage had a number of investors, helping explain its orderly conduct and its leaders' concern with the lawfulness of their acts of predation.[9] This orderliness is clearly reflected in Rogers's relationship to his crew. Far from the free privateers described by Dampier, he kept them under strict control as though the ship were "a little commonwealth."[10] Four mutinies that Rogers suppressed over the course of the voyage tested that relationship. He believed it "very necessary to bring our crew to order and discipline, which is always very difficult in privateers, and without which 'tis impossible to carry on any distant undertaking like ours."[11] This sentiment calls for some clarification, for the earlier generation of buccaneers and privateers had carried on distant undertakings with sometimes spectacular success. By "like ours," though, Rogers means a voyage conducted in a strictly lawful, orderly, and hierarchically controlled way undertaken for the benefit of investors and not, in the first place, the privateering crew themselves. This was a new face of the privateering voyage, explicitly concerned, by Rogers's account, with its ability to weather future prize court adjudication, and from which investors might have the best hope of returns on their venture.

Concerns about future adjudication similarly shaped the use of violence by Rogers and his company in a way that contrasts sharply with the earlier generation of privateers. During the sack of the port city of Guayaquil, for instance, Rogers issued strict orders regarding behavior during the attack and later reported that his men's discipline was excellent with respect to both alcohol and the treatment of women. Rogers also makes a point in his account of including a testimonial from four Spanish captives from Guayaquil as to their excellent treatment by the privateers. His keen orientation to the future context of account for his voyage is likewise displayed in his decision to bring a Spanish captive from the South Seas on the long return trip to Britain "to condemn all our prizes took there."[12] When this captive fell ill, Rogers obtained a certificate that he had witnessed the taking of various prizes by the privateers and that they were all Spanish, thus falling under Rogers's commission. This care for the future was amply rewarded. Rogers and crew took the *Nuestra Senora de la Incarnacion Disenganio*, a newly built galleon out of Manila, in December 1709; sailing westward with their rich prize, they returned home in October 1711. Their punctilious adherence to the terms of their commission enabled them to successfully navigate an extended encounter with the Dutch authorities in Batavia along the way. Moreover, once back in England, such exacting care enabled a handsome profit to the shareholders in their voyage. The expedition cost some £13,000 to outfit and cleared around £150,000 at auction in London upon its return (Beattie 2007, 149–51).

In all their violent encounters, Rogers and crew made certain to secure all ships' papers and to carefully document their actions with an eye to later adjudication. Though they could hardly have been more distant from Britain or the organizational centers of British state power, as they circumnavigated the globe they took its laws—and its interpretive infrastructure—along in anticipation of a future encounter with them. In the actions of Rogers, we see an example of the mechanism connecting institutional and semiotic changes to the temporality of maritime violence:

in even their most violent, isolated encounters, Rogers and the others in command of the voyage oriented their actions to a future context of judicial account. The Rogers case does not represent a universal new mode of privateering, and irregularities in the always suspicious trade, not to mention collusion and abuse, persisted. By the early eighteenth century, however, the new temporal horizons of privateering imposed by the new institutional and semiotic forms used to interpret it had curtailed their scope. Only fools and pirates could afford to ignore the increased risks of nonconforming maritime predation, if not at the moment of sea struggle then in an increasingly predictable future.

SEAMEN AND VIOLENCE

Similar dynamics were simultaneously at play in another area related to the flow of men into piracy: the treatment of seamen and its impact on the likelihood of discontent and even mutiny. Mutiny, abuse, and other forms of interpersonal violence at sea were structured in a like manner by the isolating characteristics of sea voyages; and over roughly the same period English state agents adopted similar mechanisms for ameliorating that isolation through the manipulation of the temporality of such encounters.

English mariners were long the objects of a complex and contradictory set of representations, hopes, and fears (Hatfield 2005). On the one hand, mariners were a crucial resource for two of the most central problems toward which English state power was directed: commerce and defense. In another sense, though, mariners were a potential threat, living much of their lives far from the corrective guidance of state, society, and religion. This menacing light, as potential pirates and mutineers, was one way that contemporaries understood the role of seamen in maritime violence.[13] But they also saw seamen as particularly vulnerable to violence and exploitation. Mariners lived much of their lives subject to the potentially capricious and violent designs of ship captains, who themselves were known to use the isolation of the high seas to establish abusive regimes of corporal punishment, purportedly to regulate their seamen. These men were also seen as particularly gullible onshore, as they were inexperienced in the ways of the terrestrial world and likely to be taken advantage of. In addition, they were legally vulnerable in that their constant movement and contractual responsibilities to a given ship made their recourse to the law for the resolution of disputes tenuous.

These understandings of seamen as both violent and vulnerable were linked in the early modern English imagination. Contemporaries were explicit in citing the abuses that seamen routinely experienced, such as harsh corporal punishment or the practice engaged in by some captains of abandoning unnecessary men in ports far from home, as primary causes of piracy and mutiny. The regulation of seamen as sources of lawless violence at sea thus entailed both the control of their violence through the definition and punishment of wrongdoing and the amelioration of their vulnerability as a likely trigger of this sort of violence. Both of these effects depended on temporal manipulations of the sort previously described.

The common objective of the pastiche of legal and institutional changes relating to the control of seamen in the later seventeenth and early eighteenth centuries was the production of the mariner as a locus of controlled violence. The curtailment of pillage as a matter of custom and law well exemplifies the semiotic-institutional-temporal-spatial mechanisms that contemporaries brought to bear on this problem. Pillage is an ancient classification that reconciled more or less uncontrolled bouts of postvictory plunder with whatever notions of order and discipline pertained at the time. This complex social arrangement was customary among English naval and privateering vessels during the seventeenth century, with the right of pillage understood to extend only to the gun deck and only to the period directly after combat. In a 1664 proclamation, for instance, Charles II affirmed "that it be lawfull for all captains, seamen, and others serving as aforesaid to take and have to themselves as pillage without further or other accompt to be given for the same, all such goods and merchandise as shal be found by them or any of them in any ship they shall take in fight as prize upon or above the gun deck of the said ship, and not otherwise" (Marsden 1916, 51–52). This proclamation confirmed a 1661 act restoring the right to pillage after its legality came into doubt under the Commonwealth regime, and it explicitly recognized pillage as an exception to the general requirement that prizes be adjudicated before captors took any cargo.[14] The practice, while of age-old provenance, weakened any system of control by enabling the perpetration of a kind of isolated, violent maritime robbery subject only to immediate local oversight with no prospects of future state-centric account.

The intrinsically uncontrollable character of pillage made it a perpetual source of tension in international maritime affairs. The exercise of pillage on prizes taken by privateers either with dubious commissions or before condemnation exacerbated this tension. Even if the captured ship was brought to a prize court and ultimately judged not a good prize—the best-case scenario for the shipowner—pillaged goods and gear were unrecoverable by the very nature of their disorderly taking. The resumption of lawful pillage by Charles II's proclamation in 1664 had by 1665 already led to such problems, identified to the king by his prize commissioners: "Your Majesty was pleased to grant [pillage] unto the seamen; of which concession use had been made, not onely on shipps taken in heat of fight, but on shipps yielding without any opposition, and on very many brought in onely on suspition, and that very light" (Marsden 1916, 65). It is in this context that we should understand the abolition of pillage and the creation of a system of punishments for those who sought to "embezzle" goods from any place on the ship. These measures were enacted by a 1692 law as a temporal intervention aimed at controlling seamen in isolated places. Though the de facto elimination of theft from prizes took much longer, this act eliminated a long-standing semiotic category of maritime predation, because it had been immune by its nature to the sovereign's retrospective authority. In addition, the act created a legal mechanism for the future punishment of what was now, by statute if not custom, unlawful theft by force.[15]

Similar developments occurred in relation to mutiny and the duty to assist in the defense of a ship in the case of attack. The reliance of captains on their crews in case of attack and the vulnerability of ships in isolated locales to mutiny were constant concerns. Indeed, the two main sources of pirates were men who joined after their vessel had been taken by pirates and those who started their careers of violence as mutineers. This fact is reflected in the provisions of the 1700 Act for the More Effectual Suppression of Piracy, which specifies the meaning of piracy to include those who engage in mutiny to run off with their ship; those who engage in combines or confederacies with pirates; and those who obstruct their officers from defending the ship, as well as those who "bring any seduceing messages from any pirate, enemy, or rebell." Avoiding mutiny, however, was not the only concern arising from violence at the intersection of piracy and the control of seamen. In the case of attack by pirates, seamen were expected to fight, and thus the law also makes provisions for rewarding seamen who assisted in the defense of their ships, to be determined by a disinterested panel of merchants.[16]

It was not all punishment and prohibition. There were also some legal efforts that reflect an understanding and concern with the vulnerability of seamen as expressed by William Fly and shared by many contemporaries. These provisions likewise depended on a temporal mechanism to counter some of the vulnerabilities to violence created by seamen's isolation. The most significant of these efforts in relation to problems of distance and isolation were developments in the colonial vice admiralty jurisdiction during the 1690s, particularly following the 1696 Navigation Act. The Admiralty Court had long understood seamen as its special charges, and this perspective shaped the jurisprudence of colonial vice admiralty courts in the matter of seamen's wage disputes (Owen and Tolley 1995, 2–3, 11). In

Owen and Tolley's review of the Maryland vice admiralty records, they find that "the seamen won all the cases in which the results can be discerned" (1995, 145). These cases typically revolved around disputes over the responsibilities of owners and captains toward their crews and vice versa. Owners and captains were within their rights to refuse wages for various reasons, such as drunkenness, mutiny, refusal to work, and neglect of duty, but these rationales also were often used to cheat seamen of their due. Crewmen, for their part, were routinely recognized as justified in refusing to work if they experienced brutal treatment, bad food, and the breach of the initial agreement over the particulars of the voyage (Andrews 1936, 25–26).

Of course, *brutal*, *bad*, and *breach* were all sites of semiotic contestation and legal interpretation. Furthermore, the experiences these terms were used to describe usually occurred in isolated locales. After the 1690s, the institutionalization of tribunals for legally adjudicating these semiotic claims throughout the English Empire again sought to manipulate the temporality of these encounters, giving seamen access to an alternative form of time-shifted social power beyond their own immediate, private, and unlawful capacities for violence (Rediker 1987, 119).[17] With the creation of the possibility of an authoritative future recounting under color of state-centric legal categories, state agents were engaged in an effort to regulate both the violence of mutinous seamen and the violence of sailing masters that had driven many to piracy. Before the 1690s—with no institutional support for authoritative interpretations of the semiotics of disputes over pay and working conditions, and abundant possibilities for escape into the as-yet-unregulated margins of the European maritime world—the prospects for private violence by all parties appeared much greater.

These dynamics are clear in the adjudication of violence against seamen in later authoritative legal contexts. A 1763 case brought before the Maryland vice admiralty court involving the *Hannah*, whose master was accused of "barbarity, inhumanity, and ill usage" toward his crew, provides a striking example of the state's ability to retroactively revisit and redefine the meaning of an event. While the alleged instances of violence on the *Hannah* occurred in shipboard isolation, the retrospection occurred in a Maryland court, presided over by a judge who had expertise in the interpretation of the semiotics of duty and violence under English admiralty law; he also had the power to make his judgment of such meanings authoritative. The judge found for the seamen and ordered the ship condemned and sold, with the wages of the righteous deserters paid out of the proceeds—a future reckoning for acts exceeding the limits of the master-crew relationship (Owen and Tolley 1995, 324).

The institutional semiotics of colonial vice admiralty courts created an

enforceable duty of captains and shipowners to their crews and a reciprocal obligation on seamen to proceed lawfully in the case of disputes. By
creating a potential future context of interpretation more favorable to seamen, the new institutional and semiotic arrangements sought to pressure
captains and shipowners to fulfill that duty by making it an enforceable
practical imperative. The prevalence of pay disputes in colonial vice admiralty courts during the eighteenth century suggests that these institutional
semiotic changes had some effect, particularly in the context of more stringent punishments for mutiny. The freedom of action of mariners and their
captains and shipowners was somewhat curtailed during the eighteenth
century, as state agents, institutions, and semiotics inveigled themselves
into their disputes even far from home, a party capable of later revisiting
the scene and determining its social meanings even though it had not
been present. These were consequential strategies, but they were nonetheless limited in their effects, particularly when it came to protecting rather
than punishing seamen. The rights of seamen, in any case, and the abuses
they suffered remained a sore point even after the golden age of piracy had
ended, becoming central disputes in the "age of maritime radicalism" that
followed later in the eighteenth century (Anderson et al. 2013).

FATALISM AND RADICALISM ON THE EDGE OF EMPIRE

All these developments in privateering commissions, prize law, and the
vice admiralty jurisdiction relating to seamen reflect and reinforce the developments in the interpretive infrastructure of British piracy institutions.
All share a common central mechanism: the creation of an interpretive
nexus sufficiently consistent in its adherence to a codified web of significance to impose meaning on even isolated maritime activity. Together they
were moving the context of private maritime violence toward the idealized
vision depicted in figure 7.1, a model of the meanings of maritime violence
organized around a clarified matrix of oppositions. Where once a chaotic
ambiguity reigned, institutional developments had gradually restructured
the semiotic realities of the English maritime world around a collection of
binary oppositions and complementarities. Actions that during the seventeenth century were mired in sheltering ambiguity were now visible
against this clearer new ground of meaning.[18]

As piracy became ever more deeply enmeshed in a suffocating semiotic
web that stole piracy's impunity and replaced it with the likelihood of
future death; stole its refuge by defining its borderlands with privateering
in a binary way; and stole its future through tightened consequences for
mutiny and a perception of greater risks for seamen, piracy began to col-

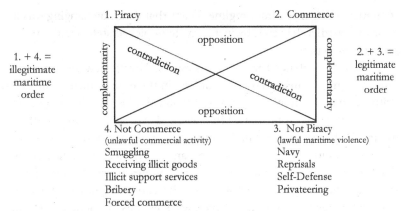

FIGURE 7.1. Greimas square illustrating the *idealized* semiotic structure relating maritime violence and commerce that the developments described in the book helped realize during the eighteenth century. This semiotic technique, developed by Algirdas Greimas (1983, 1987), visualizes how binary relations of opposition, contradiction, and complementarity imposed by state institutions clarified the meanings of forms of social action that had once been ambiguous by defining their relationship to other signifiers in this cultural system. In this idealized form, the structure remains arbitrary—they could have carved the world up differently—but is no longer ambiguous.

lapse. During this decade-long revelation of the new semiotic-institutional realities governing maritime violence, many men still turned to piracy, but they found themselves in a semiotic category offering little hope of a good end. Whereas Henry Morgan had once pillaged the Spanish in a brazenly lawless way and died a planter and vice governor of Jamaica, the men of the cohort active during the so-called golden age of piracy in the 1710s and 1720s had no hope for such an outcome. They lived close to death and inhabited the now-dangerous margins of empire with a notable fatalism and radicalism.[19]

Piracy's increasing radicalism in the early eighteenth century is further evidence that the new semiotic-institutional character of the piracy jurisdiction had penetrated mariners' mentalities by the later 1710s, thus bringing the cultural apparatus of state power into isolated maritime encounters. It is evidence, that is to say, of the changing temporality of maritime predation. While earlier cohorts of pirates had a strong incentive to hew to the ambiguous marginality in which they found substantial impunity, even isolated waters were no haven in the new institutional-semiotic context in which the pirates of the early eighteenth century operated. The unfettered powers of geographically dispersed piracy tribunals to apply the harsh semiotics of the new piracy regime meant that death by hanging was as close as a verdict delivered by just a few handpicked state agents from a poorly chosen port.

These foreshortened time horizons imposed by the new piracy institutions were most consequentially manifest in the pirates' turn against the British and their colonies. Although British colonies into the later seventeenth century often turned a blind eye and extended an open hand to pirates, by the 1710s they had become sites of danger and punishment. As alliances with colonial governors became unreliable, as public opinion in many places began to demonize them, pirates began to turn against formerly welcoming ports and sub-rosa allies, attacking British ships and towns as willingly as any other. In one suggestive episode, Benjamin Hornigold assembled a formidable group of pirates based out of the Bahamas in 1717, but his crew removed him from his position because he refused to attack English ships.[20] Hornigold's ejection typified the new radicalism of piracy in the 1710s, abandoning even the semblance of legality and national affiliation. By turning on Britain, the pirates of the early eighteenth century made a clear break with the buccaneers and privateers of the seventeenth century who still recognized some value, practical and moral, in maintaining national allegiances with their fellow Englishmen in the colonies. After Hornigold's old-fashioned nationalism led to his ouster, Blackbeard, Edward Teach, took over as captain. Teach had no similar compunctions and set himself and his crew savagely against the world, threatening to kill all New Englanders he found after a Boston piracy tribunal put "Black" Sam Bellamy to death. He perpetrated the humiliation of Charlestown described above as he careered across the western Atlantic, snapping up all ships unlucky enough to cross his path regardless of their flag. In his loyalty to none save his crew, Teach embodied this era of piracy.

The men who turned pirate in this era were themselves more violent and radical than their predecessors; even as the numbers of pirates declined, the exploits of those remaining became both more dramatic and more brutal. Edward Low was among the most infamous for engaging in luridly heinous acts of violence, such as the massacre of seventy unarmed Spanish captives that he ordered in 1723.[21] In another confrontation with a ship's captain, who had thrown gold overboard to prevent its capture: "upon hearing what a Prize had escap'd him, [Low] rav'd like a Fury, swore a thousand Oaths, and ordered the Captain's Lips to be cut off, which he broil'd before his Face, and afterwards murthered him and all the Crew, being thirty two Persons."[22] In still another episode demonstrating the shocking level of violence that pirates of this era were willing to inflict, Bartholomew Roberts captured some eleven ships by Whydah, the port

Ambiguity Lost | 173

city and slave emporium on the west coast of Africa. He ransomed ten of the ships, but the captain of one, the *Porcupine*, refused to pay, apparently thinking that his ship, apart from its consignment of enslaved people, was not worth the price demanded. Roberts then began to unload the captive Africans in order to set fire to the *Porcupine*, "but being in haste, and finding that unshackling them cost much Time and Labour, they actually set her on Fire, with eighty of those poor Wretches on board, chained two and two together, under the miserable Choice of perishing by Fire or Water: Those who jumped over-board from the Flames, were seized by Sharks, a voracious Fish, in Plenty in this Road, and in their Sight torn Limb from Limb alive."[23] The tales of mutilation, torture, and massacre from this period reflect the hostility to the world that defined pirate culture. Just as state agents, colonists, and merchants had come to define them as wild beasts in binary opposition to the civilized world order, many pirates came to agree, accepting their designation and living up to their definition as men with loyalty to none save each other and a ravenous appetite for destruction—enemies of all humankind.

These pirates' hardened stance of hostility to the milquetoast law-abiding seamen laboring under the lash of vicious captains for the benefit of unknown and undeserving owners—under the protection of the hated Royal Navy, yet—received its most memorable expression in the efflorescence of the gaudy, wild, defiant, and lawless pirate aesthetics that flourished at this time and that provide for many their first thought when they think of piracy. The chronicles of this generation of pirates are filled to the brim with accounts of shipboard dissolution and debauchery, fueled by alcohol, music, personal freedom at a fractious pitch, and mechanisms of social order tuned to preserve the bare-minimum competency for the crew to survive and pillage. This culture received its fulsome embodiment in the accounts we have of the pirates' personal style. Edward Teach, for instance, got his nickname obviously enough from his black beard. The beard, though, was just part of a bizarre and intimidating personal style his contemporaries regarded as nearly transcendent: "This Beard was black, which he suffered to grow of an extravagant Length; as to Breadth it came up to his Eyes; he was accustomed to twist it with Ribbons, in small Tails . . . and turn them about his ears: In Time of Action, he wore a Sling over his Shoulders, with three Brace of Pistols, hanging in Holsters like Bandaliers' and stuck lighted Matches under his Hat, which appearing on each Side of his Face, his Eyes naturally looking fierce and wild, made him altogether such a Figure, that Imagination cannot form an Idea of a Fury, from Hell, to look more frightful."[24] Other pirates of this generation tacked in their personal style to the wild and gaudy rather than the terrifying. Crewmen would wear the choicest bits of what they had captured, creating pastiches of assorted styles and colors.[25] At his death, Roberts, cut a striking figure, "being dressed in a rich crimson Damask Wastcoat and Breeches, a red Feather in his Hat, a Gold Chain round his neck, with a Diamond Cross hanging to it, a Sword in his Hand, and two Pair of Pistols hanging at the End of a Silk Sling, slung over his Shoulders (according to the Fashion of the Pyrates)."[26] The most iconic symbol of piracy itself reflects the aesthetics of a way of life in its death throes: the Jolly Roger, along with the whole assortment of flags that different crews used to mark themselves as pirates and so set themselves against the world. When seeking to proclaim himself and strike terror into the hearts of his adversaries, Roberts would hoist a black silk pirate's flag that "had a Death's Head on it, with an Hour-Glass in one Hand, and cross Bones in the other, a Dart by it, and underneath a Heart dropping three Drops of Blood.—The Jack had a Man pourtray'd in it, with a flaming Sword in his Hand, and standing on two Skulls, subscribed A.B.H. and A.M.H. i.e. a Barbadian's and a Martinican's Head."[27]

An hourglass on a pirate flag points to the central source of the cultural radicalism of this time: the new temporality of piracy. The hourglass in the dead man's hand on Roberts's flag represented both the fleetness of time and the keen awareness the pirates of this era had that they could not expect much of it. It was in response to this new temporal situation that pirate culture raised the general fatalism of maritime culture to its apogee. Death beckoned them now, and in their behaviors and mentalities they welcomed that proximity. Records show this commitment in the pirates' embrace of a fatalistic temporality as a defining feature of their experience and outlook. "In an honest Service," Roberts was reported to have said, "there is thin Commons, low Wages, and hard Labour; in [piracy], Plenty and Satiety, Pleasure and Ease, Liberty and Power; and who would not balance Creditor on this Side, when all the Hazard that is run for it, at worst, is only a sower Look or two at choaking [i.e., hanging]. No, a merry Life and a short one, shall be my Motto."[28] His deck was said to reflect this commitment to full and short lives, filled as it was with music, drinking, and cavorting—by men who were radically free, doomed, and knew it. Why not have another round, or raid without respect to nation, or massacre the helpless, when hell awaited and not for long?

The story with which this book began, the capture of Bartholomew Roberts's *Royal Fortune* after a bloody battle, reflects the fatalism of this mentality. In the first place, almost all aboard the *Royal Fortune* were drunk when the Royal Navy ship *Swallow* came into view, despite the dangerous waters in which they sailed. Their fatalism is further displayed in the desperate plan Roberts hatched to escape by skirting the *Swallow*, exposing the *Royal Fortune* to the full force of the navy ship's guns; as it happened, grapeshot from one of those tore out Roberts's throat, allowing him to cheat the noose as he had always hoped. The crew's fatalism reached or at least reached for its climax when, all lost, the survivors gathered by their armory and fired a pistol into the gunpowder magazine, aiming to kill themselves and take the ship with them in a last, cataclysmic act of violence undertaken on their own terms. Death before capture was a regular, defiant trope recited by pirates of the time (Rediker 2005, 148–69). Too little gunpowder was left after the furious battle for them to realize their vision, though. When they fired into the magazine, the explosion resulted in horrific injuries to some men gathered around but not the final show of defiance that they hoped for and that would have let them all cheat the state of its justice. Instead, the end came for the survivors in the powerful symbolism of their execution: on the shore by Cape Coast Castle between the floodmarks of the high and low tides indicating the limits of the admiralty's jurisdiction, dozens of sacrificial messengers from one of the most feared pirate crews of all time became heralds of the new maritime order, its signs and its consequences.

Yet to the last, many pirates stayed their course. Cheating the tone of hangings if not their fact is another constant in these records, with pirates routinely insisting on meeting their fate with cheery bravado and a fusillade of curses for all those who sought to break their necks. This adds the pirates' counterpoint to the dynamics described in the previous chapters: state agents using the pirates, their stories, and their corpses to advertise the state's new semiotically oriented powers of violence, with ministers and others seeking a share of the limelight generated by piracy trials in hopes of inspiring fear or converts by attaching their sermons to such exemplars of wickedness. The fact that many pirates refused their part in the ritual of tearful repentance and a turn to the Lord before they swung reflected the fatalism that piracy now required. William Fly's jape in the face of death, leaping to the scaffold, flower on his breast, scolding his executioner on a knot poorly tied, retying it, and lecturing the crowd on how his sentence was unjust, along with violent captains of merchant vessels who drove their men to commit murder, mutiny, and piracy, typified the piratical ethos. As for Fly's display, it was not just that of a man facing the executioner. It was a reflection of the broader culture of piratical fatalism inspired by the loss of ambiguity in the cold new light of predictable institutionalized punishment.

Fly was no hero, and there is romance to be found in his story only by ignoring the unwarranted pain he inflicted and the braggadocious glee he brought to its infliction. Upon deciding to mutiny, he and his men roused the captain of the *Elizabeth*, demanding that he come to the deck so that they would not have to scrape his blood from the cabin floor. Captain Green begged piteously and repeatedly for his life, but Fly and his men mocked him, with Fly pretending to be a parson as the captain tried to pray. The crew then threw the helpless man overboard. Captain Green managed to catch hold of the sail, hanging on for his life while dangling over the sea. One of Fly's men snatched up a cooper's broadax and lopped off the captain's hand, whereupon "he was swallowed up by the Sea." No evidence exists suggesting any violence or brutality had ever been directed by Green toward his men.

The course charted by Fly and crew continued in the cold-blooded style in which they had dispatched Green. Fly inflicted pain, death, and destruction during his piracy career with unbridled anger and pitiless scorn until one of the men he had forced to turn pirate, William Atkinson, duped him by way of a stratagem[29] and delivered him and his crew to the guards at Great Brewster Island in Boston Harbor. Fly met death with a smile on his face, a spring in his step, and an apology for nothing. Fatalistic, radical, and piratical to the last.[30]

Aside from Fly's flip scorn for the new semiotic realities facing the pirates, his story came to an end that was now predictable: he was hanged, and the authorities displayed his tarred body at the mouth of Boston Harbor. There Fly gave mute but eloquent testament to the new realities of maritime violence and maritime order. In most cases, the state now got the last word.

CONCLUSION

Pirates, Adverbs, and Institutions

The adverb is not your friend.

STEPHEN KING, *On Writing* (2000, 124)

If you were to sail past Tilbury Point near the mouth of the Thames on your way to or from London after May 1701, for some years a grisly sight would greet you: the tarred and decomposing body of Captain William Kidd, suspended in chains above the banks of the river as a warning to all mariners of the fate awaiting those who became pirates.

On May 23, Kidd was hanged at Execution Dock in Wapping. The first rope was too long and broke, so the whole procedure needed to be repeated with a shorter one (Ritchie 1986, 222–29). Why was he killed under these circumstances? In one sense, Kidd's execution can be understood as a pretty straightforward exercise of coercive state power. One of the broader points of the foregoing chapters, though, is to show that coercive state power is *not* so straightforward. Gallows are but the bitter end of a more complicated institutional reality. More particularly, even the very blunt act of coercion that Kidd encountered at the end of the short rope is so intrinsically dependent on semiotic systems and meaning-filled performances that any explanation of why Kidd was killed that does not account for these cultural questions misses too much.

GRAMMARS OF COERCION

Which brings us to adverbs. One of the key symbolic moments in the sequence of events leading to Captain Kidd's execution was his indictment. The indictment symbolically initiated the trial that led to the guilty verdict that led to Wapping Execution Dock. Kidd's indictment, like the indictments of many pirates, has a strikingly repetitive, almost ritualized adverbial phrase at its heart: "piratically and feloniously":

The Jurors for our Sovereign Lord the King, do, upon their Oath, present, That William Kidd, late of London, Mariner . . . upon the high Sea, in a certain place distant about Ten Leagues from Cutsheen in the East-Indies, and within the Jurisdiction of the Admiralty of England, did *Piratically and Feloniously* set upon, board, break, and enter a certain Merchant-Ship call'd the *Quedagh-Merchant* . . . and then and there *Piratically and Feloniously* did make an Assault in and upon certain Mariners . . . in the same Ship . . . *Piratically and Feloniously* did put the aforesaid Mariners . . . in corporal fear of their Lives . . . *Piratically and Feloniously* did Steal, Take, and Carry away the said Merchant-Ship . . . against the Peace of our said now Sovereign Lord the King, his Crown and Dignity, &c.[1]

The phrase "piratically and feloniously" bears a heavy symbolic burden in this text and the many others like it described and analyzed above. Without it, the indictment becomes a mere description. In Kidd's case this is particularly so, because the event in question occurred while he was in the East Indies on a commission from the English king to legally undertake precisely what he is accused of in the indictment: to forcibly take ships and assault mariners, but only so long as they were pirates or the French. The categories were the whole question. So especially with regard to Kidd, simply saying that he forcibly took a ship or assaulted mariners would not have specified that action with regard to English piracy law or its coercive capacities. The assertion of the adverbial phrase "piratically and feloniously" is in fact precisely the point of the indictment, trial, and execution, as well as the law that provided the whole proceeding with its conceptual structure, vocabulary, key semiotic relations, procedures, and rules. "Kidd took the *Quedagh Merchant*" is a statement. "Kidd piratically and feloniously took the *Quedagh Merchant*" is an accusation. The difference is that the latter purports to interpret Kidd's actions in light of a system of signs that attribute criminal meaning and consequent punitive action through chains of propagation to the taking for which Kidd stands accused. The conditions of possibility that enabled interpretation of Kidd's actions in light of a system of signs in a way that could generate a coordinated and violent response are, in essence, what this study has been all about.

Gilbert Ryle's comments on adverbs and thick description help clarify and extend the difference between "Kidd took . . ." and "Kidd piratically and feloniously took . . ." Ryle writes about a military command to illustrate his point:

Sloping arms in obedience to an order differs, but does not differ in number of actions from just sloping arms. It is not a conjunction of a bit of sloping arms with a separately do-able bit of obeying. It is obeying by sloping arms; it is obediently sloping arms. This adverb 'obediently' does import a big difference, but not by recording any something else . . . that the soldier also did. (1968, 6)

What the indictment and the jury that convicted Kidd are doing is essentially what Ryle calls "thick description," or interpreting the meaning of Kidd's actions with respect to a semiotic code ("structures of signification," as Geertz puts it [1977b, 9]). By accepting "piratically and feloniously" as a correct description, the judge and jury ascribe a set of meanings to those actions that, in the semiotic code of the English state in 1701, entailed execution.

Accounting for Kidd's demise helps demonstrate the importance of thick descriptive efforts to articulate not just action but meaningful action. "They hanged Kidd" is accurate but insufficient. It is like saying, to use examples from Ryle, "He twitches his eye" when normally we would say "He winks at me," or "She moves the pen across the paper" when normally we would say "She signs a peace treaty" (Geertz 1977b, 6–7, 9; Ryle 1968, 20). "They hanged Kidd" is similarly thin. It is not wrong, but it is also not all the executioner does in terms of the social significance of the action. In order to bring in that significance, we need to extend the thinness of bare behavioralism to say something like "They executed Kidd," which by placing the act in the context of a code of legal meanings says and implies and demands something different and more from the analysis.

Actors of the period were aware and precise with exactly these distinctions. In a pardon issued in an attempt to reduce piracy in the East Indies, for example, William III proclaimed that those who refused "our royal mercy" and "continued obstinate" as pirates would be subject to "the severest punishment according to law."[2] In this direct invocation of coercive state power by the English sovereign, the thick/thin distinction is necessary to work out what is going on and how that threat becomes real. The king doesn't threaten generic violence but rather threatens to punish, and further, to lawfully punish. He threatens to inflict harm under color of law and through an apparatus of coordinated actions by multiple actors that will propagate and reproduce those lawfully determined meanings. How seriously to take that threat, how real the power its associated interpretive infrastructure could concoct, depended on the dynamics described in the preceding chapters.

William's and his successors' and subsidiaries' threats against pirates fall squarely in Ryle's category of "constitutionally adverbial verbs" (1968, 11)—that is, descriptions of action that refer to and only become legible within a web of significance, a cultural system. Punishment requires some violation of norms, laws, or some other proscription as well as the interpretive infrastructure that makes codes real in the social world; the adverb "lawfully" implies another network of rules, procedures, and definitions. There is a really critical sociological difference between the material thinness of "He (the executioner) hangs Kidd" and "He lawfully punishes Kidd." But we must recall Ryle's other point: it is crucial to understanding this difference that these are not descriptions of *separate* things, one material, the other cultural. The executioner did not push Kidd off a ladder and separately "lawfully punish" him. He lawfully punished him by pushing him off a ladder. And, as the examples of previous chapters abundantly demonstrate, the executioner was only in a position to do so because of the coordinated actions of many other state agents who had behaved in ways oriented toward the same system of meanings, who propagated and ratified previous interpretations and meaningful action in order to collectively generate a thick description of Kidd's actions and to translate that interpretation into patterns of reinforcing action. The material action is necessarily wrapped up in the semiotic networks of its thick description, and the cultural dimension is what makes Kidd's execution punishment rather than mere violence—in its meaning but also, and not separately, in coordinated, violent social fact.

We can say even more about the semiotic and sociological dynamics of this case by turning to John Austin's theory of performative speech acts. In one sense, Kidd was a pirate because he took ships and stole goods that didn't belong to him. In another, though, he became a pirate precisely at the moment when the Clerk of Arraigns says, "William Kid, hold up thy Hand (which he did) Look upon the Prisoner: How say you? Is he Guilty of the Piracy and Robbery whereof he stands Indicted by the first Indictment, or not Guilty?" "Guilty," responds the foreman.[3] As Austin writes, in order for the foreman's word to have the performative capacity to transmute an accused ship captain awaiting trial into a guilty pirate awaiting execution, "there must exist an accepted conventional procedure having a certain conventional effect, that procedure to include the uttering of certain words by certain persons in certain circumstances, and further . . . the procedure must be executed by all participants both correctly and . . . completely" (1962, 14–15). The illocutionary, or performative, force of the foreman's "guilty" depends on these conventional procedures—classification rituals. They are among the keys for understanding the propagation of the guilty

CONCLUSION | 181

verdict through networks of state agents who ratify and further propel it along the trajectory from word to fatal social fact.

The performance of meaning in a situation like Kidd's trial draws from a network of other semiotic structures, techniques, definitions, prior performances, and otherwise thick, adverbial actions. The system of definitions, procedures, and meanings defining piracy and the limits of private maritime violence were the real strategic battleground of the trial. Here, Kidd and his accusers fought for the interpretive high ground on questions like who said what, when; who fired first; and whether there was a credible threat of mutiny, along with the significance of a vote that Kidd held on whether to take the *Quedah Merchant*. Two strategic constructions were particularly important in this contestation. First, there was extensive discussion of the situated meaning of Kidd's commissions to take French and pirate ships as legal prizes. If indeed the conditions of these commissions were met, then Kidd was acting as a privateer and was authorized to take ships on behalf of the king in pursuit of his foreign policy objectives. While Kidd attempted to describe his actions as justified under these commissions, the solicitor argued that he had failed to meet the necessary conditions to make his actions lawful. A second and related construction was the question of passes. The crew of the ship that Kidd took was a mix of Armenians, French, English, Berbers, and others. Whether the ship was French, and therefore whether it fell under the terms of Kidd's commission, depended on the passes that its captain produced. Kidd insisted that he had taken French passes from the ship and was thus justified in taking it. The passes could not be produced, however. The pass is a semiotic construct used by many early eighteenth-century states to locate people and ships within a framework of national affiliation and thus cooperation and contention. Its connection, in Kidd's case, to his commissions on the one hand and his trial and execution on the other suggests a much more complex network of signs and symbolic technologies that constituted the social environment in which accused and accuser had to persuasively perform social meaning, and which the jury had to interpret.

Ryle argues that any thick action relies on a series of preconditions. What I have sketched here is some of the semiotic and coordination preconditions of the adverbial phrase "piratically and feloniously," of the successful performance of piratical guilt or innocence and thus of Kidd's execution. This is in contrast to the primary association of coercion with materiality. The case encapsulates the broader point that the materiality of violence, though very real and relevant, can only ever be a thin description of coercion, and that its embeddedness in meaning structures is what makes coercion matter as a characteristic of institutionalized forms of power, including state power. Think again of Kidd's body hanging in chains at Tilbury Point. In material terms, one can only say "Kidd's body hung in chains," but to make sharper sociological sense of this display as coercion, we can further specify it adverbially: "Kidd's body threateningly hung in chains." Our thick description reflects theirs. His body was not just a body but a performance of a threat and a warning because it signified the force of the coordinating semiotic assemblages that state agents had constructed, defining the meaning of piracy and the potential for violence organized by various permutations of the adverb *piratically*. What I have suggested here is that the hangman's rope was indeed just the bitter end of a more involved story.

INSTITUTIONS AND INTERPRETIVE INFRASTRUCTURES

Coercion is a clear example of the significance of distribution, who gets what, for institutional order. As far as incentives go, being hanged not once but twice after the first rope breaks seems strong. The point of this study, however, boiled down to its essence, is that the apparent simplicity of the distributional enforcement of institutional order through the infliction of violence against pirates belies a more complex reality. For this enforcement wasn't just violence, just as winking is not just blinking. It was a cultural, material, organizational, and legal system capable of producing collective violence throughout a global empire in a rapid and decisive way against those it labeled pirates. Coordination played a crucial role in the transformation of English piracy institutions. As the study further demonstrates, coordination itself was complex, and actors found themselves struggling over, negotiating, and remaking it on the basis of what already existed. A key part of the reason that they had no choice but to work with what there was is that coordination depends on the kind of "magic" that Bourdieu (1985, 742, 1999b), Geertz (1981, 130), and others have noted in their observations of coordinated state power. That magic, essentially, is that even extremely powerful and large-scale effects depend on the myriad actions undertaken by different people facing a potentially wide variety of circumstances, across a potentially wide range of times, places, and concrete situations (Weber 1981, 158). Even though those actors in a very real sense have a tremendously wide scope of possible action, in aggregate they behave in ways that coordinate to produce stable patterns of institutionalized power. They behave in rule-based ways, even though the rules are nothing but the similarly institutionally oriented behaviors of others who themselves could choose to do otherwise but normally—at least in circumstances of institutional stability—don't. As Goffman, Wittgenstein, and Geertz have all shown, among other things rules are meanings. Cultural sociologists interested in these phenomena cannot be content to think of culture as a matter of values, beliefs, or even just semiotic structures. It is these things, but it is also an analytical framework that moves from minds to action to interaction as it attempts to trace the circuits of meaning making. Cultural sociologists can't concede guns and gallows to some other, material part of the analysis (Geertz 1981, 135–36). For one of the main starting points of the cultural sociological enterprise is that for the people wielding the guns and manning the gallows, as well as for their targets, what they do with those things is always enmeshed in a universe of meaning. Mead writes that meaning, paraphrasing a bit, is "What are you going to do about it?" (Mead 2015, 49) While this is not all that meaning is, it is a key part of why an analysis like this one that seeks to embed brutal violence in the universe of signs that made it possible and shaped its course is not some filigree but an important part of the explanation of the powers and violence produced.

In particular, this study has focused on the development of an important part of this broader tie-up between institutions and culture, the interpretive infrastructure of an institution. I argued at the beginning that this is an especially important part of institutional power to look at because it is the part explicitly focused on creating and maintaining a collective capacity to define, label, and classify the social world and to make its classificatory model real through chains of coordinated action undertaken by people in concrete situations that were oriented toward institutionalized structures of power and meaning, models of what mattered in the situations that they faced and models for what to do about it. Interpretive infrastructures are not all that matters in understanding institutions, or even for developing a more robust understanding of the cultural dimensions of institutional orders than many studies of institutions adopt. They are of great strategic importance, however, acting as a key transmission mechanism through which institutional models of and for the world, institutional rules, become real in their consequences, including in their distributional consequences.

The piracy case examined here also demonstrates that the cultural dimensions of institutions, including their interpretive infrastructures, have specific dynamics and histories that can only be properly understood through an analysis that incorporates them. The interpretive, and more broadly cultural, infrastructures of institutions play a powerful and important role in the creation, dissolution, stabilization, and change of all institutional orders. Reducing culture to simplistic concepts like values or beliefs, or folding it into a more general analysis of an institution's trajectory, or using it as an explanation for an institution's irrational anomalies is to risk missing a major driver of historical and institutional change.

In the case of piracy in the early modern British Empire, a focus on interpretive infrastructures opens a well-positioned analytical window on a fundamental transformation of the political-economic model of the empire, a concomitant transformation of its coordinating and regulating institutions, and the coordinated performances of the new meaning of piracy that comprised the bloody history of the war against the pirates. Viewed through that window, here is how the story ends: once British state agents could collectively classify pirates wherever they found them, and once they began using that interpretive power to perpetrate a sustained, coordinated, global bloodletting, the implication was clear. Though the ocean abided, much else in the colonial maritime world had changed. The pirate life wasn't what it used to be.

Acknowledgments

I've been working on this book a bit at a time, and the time has flown. All along the way, I've had help: fellowship, guidance, assistance, and occasionally apt cutting words. For all I offer thanks.

Jeff Alexander was the instigator of all this. His work introduced me to sociology and induced me to apply to graduate school, a touchstone always. Generosity, vision, direction, and care.

Julia Adams, Ron Eyerman, Phil Gorski, and the indefatigable Phil Smith have guided this project from the beginning, taught me the ropes, shown me multiple ways to proceed and think. What guides! Particularly important for this study was Julia making historical sociology at first intriguing to me and then inevitable.

As for the communal parts of writing a book, the Center for Cultural Sociology at Yale was the cornerstone that shaped this and everything I do, highlighted by its comradeship and sparkling exchange every Friday. My special thanks to Nadine Amalfi for all that she does to make it all happen. The Comparative Research and the Transitions to Modernity workshops propelled me down the substantive trails that led to this book: sounding board, reality check, historical and methodological education.

Since this book was long in the works, many people and places allowed me to present parts of it in speech and writing and have engaged, challenged, and driven the arguments forward. Emily Barman, Claudio Benzecry, Clayton Childress, Emily Erikson, Alison Gerber, Julian Go, Fiona Greenland, John Hall, Sarah Kinkel, Joe Klett, George Lawson, Ryan Light, Jim Mahoney, Isaac Martin, Jason Mast, Damon Mayrl, Steve Pincus, Sarah Quinn, Isaac Reed, Adam Slez, Lyn Spillman, Robin Wagner-Pacifici, and Nick Wilson have all helped the project along in different and important ways. I've presented parts of it at American Sociological Association meetings, at Social Science History Association meetings, and at the University of Virginia's SWAMP workshop. Good points and questions and challenges and doubts and enthusiasms for bits and pieces of this book have abounded. I thank the questioners and commenters, even if I can't name them all. Speaking of community, my colleagues at the University of Oregon, all of whom I can name but won't here, have created and sustained a rich and welcoming intellectual and professional environment. I am still routinely amazed that I wound up as a working sociologist in such a great place with such wonderful people.

I must devote a special paragraph of thanks to Dave, Elaine, Mary, Mary, and Vinny—friends to the point of family. They have put me up (and put up with me) during four extended visits to London for archival work. I suppose that as far as methodological advice goes, making a childhood friend who will continue to be wonderful and surround himself with a wonderful(er) family and who will move within a Tube ride of the main archives you want to use is hardly generalizable—but it's good advice if you can manage it.

At the University of Chicago Press, Doug Mitchell's enthusiasm when we first talked about this project launched me, and Elizabeth Branch Dyson's encouragement kept me going when doubts and topic fatigue crowded in. The anonymous reviewers for the project were to a person kind, incisive, and generous with their time and intelligence. Whoever you are, I pored over your responses to my text and did my best to reflect your guidance, grateful to have had such thoughtful first readers. My thanks also to Sandy Hazel, who copyedited the manuscript. Every page, every one, is better for her work.

Most of all, I am grateful for my family. The Massachusetts wing, and especially mum and dad, for . . . how can I even start? Home, life, love, lift. Last because most, Oscar and Julius—heart's delight, the most interesting people I know—and Emmy—beloved. It sounds like they are up to something fun downstairs right now, so I'll end this here to investigate.

(Oh, and to everyone who has aimed a pirate joke in my direction—arr, mateys, arrr!)

Notes

Primary sources are not listed in the References section but are cited in full in the notes at their first mention in any given chapter. Subsequent citations of the same source in a chapter are also given in full if they do not occur near the first citation. Secondary sources are listed in the References section and are cited mainly in the text using the author-date documentation system.

ABBREVIATIONS

CSPC Calendar of State Papers, Colonial, America and West Indies. All references are to the online version, accessible at https://www.british-history.ac.uk/search/series/cal-state-papers--colonial--america-west-indies.

CO Records of the Colonial Office, Commonwealth and Foreign and Commonwealth Offices, Empire Marketing Board, and related bodies pertaining to the administration of Britain's colonies. The National Archives, London.

PC Records of the Privy Council, and its secretariat the Privy Council Office, reflecting its changing role as an advisory body to the monarch. The National Archives, London.

INTRODUCTION

1. *A Full and Exact Account of the Tryal of all the Pyrates Lately taken by Captain Ogle On Board the Swallow Man of War, on the Coast of Guinea.* 1723. London: J. Roberts.

2. Samuel Taylor Coleridge, "The Rime of the Ancient Mariner," http://www.poetryfoundation.org/poem/173253. Accessed March 11, 2022.

3. For a more detailed consideration of this question, see Rediker 1987, 2005.

CHAPTER ONE

1. Which is not to say that institutional or other sorts of sociological analysis should limit themselves to comparisons between nation-states. For more on the limitations of approaches that take national boundaries for granted as units of comparison, see Go and Lawson 2017.

2. While they think that norms, beliefs, and values "sometimes support institutional differences" and that they "can be hard to change," culture, as they understand it, is "mostly an outcome of institutions, not an independent cause" (Acemoglu and Robinson 2013, 57).

3. For an alternative and complementary approach to thinking about the production of meaning through performances and the propagation of meaning through enchained action sequences, see Reed 2020.

4. https://www.bls.gov/ooh/business-and-financial/loan-officers.htm, accessed March 11, 2022.

5. Mayrl and Quinn (2016) provide an extended discussion of how state boundaries of this kind are created and maintained.

6. For a lucid and lively discussion of Peirce on semiosis, see Liszka 1996. For my effort to develop Peirce's framework in a theoretical direction aligned with the current argument, see Norton 2019.

7. This effect, in Peirce's scheme, is itself a sign. To continue the example, the punished pirate signifies state power to punish piracy. For more on punishment as a signifier, see Garland 1991; Smith 2008.

CHAPTER TWO

1. Hakluyt, Richard. 1599. *The Principal Nauigations, Voyages, Traffiques and Discoueries of the English Nation*. Imprinted at London: George Bishop, Ralph Newberie, and Robert Barker; Hakluyt, Richard. (1582) 2010. *Divers Voyages Touching the Discovery of America and the Islands Adjacent*, ed. J. W. Jones. Farnham, England: Ashgate.

2. Andrews (1966, 134) identifies 271 known privateering voyages from 1589 to 1591.

3. Molloy, Charles. 1722. *De Jure Maritimo et Navali: Or a Treatise of Affairs Maritime and of Commerce*, 7th ed. (London: Printed for John Walthoe Junior), pp. 24–72.

4. The exact profitability of privateering voyages as a class of economic activity is hard to estimate. At the very least, it is clear that it was generally profitable (Andrews 1966, 229; Zahedieh 1990, 153).

5. Exquemelin, Alexander O. 1684. *The Buccaneers of America: A True Account of the Most Remarkable Assaults Committed of Late Years Upon the Coast of the West Indies by the Buccaneers of Jamaica and Tortuga, Both English and French. Wherein Are Contained More Especially the Unparalleled Exploits of Sir Henry Morgan . . .* , ed. W. S. Stallybrass. Williamstown, MA: Corner House.

6. Raleigh, Sir Walter. 1829. *The Works of Sir Walter Ralegh, Kt: Miscellaneous Works*. Vol. 8, ed. W. Oldys and T. Birch (Oxford: Oxford University Press), 325.

7. The state played a major role in these developments by erecting statutory barriers around this trading system, beginning with the Navigation Acts in 1651. This aspect of imperial transformation is discussed below.

8. The Staples Act of 1663 and the Naval Stores Act of 1705 complemented the main Navigation Acts and contributed to their general theme of centralizing administrative control.

NOTES TO PAGES 48–63 | 189

9. Zahedieh (2010, 281) notes that the capacity of the central state was not sufficient to vigorously enforce the Navigation Acts, and concludes that the acts merely "nudged" the commercial system.

10. Davenport, Frances Gardiner. 1917. *European Treaties Bearing on the History of the United States and Its Dependencies to 1648*. Vol. 1 (Washington, DC: Carnegie Institution of Washington), 220–21, 306–7.

11. Davenport, Frances Gardiner. 1929. *European Treaties Bearing on the History of the United States and Its Dependencies*. Vol. 2 (Washington, DC: Carnegie Institution of Washington), 194.

CHAPTER THREE

1. Exquemelin, Alexander O. 1684. *The Buccaneers of America: A True Account of the Most Remarkable Assaults Committed of Late Years Upon the Coast of the West Indies by the Buccaneers of Jamaica and Tortuga, Both English and French. Wherein Are Contained More Especially the Unparalleled Exploits of Sir Henry Morgan . . .* , ed. W. S. Stallybrass (Williamstown, MA: Corner House), p. 152.

2. Jameson, John Franklin, ed. 1923. *Privateering and Piracy in the Colonial Period: Illustrative Documents* (New York: Macmillan), p. 84.

3. Jameson 1923, 84.

4. The treaty itself is both important on its own terms and a convenient, conventional marker of a broader turn of English political and merchant elites against piracy. It is but part of that broader turn, though it conveniently demarcates it.

5. CSPC, 1696–97, nos. 149, 149 I.

6. CSPC, 1697–98, no. 223.

7. CSPC, 1696–97, no. 894.

8. CSPC, 1696–97, no. 896.

9. CSPC, 1696–97, nos. 149, 1203.

10. CSPC, 1696–97, no. 1178X.

11. CSPC, 1696–97, nos. 373, 1028.

12. This is not to say that the metropole never got its cut. A ship from Jamaica arrived in London "laden upon the King and Duke's account, having £50,000 worth of gold and plate for the tenths and fifteenths of prizes taken about those islands" (CSPC, 1661–68, no. 1199, 7 May 1666).

13. This perception of dependence is exemplified by a letter from Governor Carlisle of Jamaica. He writes: "About 1,200 privateers abroad, but some come in since his arrival, and more hoped for from the encouragement he has given them to stay; they have generally French commissions. . . . If a war with France, this island will stand in need of their assistance, for we have not above four thousand whites able to bear arms, a secret not fit to be made public" (CSPC, 1677–80, no. 815, 24 October 1678).

14. CSPC, 1661–68, no. 942, 20 February 1665.

15. CSPC, 1696–97, no. 1187.

16. CSPC, 1697–98, no. 94.

17. CSPC, 1696–97, no. 517I. See also CSPC, 1696–97, no. 1178X.

18. CSPC, 1696–97, no. 517 I.

19. CSPC, 1696–97, no. 517 III.

20. See, for example, Van Broeck, Adrian. 1709. *The life and adventures of Capt. John Avery the famous English pirate, (rais'd from a cabbin-boy, to a King) now in possession of Madagascar* (London: Printed, and sold by the booksellers); Johnson, Captain Charles. (1724) 1999. *A General History of the Pyrates* (reprint, Mineola, NY: Dover, 1999), pp. 49–62; *The Famous Adventures of Captain John Avery, of Plymouth: A Notorious Pirate*. 1809 (Falkirk: Printed by T. Johnston); and the late eighteenth-century ballads "Bold Captain Avery" and "Captain Ivory, the Bold English Pirate" (Baer 2007, 4:369–70).

21. CSPC, 1675–76, no. 993.

22. It is possible that Browne's trial is one of the reasons for the clause of the Jamaica Piracy Act stating that "all tryalls heretofore had against such criminall or criminals before any judge or judges, by vertue of commission or authority at any time heretofore granted, and all proceedings thereupon, are hereby rattified, confirmed and adjudged lawfull; and all such judges, with all and every the inferior officers that have acted thereby, are hereby indeminfyed to all intents and purposes whatsoever" (Trumbull 1859, 153).

23. CSPC, 1677–80, nos. 375, 383, 1512.

24. CSPC, 1681–85, no. 2067.

25. CSPC, 1685–88, no. 1041.

26. CSPC, 1685–88, no. 1127.

27. Ritchie's *Captain Kidd and The War against the Pirates* is the definitive source on Kidd (Ritchie 1986).

28. CSPC, 1696–97, no. 1331.

29. Justice, Alexander. 1710. *A General Treatise of the Dominion of the Sea and a Compleat Body of the Sea- Laws: . . . The Third Edition, with Large Additions, and Improvements. And a New Appendix, Containing Several Eminent Lawyers Opinions in Important Marine Cases . . .* (London: Printed for the executors of J. Nicholson; J. and B. Sprint; and R. Smith), p. 472.

30. *Piracy Destroy'd: Or, a Short Discourse Shewing the Rise, Growth and Causes of Piracy of Late; . . . In a Letter from an Officer of an East-India Ship . . . to the Deputy Governour of the East-India-Company, London.* 1701 (London: Printed and sold by John Nutt), pp. 2–3.

31. Justice 1710, p. 482.

32. As Thomson (1994, 70–71) notes, however, it was not until the abolition of privateering with the 1856 Treaty of Paris that this source of ambiguity was more permanently resolved.

33. 4 Will. & Mary, c. 25: "If Torture, Cruelty, or any Barbarous Usage happens, after the capture, to be done to the persons taken in the prize . . . [those involved should] discharge such a prize tho' she was lawful; and the captains should lose their commissions, and both they and the offenders be subject to punishment"; Justice 1710, *General Treatise of the Dominion of the Sea*, p. 472. The use of foreign commissions was a long-standing problem for English state agents, addressed by proclamations in 1668, 1674, 1676, and 1684 as well as in the 1692 statute and again in the piracy act of 1700, An Act for the More Effectual Suppression of Piracy.

NOTES TO PAGES 78–80 | 191

34. Although admiralty courts adjudicated both prize cases—trials relating to ships seized in wartime—and instance cases—trials relating to commercial disputes, collision, salvage, etc.—the legal frameworks of the two types of cases were totally distinct.

35. A report on English prize law procedure from 1753 provides a lucid description of the principle: "By the maritime law of nations, universally and immemorially received, there is an established method of determination, whether the capture be, or be not, lawful prize. Before the ship or goods can be disposed of by the captor, there must be a regular judicial proceeding, wherein both parties may be heard, and condemnation thereupon as prize, in a court of admiralty, judging by the law of nations and treaties. The proper and regular court for these condemnations is, the court of that State to whom the captor belongs" (Moore 1931, 44).

36. These developments took time. An order of Queen in Council from 1703 reflects the ongoing struggle to consolidate control over colonial maritime violence. The order complains "that notwithstanding there are regular Courts of Admiralty established for trying prizes there, yet the Governors do not only pretend to an authority, but actually doe dispose of the prizes without giving any accompt of their produce, and proposing that H.M. strictly enjoin them not only to permit prizes to be legally tried and condemned by the Courts of Admiralty settled there, but that they do take an especial care, as they will answer the contrary, there be not anything whatever belonging to the prizes embezzled" (CSPC, 1702–3, no. 1279).

37. Justice 1710, *General Treatise of the Dominion of the Sea*, pp. 471, a92–93.

38. Justice 1710, 688–90.

39. The system of neutral passports emerged in the wake of the First Anglo-Dutch War, with Sweden pushing for the inclusion of provisions in the Treaty of Uppsala of 1654 for neutral parties to assert their ineligibility for capture and condemnation under the currently prevalent doctrine that enemy ships inherently mean enemy goods (Deák and Jessup 1933, 490–510, 515–26; 1934b, 823–24).

40. Admiralty judges were known to push back when pressured in prize matters. Charles Hedges wrote in 1689 of his reasons for refusing to condemn Hamburg ships for trading with France as follows: "The court of Admiralty is a court of justice, and the judge sworn to administer it . . . is as much obliged to observe the laws of nations . . . as the judges of the courts at Westminster are bound to proceed according to statutes and the common law." For a similar case, see the reply of the admiralty judge Leoline Jenkins against new prize rules. The independence of the prize courts only gradually and partially emerged in colonial vice admiralty courts. Even as an occasionally biased institution, however, it represented a sea change in private maritime violence in distant waters to have any serious scrutiny and judgment (Marsden 1916, 132, xii–xiii).

41. The case of the ship *François*, seized in 1705 by Edward Ratchdale, master of the *Elizabeth*, exemplifies a typical interaction of a commissioned ship with the prize system. Ratchdale brought the *François* to Maryland for condemnation. After he produced his letter of marque, it was judged a lawful prize and ordered to be appraised.

192 | NOTES TO PAGES 81–97

42. Rogers, Woodes. (1712) 1928. *A Cruising Voyage Round the World* (New York: Longmans, Green), 3.

CHAPTER FOUR

1. CSPC, 1661–68, no. 744, 25 May 1664.

2. Labaree, Leonard Woods, ed. 1935. *Royal Instructions to British Colonial Governors, 1670–1776*. Vol. 1 (New York: D. Appleton-Century), p. 453.

3. CO 323/2, ff. 590–93.

4. CO 324/7, ff. 166–69. Ten months earlier, in January of 1699, the board had laid out an even more specific vision, indicating the sizes of warships it thought should be assigned to different colonial governors to use as they saw fit, to "suppress and pursue pyrates, prevent illegal traders, and hinder the encroachments of forreigners in our fishery and otherwise" (CO 324/7, ff. 4–7).

5. CO 389/17, f. 33.

6. CO 391/11, f. 131.

7. CO 391/11, f. 132.

8. CO 389/17, ff. 34–35.

9. *Statutes of the Realm* 1509–1545, 3:671.

10. CO 139/8, ff. 11–13; CSPC, 1681–85, no. 160.

11. CO 138/3, ff.192–94.

12. CO 139/8, f. 12.

13. The trial of some of the crewmen of the infamous Henry Every in London in 1696 resulted in an unexpected acquittal. This verdict had the potential to seriously undermine the trading relations of the East India Company, as Every and his men had preyed with great success on the ships of the Mughal emperor. The acquitted men were quickly tried for another crime and then executed.

14. CO 324/4, f. 103.

15. E.g., Jenkins wrote to Connecticut with the demand to pass the enclosed Jamaica law (CO 324/4, f. 104), and Connecticut did so on July 5, 1684 (Trumbull 1859, 150–55). The connection between the two laws couldn't be clearer; the Connecticut statute is a nearly verbatim copy of the Jamaica Piracy Act.

16. CO 1/54, f. 190.

17. Ruffhead, Owen. 1761a. *The Statutes at Large: From Magna Charta, to the End of the Last Parliament, 1761*. Vol. 3 (London: Printed by Charles Eyre and Andrew Strahan; and by William Woodfall and Andrew Strahan), 611.

18. CSPC, 1697–98, no. 55.

19. CSPC, 1697–98, no. 56.

20. CSPC, 1697–98, no. 94.

21. CSPC, 1697–98, nos. 115, 234, 235, contain detailed accounts of the threat East India Company agents and officials felt that piracy posed to their and England's trading interests in the region.

22. CO 324/7, ff. 90–92.

23. CSPC, 1699, preface, p. x.

24. CSPC, 1697–98, no. 351.

NOTES TO PAGES 97–108 | 193

25. CO 324/7, ff. 67–71, 93, 96; CO 389/17, ff. 155–56.

26. 11&12 William III, c. 7 (in Ruffhead, Owen. 1761b. *The Statutes at Large: From Magna Charta, to the End of the Last Parliament, 1761.* Vol. 4 [London: Printed by Charles Eyre and Andrew Strahan; and by William Woodfall and Andrew Strahan], 43–46).

27. One further element of note: section 15 of the act responds to the widespread knowledge that the proprietary and charter colonies were particularly active in supporting pirates and particularly likely to regard themselves as above the law by threatening these colonies with the revocation of their charters should they not comply.

28. Coke, Edward. 1644. *The Fourth Part of the Institutes of the Laws of England Concerning the Jurisdiction of Courts* (London: M. Flesher for W. Lee, and D. Pakeman); translation from p. 1058 of Coke, Edward. 2003. *The Selected Writings and Speeches of Sir Edward Coke.* Vol. 2, ed. and trans. S. Sheppard. Indianapolis: Liberty Fund.

29. Coke, Edward. 1670. *The Third Part of the Institutes of the Laws of England Concerning High Treason and Other Pleas of the Crown and Criminal Causes* (London : Printed by John Streater, James Flesher, Henry Twyford, assigns of Richard Atkyns and Edward Atkyns), B–B2.

30. It should be noted that Coke was no neutral observer of jurisdictional issues but rather wrote as the preeminent partisan of the common law. His writing on the subject of jurisdiction was a sally in his vigorous battle to reshape the lines of jurisdiction in favor of common law and at the expense, especially, of civil law courts.

31. CSPC, 1675–76, no. 993.

32. Benton (2010, 104–61) pushes this point further, arguing that the struggle between pirates and sovereigns over jurisdictional claims played a central role in establishing state claims to sovereignty over the seas and to the emergence of oceans as distinctive regions in the legal structures of empire.

33. *Statutes of the Realm* 1509–1545, 3:671.

34. Interestingly, the effect of the law was *not* to make piracy a felony by the common law. As Coke wrote, "This statute did not alter the offence, or make the offence felony, but leaveth the offence as it was before this Act, viz., felony only by the Civil Law, but giveth a mean[s] of trial by the Common Law . . . although the King may pardon this offence, yet being no felony in the eye of the law of the Realm, but only by the Civil Law, the pardon of all felonies generally extendeth not to it, for this is a special offence, and ought to be especially mentioned" (1670. *The Third Part of the Institutes of the Laws of England*, 112). The law, in other words, associated common law procedure with the special piracy court, but it did not otherwise change the legal-structural position of piracy as a crime that occurred under special maritime circumstances.

35. CSPC, 1675–76, no. 994.

36. CSPC, 1681–85, no. 1578.

37. CSPC, 1720–21, no. 117.

38. Trumbull 1859, 152; the Jamaica Act uses the same mechanism.

39. *Statutes of the Realm* 1695–1701, 7:590–94.

194 | NOTES TO PAGES 114–119

CHAPTER FIVE

1. All citations of 11&12 William III, c. 7, in this section are to Ruffhead, Owen. 1761b. *The Statutes at Large: From Magna Charta, to the End of the Last Parliament, 1761.* Vol. 4 (London: Printed by Charles Eyre and Andrew Strahan; and by William Woodfall and Andrew Strahan), 43–46.

2. CO 323/2, B32, ff. 610.

3. CO 323/2, B32, ff. 612.

4. *The Trials of Eight Persons Indited for Piracy &c.* 1718 (Boston: B. Green, for John Edwards), p. 20.

5. Eyewitness testimony was the predominant form of evidence in early modern English criminal trials, including piracy trials. The concept of forensic evidence did not yet exist. Justice's discussion of procedures for securing evidence in piracy cases strongly supports this view, as for Justice, securing evidence was entirely a matter of securing witnesses. Justice, Alexander. 1710. *A General Treatise of the Dominion of the Sea and a Compleat Body of the Sea- Laws: . . . The Third Edition, with Large Additions, and Improvements. And a New Appendix, Containing Several Eminent Lawyers Opinions in Important Marine Cases . . .* (London: Printed for the executors of J. Nicholson; J. and B. Sprint; and R. Smith), pp. 482–84.

6. CO 323/2, B32, f. 614.

7. Oddly, given the well-known complicity of many merchants, officials, and others with pirates, the act specifies that accessories to piracy will be tried as principals, but only in England under the 1536 law, Act for Punishment of Pirates and Robbers of the Sea. This may be because under the civil law that the 1700 act institutes, only accessories before the fact can be treated as principals (Prichard and Yale 1993, cxcii), or it may simply be a limit on the reach and power of already powerful commissions (CO 389/17, ff. 50–51).

8. CO 389/17, f. 241; PC 5/2, ff. 84–85.

9. CO 389/17, f. 242.

10. CO 390/12, f. 370. For the entire procedure, see "Method of proceedings for holding Courts of Admiralty in the Plantations, according to what was left by Mr. Larkin at Bermuda in 1703," CO 390/12, ff. 360–85.

11. Concern for the successful execution of the new law was evident across many different bodies. For example, see the Board of Trade's report to the House of Commons updating it on the implementation of the new law: CO 389/17, ff. 165–66.

12. PC 5/2, f. 86.

13. Larkin had already departed Massachusetts by the time of the trial, though he noted in his report to the Board of Trade that given the encouragement Boston routinely showed to illegal trade and piracy, "he doubts whether the act will be duly complied with in its execution" (CO 389/17, f. 242). Baer (2007, 2:257) suggests that the precision of the trial, and the precision of the trial report, could indeed have been meant to signal the intentions of state agents in Massachusetts to comply with the law.

14. *The Arraignment, Tryal, and Condemnation, of Capt. John Quelch, And Others of his Company, &c.* 1704 (London: Printed for Ben. Bragg), p. 1.

NOTES TO PAGES 119–126 | 195

15. One major exception that proves this general observation is the trial of Stede Bonnet and his men in 1718 in Charlestown, South Carolina. The 1700 Act for the More Effectual Suppression of Piracy had briefly lapsed in 1717, but 4 Geo. I, c. 11, gave admiralty commissions in the colonies the option of using the jury-based proceedings of the 1536 piracy law, Act for the Punishment of Pirates and Robbers of the Sea—still the law by which piracy trials in England were organized. Even in this case, which followed a very different procedure, the procedure had a clear legal basis, and the judge, Nicholas Trott, followed it precisely. See *The Tryals of Major Stede Bonnet, and other Pirates*. 1719. London: Printed for Benj. Cowse.

16. Quelch's trial was the first to employ the new commissions, so it occupies a particularly important position in the standardization of both procedural and jurisprudential aspects of the new courts.

17. 28 Henry VIII, c. 15, *Statutes of the Realm* 1509–1545, 3:671.

18. *The Arraignment, Tryal, and Condemnation, of Capt. John Quelch, And Others of his Company, &c.* 1704 (London: Printed for Ben. Bragg), p. 13.

19. *The Arraignment, Tryal, and Condemnation, of Capt. John Quelch*, 1704, p. 14.

20. *The Arraignment, Tryal, and Condemnation, of Capt. John Quelch*, 1704, p. 14.

21. *The Arraignment, Tryal, and Condemnation, of Capt. John Quelch*, 1704, p. 14.

22. *A Full and Exact Account of the Tryal of all the Pyrates Lately taken by Captain Ogle, On Board the Swallow Man of War, on the Coast of Guinea.* 1723 (London: J. Roberts), p. 5.

23. *The Trials of Eight Persons Indited for Piracy &c.* 1718 (Boston: B. Green, for John Edwards), p. 8.

24. *The Arraignment, Tryal, and Condemnation, of Capt. John Quelch*, 1704, p. 6.

25. *A Full and Exact Account of the Tryal of all the Pyrates Lately taken by Captain Ogle*, 1723, pp. 84–85.

26. *The Tryals of Captain John Rackam, and other Pirates.* 1721 (Jamaica: Robert Baldwin), p. 19.

27. *The trials of five persons for piracy, felony and Robbery.* 1726 (Boston: T. Fleet, for S. Gerrish), p. 13. The defense counsel goes on to counter an anticipated objection: "It cannot be expected I should produce any evidence of the age of this lad, who was born and educated in the woods among the wild and sa[vage] Indians, where no Register of Births or Burials is kept; he knows not his own age, but by the information of his father, who here declares in publick court, his son is but fourteen this fall; there is no evidence to disprove him in this assertion, and where the scale is but even, your honours will give the balance in favour of life" (13).

28. *The trials of five persons for piracy, felony and Robbery*, 1726, p. 18. In the same case, the defense counsel provides another reason for acquittal, making the argument that in fact the accused could not be classified as criminals and pirates because they had, when they took the ship, been engaged in acts of war against the English. This argument went nowhere, though, because a peace treaty had been concluded weeks before the attack, though whether the accused knew this was contentious.

29. *The Tryals of Major Stede Bonnet, And Other Pirates.* 1719 (London: Printed for Benj. Cowse), pp. 18–19.

196 | NOTES TO PAGES 126–127

30. *The Tryals of Sixteen Persons for Piracy, &c.* 1726 (Boston: Joseph Edwards), p. 14. Also see the trial of Edward Low: *Tryals of Thirty-Six Persons for Piracy.* 1723 (Boston: Samuel Kneeland), p. 4, "Their Plea of constraint or force, (in the mouth of every Pirate) can be of no avail to them, for if it but could Justify or Excuse, No Pirate would ever be Convicted."

31. *The Tryals of Sixteen Persons for Piracy, &c.* 1726.

32. *New England Courant,* June 18, 1722.

33. Johnson, Captain Charles. (1724) 1999. *A General History of the Pyrates* (reprint, Mineola, NY: Dover), p. 365.

34. *Petition of William Davis.* 1717. Reprinted in Jameson, John Franklin, ed. 1923. *Privateering and Piracy in the Colonial Period: Illustrative Documents* (New York: Macmillan), 311.

35. *The Trials of Eight Persons Indited for Piracy &c.* 1718 (Boston: B. Green, for John Edwards), p. 22. The jurisprudence of early eighteenth-century piracy tribunals when it came to forced men was often unsympathetic, however. Many men who were abducted by pirates and forced to assist them were hanged. The signs discussed in this section were an important part of the broader semiotic clarification of the category of piracy, but they were hardly a free pass.

36. CSPC, 1700, no. 523 ii.

37. CSPC, 1700, no. 523 xiv (2); Captain Passenger's account of the taking of the *La Paix* is such a ripping yarn that I reproduce it here in full: "Hearing from a merchant ship, on Sunday, April 28, at Kiquotan, news of a pirate in Lynnhaven Bay, that had taken some Virginiamen bound out of the Capes, I set sail, and the wind being contrary and night coming on, anchored about three leagues short of the pirate. About ten at night H.E. Francis Nicholson came on board with Capt. Aldred of the *Essex* prize and Peter Heyman, Esq., who remained on board during the whole action. At four next morning I came within half a mile of the pirate. He got under sail, with a design to get to windward and board us, and said 'This is but a small fellow, we shall have him presently.' I guessed his intention and kept to windward, fires one shot at him, he immediately hoists a Jack, ensign, with a broad pendent all red, and returned me thanks. So then the dispute began and continued till three in the afternoon, the major part of which time within pistol shot of one another. It was a fine top gallant gale of wind, and I sailing something better than the pirate, so that he could not get the wind of me to lay me on board, which was his design. After we had shot all his masts and rigging to shatters, unmounted several guns and hull almost beaten to pieces, and being very near the shore, he put his helm a-lee, so the ship came about, but he having no braces, bowlines nor sheets to haul his sails about, and we playing small shot and partrige so fast that all his men run into the hold, so the ship drove on shore with all her shattered sails aback. I let go my anchor in three fathoms of water, so he struck his ensign. I left off firing. They had laid a train to thirty barrels of powder and threatened to blow the ship up, so the English prisoners, that were on board, interceded for one to swim on board of me to acquaint me of his design and desire they might have some promise of quarter, otherwise those resolute fellows would certainly blow up the ship. His Excellency the Governor being on board, in regard of so many prisoners that were His Majesty's subjects,

thought fit to send them word under his hand and lesser seal they should be all referred to the King's mercy, with the proviso they would quietly yield themselves up prisoners of war. *Signed*, W. Passenger" (CSPC, 1700, no. 523 ii).

38. CSPC, 1700, no. 523.

39. Johnson, Captain Charles. (1724) 1999. *A General History of the Pyrates* (reprint, Mineola, NY: Dover), p. 40.

40. CO 23/1/18, ff. 75–82. Edward Teach (also spelled Thatch, a.k.a. Blackbeard), and Stede Bonnet, both notorious pirates, likewise sought a pardon as a temporary reprieve before going back on the account. The pardon was not always so sure a thing. During the trial of several men captured with Captain William Kidd, three claimed that they had surrendered in accordance with an earlier proclamation and should therefore be pardoned instead of tried. One of the judges, Sir Edward Ward, had the proclamation read, and then he objected that the three men were ineligible for pardons. "The Proclamation says they must surrender themselves to such and such persons by name . . . here are several qualifications mention'd; you must bring your selves under them, if you would have the benefit of it." He goes on, specifying, "now there are four commissioners named [in the proclamation], that you ought to surrender to, but you have not surrendered to any one of these, but to Col. Bass, and there is no such man mention'd in this proclamation." On these narrow technical grounds, the pardon was denied, and the jury subsequently found them guilty (*The Arraignment, Tryal, and Condemnation of Captain William Kidd, for Murther and Piracy*. 1701 [London: J. Nutt], pp. 15–16).

41. CSPC, 1716, nos. 240, 240 i.

42. CSPC, 1717, nos. 64, 286.

43. CSPC, 1717, nos. 249, 250.

44. CSPC, 1717, nos. 255, 287.

45. CSPC, 1718, no. 737.

46. Rogers reports in October of 1718 that "above 100 men that accepted H.M. Act of Grace in this place are now out pirating again" (CSPC, 1718, no. 737).

47. Johnson, Captain Charles. (1724) 1999. *A General History of the Pyrates*. Vol. 2, chap. 18, "The Tryal of the Pyrates at Providence" (reprint, Mineola, NY: Dover), p. 643.

48. "Notwithstanding [that Governor Rogers] has made known to us, that he has no direct Commission for Tryal of Pyrates; yet according to the Intent and Meaning of the sixth Article of the Governor's Instructions, which, in this Case, refers to the fourth Article in those given to the Governor of *Jamaica*, a Copy of whose Instructions he has for his Directions to govern himself by, as near as the Circumstances of the Place will admit. This corroborated with the Power in the Governor's Commission of Governor, Captain-General, and Vice-Admiral of the Bahama Islands, shew the Intention of his Majesty, for such Authority here" (Johnson [1724] 1999, 643).

49. Johnson (1724) 1999, p. 644.

50. Johnson (1724) 1999, pp. 646–47.

51. Johnson (1724) 1999, pp. 656–57.

52. Johnson (1724) 1999, pp. 657–58.

53. Johnson (1724) 1999, p. 659.

198 | NOTES TO PAGES 134–145

54. CSPC, 1718, no. 807.

55. Johnson (1724) 1999, p. 658.

56. CSPC, 1697–98, no. 1007.

57. CSPC, 1697–98, no. 1077.

58. See CSPC, 1697–98, preface, pp. 5–34.

CHAPTER SIX

1. *Boston Gazette*, from Monday, June 1, to Monday, June 8, 1724, issue 237, p. 2.

2. Quoted in Jameson, John Franklin, ed. 1923. *Privateering and Piracy in the Colonial Period: Illustrative Documents* (New York: Macmillan), 345.

3. *The Trials of Eight Persons Indited for Piracy &c.* 1718 (Boston: B. Green, for John Edwards), p. 6. Italics in original. The phrase is often provided in Latin, *hostis humani generis*, "an enemy of mankind." This exact formulation seems to come from Coke's *Institutes*, and it became a standard trope for defining the crime of piracy.

4. Coke, Edward. 1644. *The Fourth Part of the Institutes of the Laws of England Concerning the Jurisdiction of Courts* (London: M. Flesher for W. Lee, and D. Pakeman), p. 147.

5. Another common trope in piracy trials was, to cite the Bellamy prosecutor again, "that the unhappy persons on whom [piracy] is acted are the most innocent in themselves and the most useful and beneficial to the publick, whose indefatigable industry conveys amidst innumerable dangers . . . blood into the veins of the body politick and nourishes every member" (*The Trials of Eight Persons Indited for Piracy &c.* 1718, p. 7). As noted in chapter 2, many contemporaries recognized commerce as the lifeblood of the empire and the source of its wealth, stability, and martial prowess.

6. *The trials of five persons for piracy, felony and Robbery.* 1726. Boston: T. Fleet, for S. Gerrish.

7. *Boston News-Letter*, Thursday, September 8, to Thursday, September 15, 1726, issue 1181, p. 2; *Boston News-Letter*, Thursday, September 29, to Thursday, October 6, 1726, issue 1184, p. 2.

8. *Boston News-Letter*, Thursday, October 27, to Thursday, November 3, 1726, issue 1188, p. 2.

9. *The Tryals of Captain John Rackam, and other Pirates.* 1721 (Jamaica: Robert Baldwin), p. 41.

10. Ruffhead, Owen. 1761b. *The Statutes at Large: From Magna Charta, to the End of the Last Parliament, 1761.* Vol. 4 (London: Printed by Charles Eyre and Andrew Strahan; and by William Johnson Woodfall and Andrew Strahan), p. 43.

11. Ruffhead 1761b, p. 44.

12. Johnson, Captain Charles. (1724) 1999. *A General History of the Pyrates* (reprint, Mineola, NY: Dover), p. 281.

13. *The Trials of Eight Persons Indited for Piracy &c.* 1718 (Boston: B. Green, for John Edwards), p. 14.

14. The silver oar was the symbol of the admiralty, and when available was used to mark the proceedings as under the admiral's jurisdiction—though as

discussed here, jurisdiction over piracy had not been exercised under the authority of the admiral for some time. There was still a strong connection between the admiralty, jurisdiction over the sea, and piracy, of course, and much of the procedural and other jurisdictional machinery of the admiralty was incorporated into the piracy courts, which is probably why the symbol seemed appropriate.

15. *An Account of the Behaviour and last Dying Speeches of the Six Pirates, that were Executed on Charles River, Boston side, on Fryday June 30th, 1704.* 1704 (Boston: Nicholas Boone), pp. 1–2.

16. S. Sewall, *Diary of Samuel Sewall*, 2:135. Quoted in Baer 2007, 2:259.

17. *An Account of the Behaviour and last Dying Speeches of the Six Pirates*, 1704, p. 2.

18. CSPC, 1704–5, no. 1274.

19. *A Full and Exact Account of the Tryal of all the Pyrates Lately taken by Captain Ogle, On Board the Swallow Man of War, on the Coast of Guinea.* 1723 (London: J. Roberts), p. 53.

20. Mather, Cotton. 1704. *Faithful Warnings to Prevent Fearful Judgments Uttered in a Brief Discourse, Occasioned, by a Tragical Spectacle, in a Number of Miserables under a Sentence of Death for Piracy. At Boston in N.E. Jun. 22. 1704* (Boston: Printed & sold by Timothy Green, at the north end of the town), p. 11.

21. Colman, Benjamin. 1726. *It Is a Fearful Thing to Fall into the Hands of the Living God a Sermon Preached to Some Miserable Pirates July 10. 1726. On the Lord's Day, before Their Execution* (Boston, N.E.: Printed for John Phillips and Thomas Hancock, and sold at their shops), p. 8.

22. Mather, Cotton. 1726. *The Vial Poured out upon the Sea. A Remarkable Relation of Certain Pirates Brought unto a Tragical and Untimely End. Some Conferences with Them, after Their Condemnation. Their Behaviour at Their Execution. And a Sermon Preached on That Occasion* (Boston: Fleet for Belknap), pp. 42–43.

23. Mather, Cotton. 1723. *Useful Remarks. An Essay upon Remarkables in the Way of Wicked Men. : A Sermon on the Tragical End, unto Which the Way of Twenty-Six Pirates Brought Them ; at New Port on Rhode-Island, July 19, 1723. : With an Account of Their Speeches, Letters, & Actions, before Their Execution* (New London: T. Green), p. 20. Also see p. 35.

24. Mather 1704, *Faithful Warnings to Prevent Fearful Judgments*, p. 37.

25. Mather 1723, *Useful Remarks*, p. 1.

26. Mather had a gentle moral message for kids: "Shall this confession make no impression on you, o wicked and woful children, who break the hearts of your parents, with your ungodly courses? You cannot but know, that it kills your distressed parents, & makes their hearts even to stoop with heaviness, to see that you are irreclameable from your enormities, and that none of their commands or counsels will prevail with you, to reform your disorderly living. O Murderers of your parents, can you think, that you shall escape unpunished? Will you not hearken to the voice of your parents; the LORD will do something worse than slay you, for this disobedience! Tis a sign, that GOD has a terrible thing to do upon you. Wretches, leave off your impieties, & be no longer an heaviness unto your parents; or GOD will do a terrible thing upon you" (Mather 1723, *Useful Remarks*, p. 24).

27. Mather 1723, pp. 23–28.

28. Mather 1723, p. 30.

200 | NOTES TO PAGES 150–152

29. Mather, Cotton. 1724. *The Converted Sinner the Nature of a Conversion to Real and Vital Piety: And the Manner in Which It Is to Be Pray'd & Striv'n for. : A Sermon Preached in Boston, May 31, 1724. In the Hearing and at the Desire of Certain Pirates, a Little before Their Execution. : To Which There Is Added, a More Private Conference of a Minister with Them* (Boston: Printed for Nathaniel Belknap, and sold at his shop the corner of Scarletts-Wharff), p. 35.

30. Colman, Benjamin. 1726. *It Is a Fearful Thing to Fall into the Hands of the Living God a Sermon Preached to Some Miserable Pirates July 10. 1726. On the Lord's Day, before Their Execution* (Boston, N.E.: Printed for John Phillips and Thomas Hancock, and sold at their shops), pp. 26–28.

31. Colman 1726, p. 27.

32. Woodward, Josiah. 1723. *The Seaman's Monitor, or, Advice to Sea-Faring Men : With Reference to Their Behaviour before, in, and after Their Voyage : With Prayers for Their Use, and an Address to the Officers and Seamen in His Majesty's Royal Navy, with a Caution to Prophane Swearers.* London: Printed and sold by J. Downing. Also see *The Mariner's Divine Mate*, reprinted in Baer 2007, 4:103–24. It attempts to link common experiences that mariners could be expected to have, such as storms, pirates, and so on, to moral virtues and Christian religion.

33. Mather, Cotton. 1726. *The Vial Poured out upon the Sea. A Remarkable Relation of Certain Pirates Brought unto a Tragical and Untimely End. Some Conferences with Them, after Their Condemnation. Their Behaviour at Their Execution. And a Sermon Preached on That Occasion* (Boston: Fleet for Belknap), p. 50.

34. Mather 1726, p. 43.

35. Mather, Cotton. 1717. *Instructions to the Living, from the Condition of the Dead a Brief Relation of Remarkables in the Shipwreck of above One Hundred Pirates, Who Were Cast Away in the Ship Whido, on the Coast of New-England, April 26. 1717. And in the Death of Six, Who after a Fair Trial at Boston, Were Convicted & Condemned, Octob. 22. And Executed, Novemb. 15. 1717. : With Some Account of the Discourse Had with Them on the Way to Their Execution. And a Sermon Preached on Their Occasion* (Boston: Printed by John Allen, for Nicholas Boone, at the Sign of the Bible in Cornhill), p. 39.

36. For an extended account of these conditions and their connections to piracy, see Rediker 1987, 2005.

37. Mather 1726, *The Vial Poured out upon the Sea*, p. 21.

38. Mather 1726, p. 48.

39. Anon. 1701. *Piracy Destroy'd: Or, a Short Discourse Shewing the Rise, Growth and Causes of Piracy of Late; . . . In a Letter from an Officer of an East-India Ship . . . to the Deputy Governour of the East-India-Company, London* (London: Printed and sold by John Nutt); see also Anon. 1726. *A Discourse of the Laws Relating to Pirates and Piracies, and the Marine Affairs of Great Britain* (London: Printed by W. Wilkins, for J. Peele), pp. 35–39.

40. Anon. 1701, *Piracy Destroy'd*, p. 9.

41. Anon. 1701, p. 10.

42. Mather, Cotton. 1723. *Useful Remarks. An Essay upon Remarkables in the Way of Wicked Men. : A Sermon on the Tragical End, unto Which the Way of Twenty-Six Pirates Brought Them ; at New Port on Rhode-Island, July 19, 1723. : With an Account*

of Their Speeches, Letters, & Actions, before Their Execution (New London: T. Green), p. 39; see also p. 41.

43. Woodward, Josiah. 1723. *The Seaman's Monitor, or, Advice to Sea-Faring Men : With Reference to Their Behaviour before, in, and after Their Voyage : With Prayers for Their Use, and an Address to the Officers and Seamen in His Majesty's Royal Navy, with a Caution to Prophane Swearers.* (London: Printed and sold by J. Downing), pp. 68–69.

44. Woodward 1723, pp. 69–70.

45. E.g., Justice, Alexander. 1710. *A General Treatise of the Dominion of the Sea and a Compleat Body of the Sea-Laws: . . . The Third Edition, with Large Additions, and Improvements. And a New Appendix, Containing Several Eminent Lawyers Opinions in Important Marine Cases . . .* (London: Printed for the executors of J. Nicholson; J. and B. Sprint; and R. Smith), p. 475; *The Arraignment, Tryal, and Condemnation, of Capt. John Quelch, And Others of his Company, &c.* 1704 (London: Printed for Ben. Bragg), p. 6; *The Trials of Eight Persons Indited for Piracy &c.* 1718 (Boston: B. Green, for John Edwards), p. 6; Mather, Cotton. 1704. *Faithful Warnings to Prevent Fearful Judgments Uttered in a Brief Discourse, Occasioned, by a Tragical Spectacle, in a Number of Miserables under a Sentence of Death for Piracy. At Boston in N.E. Jun. 22. 1704* (Boston: Printed & sold by Timothy Green, at the north end of the town), p. 22; Mather, Cotton. 1717. *Instructions to the Living, from the Condition of the Dead a Brief Relation of Remarkables in the Shipwreck of above One Hundred Pirates, Who Were Cast Away in the Ship Whido, on the Coast of New-England, April 26. 1717. And in the Death of Six, Who after a Fair Trial at Boston, Were Convicted & Condemned, Octob. 22. And Executed, Novemb. 15. 1717 : With Some Account of the Discourse Had with Them on the Way to Their Execution. And a Sermon Preached on Their Occasion* (Boston: Printed by John Allen, for Nicholas Boone, at the Sign of the Bible in Cornhill), p. 4; Mather, Cotton. 1724. *The Converted Sinner the Nature of a Conversion to Real and Vital Piety: And the Manner in Which It Is to Be Pray'd & Striv'n for. : A Sermon Preached in Boston, May 31, 1724. In the Hearing and at the Desire of Certain Pirates, a Little before Their Execution. : To Which There Is Added, a More Private Conference of a Minister with Them* (Boston: Printed for Nathaniel Belknap, and sold at his shop the corner of Scarletts-Wharff), p. i; Mather, Cotton. 1726. *The Vial Poured out upon the Sea. A Remarkable Relation of Certain Pirates Brought unto a Tragical and Untimely End. Some Conferences with Them, after Their Condemnation. Their Behaviour at Their Execution. And a Sermon Preached on That Occasion* (Boston: Fleet for Belknap), pp. 1, 16, 18, 44; Woodward 1723, *The Seaman's Monitor*, pp. i–ii.

46. *The Trials of Eight Persons Indited for Piracy &c.* 1718 (Boston: B. Green, for John Edwards), p. 6.

47. E.g., *The Arraignment, Tryal, and Condemnation, of Capt. John Quelch*, 1704, p. 5.

48. *Tryals of Thirty-Six Persons for Piracy.* 1723 (Boston: Samuel Kneeland), p. 3.

49. *Tryals of Thirty-Six Persons for Piracy*, 1723, p. 3.

50. *The Arraignment, Tryal, and Condemnation, of Capt. John Quelch*, 1704, p. 5.

51. *The Trials of Eight Persons Indited for Piracy &c.* 1718 (Boston: B. Green, for John Edwards), p. 7.

202 | NOTES TO PAGES 153–154

52. Mather, Cotton. 1717. *Instructions to the Living, from the Condition of the Dead a Brief Relation of Remarkables in the Shipwreck of above One Hundred Pirates, Who Were Cast Away in the Ship Whido, on the Coast of New-England, April 26. 1717. And in the Death of Six, Who after a Fair Trial at Boston, Were Convicted & Condemned, Octob. 22. And Executed, Novemb. 15. 1717. : With Some Account of the Discourse Had with Them on the Way to Their Execution. And a Sermon Preached on Their Occasion* (Boston: Printed by John Allen, for Nicholas Boone, at the Sign of the Bible in Cornhill), pp. 3–4.

53. *The Trials of Eight Persons Indited for Piracy &c*, 1718, p. 7.

54. Mather, Cotton. 1726. *The Vial Poured out upon the Sea. A Remarkable Relation of Certain Pirates Brought unto a Tragical and Untimely End. Some Conferences with Them, after Their Condemnation. Their Behaviour at Their Execution. And a Sermon Preached on That Occasion* (Boston: Fleet for Belknap), p. 11.

55. Mather 1726, p. 21; see also *The Arraignment, Tryal, and Condemnation, of Capt. John Quelch.* 1705, p. 6; Mather, Cotton. 1724. *The Converted Sinner the Nature of a Conversion to Real and Vital Piety: And the Manner in Which It Is to Be Pray'd & Striv'n for. : A Sermon Preached in Boston, May 31, 1724. In the Hearing and at the Desire of Certain Pirates, a Little before Their Execution. : To Which There Is Added, a More Private Conference of a Minister with Them* (Boston: Printed for Nathaniel Belknap, and sold at his shop the corner of Scarletts-Wharff), pp. i, 8, 30.

56. Woodward, Josiah. 1723. *The Seaman's Monitor, or, Advice to Sea-Faring Men : With Reference to Their Behaviour before, in, and after Their Voyage : With Prayers for Their Use, and an Address to the Officers and Seamen in His Majesty's Royal Navy, with a Caution to Prophane Swearers.* London: Printed and sold by J. Downing), pp. iii, 73.

57. *Tryals of Thirty-Six Persons for Piracy.* 1723 (Boston: Samuel Kneeland), p. 10.

58. Mather 1724, *The Converted Sinner*, pp. 40–41.

59. Mather, Cotton. 1704. *Faithful Warnings to Prevent Fearful Judgments Uttered in a Brief Discourse, Occasioned, by a Tragical Spectacle, in a Number of Miserables under a Sentence of Death for Piracy. At Boston in N.E. Jun. 22. 1704* (Boston: Printed & sold by Timothy Green, at the north end of the town), p. 46.

60. Mather 1704, p. 46.

61. Mather, Cotton. 1726. *The Vial Poured out upon the Sea. A Remarkable Relation of Certain Pirates Brought unto a Tragical and Untimely End. Some Conferences with Them, after Their Condemnation. Their Behaviour at Their Execution. And a Sermon Preached on That Occasion* (Boston: Fleet for Belknap), p. 19.

62. Mather, Cotton. 1717. *Instructions to the Living, from the Condition of the Dead a Brief Relation of Remarkables in the Shipwreck of above One Hundred Pirates, Who Were Cast Away in the Ship Whido, on the Coast of New-England, April 26. 1717. And in the Death of Six, Who after a Fair Trial at Boston, Were Convicted & Condemned, Octob. 22. And Executed, Novemb. 15. 1717. : With Some Account of the Discourse Had with Them on the Way to Their Execution. And a Sermon Preached on Their Occasion* (Boston: Printed by John Allen, for Nicholas Boone, at the Sign of the Bible in Cornhill), pp. 6–7.

63. Mather, Cotton. 1724. *The Converted Sinner the Nature of a Conversion to Real and Vital Piety: And the Manner in Which It Is to Be Pray'd & Striv'n for. : A Sermon*

Preached in Boston, May 31, 1724. In the Hearing and at the Desire of Certain Pirates, a Little before Their Execution. : To Which There Is Added, a More Private Conference of a Minister with Them (Boston: Printed for Nathaniel Belknap, and sold at his shop the corner of Scarletts-Wharff), p. i.

64. Mather 1717, *Instructions to the Living*, p. 10.

65. Mather 1726, *The Vial Poured out upon the Sea*, p. 10.

66. Mather 1724, *The Converted Sinner*, p. 48.

67. Mather 1726, *The Vial Poured out upon the Sea*, p. 5.

68. Mather 1726, p. 22.

69. Mather 1726, pp. 47–48.

70. Mather 1726, p. 48.

71. Mather 1726, p. 49; for an alternative account of the confrontation between Mather and Fly, see Williams 1987.

CHAPTER SEVEN

1. My thanks to Sarah Kinkel for suggesting this sentence and for her help in clarifying these points about temporality.

2. *The Tryals of Major Stede Bonnet, And Other Pirates* 1719 (London: Printed for Benj. Cowse), p. 8.

3. *The Tryals of Major Stede Bonnet*, 1719, p. 10.

4. *The Trials of Eight Persons Indited for Piracy &c.* 1718 (Boston: B. Green, for John Edwards), p. 6. A 1696 act from Massachusetts provides another good example of this theme of isolation. In its preamble the act reads, "Whereas, also, divers of his majesty's subjects have and do commit divers inhumane and hostile acts and depradations upon the subjects and allies of divers princes and states in foreign parts, in amity with his majesty, which by reason of the remoteness of the place where the fact was committed can very rarely be proved by witness indifferent, and many times kill and murder such persons, being in the ship or boat where such offences are perpetrated, which should bear witness against them in that behalf" (Clifford, John Henry, William Cross Williamson, and Melville Madison Bigelow, eds. 1869. *The Acts and Resolves, Public and Private, of the Province of the Massachusetts Bay: To Which Are Prefixed the Charters of the Province* [Boston, 1869], 245).

5. *The Trials of Eight Persons Indited for Piracy &c*, 1718, p. 5.

6. Dampier, William. (1697) 2007. *A New Voyage Round the World* (Warwick, NY: 1500 Books, 2007), p. 36.

7. Dampier (1697) 2007, p. 43.

8. There is a direct line connecting these two cases. Dampier signed on to Rogers's expedition as a pilot for the South Seas. Rogers acted in direct response to a law passed in 1708 that set out new legal incentives encouraging privateers to pursue state-centric goals. 6 Anne, c. 13.

9. At one point, the resident British vice-consul to the Canary Islands demanded that Rogers return a Spanish bark taken as prize in light of an alleged arrangement whereby a trade to the islands was allowed to proceed without intervention by warships or privateers. Rogers responded, "You ought to have sent

us a copy of her majesty's orders or proclamation. . . . We are requir'd to be accountable no farther than we are oblig'd by our instructions, which we have given sufficient security already to follow, and don't fear a premunire [forfeit of bond] when we comply with them. We know fishing boats are excus'd on both sides, and all trading vessels from Rio la Hache to the River of Chagre in the Spanish West-Indies . . . and we know the English ships are protected no farther than in anchor-ground: and since we took this vessel at sea, we shan't part with her unless on our own terms. . . . and if it be her Majesty of Great Britain's pleasure, and we are better inform'd in England, then we can justify our conduct to the gentlemen that imploy'd us, and you will be again reimburs'd." Rogers's response makes a fortuitously explicit case of the introduction of a judicially mediated future into the present of maritime violence. Rogers, Woodes. (1712) 1928. *A Cruising Voyage Round the World* (New York: Longmans, Green), pp. 13–14.

10. Rogers (1712) 1928, pp. 161, 227.

11. Rogers (1712) 1928, p. 11.

12. Rogers (1712) 1928, pp. 131, 135–36, 223, 267.

13. *Piracy Destroy'd: Or, a Short Discourse Shewing the Rise, Growth and Causes of Piracy of Late; . . . In a Letter from an Officer of an East-India Ship . . . to the Deputy Governour of the East-India-Company, London.* 1701 (London: Printed and sold by John Nutt); Peregrine Osborne, *Reasons for Reducing the Pyrates at Madagascar.* In Baer 2007, 3:419–22.

14. 13 Charles II, c. 9, s. 7; see also Marsden 1911, 41.

15. 4 William & Mary, c. 25, s. 14. In a 1727 letter, Sir Charles Wager complains of the ongoing problem of embezzlement from prizes, "everybody thinking they have a right to get what they can, especially if they belong to the ship that took her" (Marsden 1916, 266).

16. By a similar token, the various prize acts can be seen as an inducement to state-centric violence by formally defining the shares seamen in privateers could expect from prizes. The act also provided rewards for informants who revealed conspiracies to run away with ships. 11&12 William III, c. 7.

17. The favorability of admiralty courts to seamen was not just temperamental. They also presented practical procedural advantages, such as the seamen's ability to present a libel against the owners of a vessel as a group rather than individually, as well as proceed in rem against their ships and goods rather than in personam against the owners. Woodes Rogers is explicit in his recommendation that the restive seamen on his voyage look to a future reckoning, exhorting the crew "to believe they would have justice in England, should any thing seem uneasy to them now, or in the whole course of the voyage" (Andrews 1936, 27).

18. Though it was hardly perfectly clear. The control of maritime violence continued to be a vividly important and constantly evolving question in an empire based on merchant capitalist trade and naval supremacy (Thomson 1994; Anderson et al. 2013; Rediker 1987; Kinkel 2018).

19. The collective identity of pirates, their efforts to create alternative symbolic systems and counterrepresentations in their battle with the powers that state agents brought against them after the war years is ground well covered by others. For more details of pirate culture, their counterperformances to state authority,

NOTES TO PAGES 172–180 | 205

their systems of governance and coordination, and other aspects of the performance of piracy, see Cordingly 2006; Gosse 1932; Leeson 2009; Rediker 1987, 2005; Ritchie 1986. See also Johnson, Captain Charles. (1724) 1999. *A General History of the Pyrates* (reprint, Mineola, NY: Dover).

20. Edward Teach (aka Blackbeard) was Hornigold's second in command until they parted ways. Hornigold's navigation of the changing world of piracy continued in this direction upon the arrival of Woodes Rogers the following year. Hornigold accepted the king's pardon and Rogers's commission to hunt pirates from the Bahamas, capturing the ten men whose trial is described in chapter 5.

21. Johnson, Captain Charles. (1724) 1999. *A General History of the Pyrates* (reprint, Mineola, NY: Dover), p. 326.

22. Johnson (1724) 1999, p. 377.

23. Johnson (1724) 1999, p. 236.

24. Johnson (1724) 1999, pp. 84–85.

25. Johnson (1724) 1999, p. 241.

26. Johnson (1724) 1999, p. 243.

27. Johnson (1724) 1999, p. 234, italics removed.

28. Johnson (1724) 1999, p. 244, italics removed.

29. Essentially, Atkinson pretended to see some ships. Fly came forward to take a look, leaving his weapons behind (Atkinson had spent days pretending to be enthusiastic about piracy), whereupon Atkinson and some confederates overpowered him. They and others of the forced men then infiltrated and retook the other ships in their small fleet and surrendered to the nearest authorities they could find.

30. Johnson, Captain Charles. (1724) 1999. *A General History of the Pyrates* (reprint, Mineola, NY: Dover), 608, 613; *The Tryals of Sixteen Persons for Piracy, &c.* 1726 (Boston: Joseph Edwards), esp. pp. 19–24.

CONCLUSION

1. *The Arraignment, Tryal, and Condemnation of Captain William Kidd, for Murther and Piracy.* 1701 (London: J. Nutt), p. 14. Italics mine.

2. *The Arraignment, Tryal, and Condemnation,* 1701, p. 15.

3. *The Arraignment, Tryal, and Condemnation,* 1701, p. 51.

References

Abbott, Andrew. 2001a. "Temporality and Process in Social Life." In *Time Matters: On Theory and Method*, 209–39. Chicago: University of Chicago Press.

———. 2001b. *Time Matters: On Theory and Method*. Chicago: University of Chicago Press.

Acemoglu, Daron, and James A. Robinson. 2013. *Why Nations Fail: The Origins of Power, Prosperity, and Poverty*. London: Profile.

Adams, Julia. 1996. "Principals and Agents, Colonialists and Company Men: The Decay of Colonial Control in the Dutch East Indies." *American Sociological Review* 61 (1): 12–28.

———. 1999. "Culture in Rational-Choice Theories of State Formation." In *State/Culture: State-Formation after the Cultural Turn*, edited by G. Steinmetz, 98–122. Ithaca, NY: Cornell University Press.

———. 2007. *The Familial State: Ruling Families and Merchant Capitalism in Early Modern Europe*. Ithaca, NY: Cornell University Press.

Adams, Julia, Elisabeth S. Clemens, and Ann Shola Orloff. 2005. Introduction to *Remaking Modernity: Politics, History, and Sociology*. Durham, NC: Duke University Press.

Alexander, Jeffrey C. 1987. "Action and Its Environments." In *The Micro-Macro Link*, edited by J. C. Alexander, B. Giesen, R. Münch, and Neil J. Smelser, 289–318. Berkeley: University of California Press.

———. 2004. "Cultural Pragmatics: Social Performance between Ritual and Strategy." *Sociological Theory* 22 (4): 527–73. https://doi.org/10.1111/j.0735-2751.2004.00233.x.

Alexander, Jeffrey C., and Philip Smith. 2003. "The Strong Program in Cultural Sociology: Elements of a Structural Hermeneutics." In *The Meanings of Social Life: A Cultural Sociology*, 11–26. New York: Oxford University Press.

Alvard, Michael S., and David A. Nolin. 2002. "Rousseau's Whale Hunt?: Coordination among Big-Game Hunters." *Current Anthropology* 43 (4): 533–59. https://doi.org/10.1086/341653.

Anderson, Clare, Niklas Frykman, Lex Heerma van Voss, and Marcus Rediker. 2013. *Mutiny and Maritime Radicalism in the Age of Revolution*. Cambridge: Cambridge University Press.

Andrews, Charles M. 1908. *British Committees, Commissions, and Councils of Trade and Plantations, 1622–1675.* Project Gutenberg, https://www.gutenberg.org/ebooks/33313.

———. 1936. "Vice-Admiralty Courts in the Colonies." In *Records of the Vice-Admiralty Court of Rhode Island, 1716–1752,* edited by D. S. Towle, 1–79. Washington, DC: American Historical Association.

Andrews, Kenneth R. 1966. *Elizabethan Privateering: English Privateering during the Spanish War, 1585–1603.* Cambridge: Cambridge University Press.

———. 1984. *Trade, Plunder and Settlement: Maritime Enterprise and the Genesis of the British Empire, 1480–1630.* Cambridge: Cambridge University Press.

Appleby, John C. 1998. "War, Politics, and Colonization, 1558–1625." In Canny 1998b, 55–78.

———. 2009. *Under the Bloody Flag: Pirates of the Tudor Age.* London: History Press.

Austin, J. L. 1976. *How to Do Things with Words: The William James Lectures Delivered in Harvard University in 1955.* London: Oxford Paperbacks.

Baer, Joel, ed. 2007. *British Piracy in the Golden Age: History and Interpretation, 1660–1730.* 4 vols. London: Pickering and Chatto.

Barkey, Karen. 1997. *Bandits and Bureaucrats: The Ottoman Route to State Centralization.* Ithaca, NY: Cornell University Press.

Barrow, Thomas C. 1967. *Trade and Empire: The British Customs Service in Colonial America, 1660–1775.* Cambridge, MA: Harvard University Press.

Beattie, Tim. 2007. "Adventuring Your Estate: The Origins, Costs and Rewards of Woodes Rogers's Privateering Voyage of 1708–11." *Mariner's Mirror* 93 (2): 143–55.

Benton, Lauren. 1999. "Colonial Law and Cultural Difference: Jurisdictional Politics and the Formation of the Colonial State." *Comparative Studies in Society and History* 41 (3): 563–88.

———. 2001. "Making Order out of Trouble: Jurisdictional Politics in the Spanish Colonial Borderlands." *Law and Social Inquiry* 26 (2): 373–401.

———. 2002. *Law and Colonial Cultures: Legal Regimes in World History, 1400–1900.* Cambridge: Cambridge University Press.

———. 2010. *A Search for Sovereignty: Law and Geography in European Empires, 1400–1900.* Cambridge: Cambridge University Press.

Bilder, Mary. 2008. *The Transatlantic Constitution : Colonial Legal Culture and the Empire.* Cambridge, MA: Harvard University Press.

Bourdieu, Pierre. 1985. "The Social Space and the Genesis of Groups." *Theory and Society* 14 (6): 723–44.

———. 1994. "Rethinking the State: Genesis and Structure of the Bureaucratic Field." *Sociological Theory* 12 (1): 1–18. https://doi.org/10.2307/202032.

———. 1999a. *Language and Symbolic Power.* Cambridge, MA: Harvard University Press.

———. 1999b. "Rethinking the State: Genesis and Structure of the Bureaucratic Field." In *State/Culture : State-Formation after the Cultural Turn,* edited by G. Steinmetz, 53–75. Ithaca, NY: Cornell University Press.

———. 2015. *On the State: Lectures at the Collège de France, 1989—1992.* Cambridge: Polity.

Bowen, H. V., Elizabeth Mancke, and John G. Reid. 2012. "Introduction: Britain's

Oceanic Empire." In *Britain's Oceanic Empire: Atlantic and Indian Ocean Worlds, c. 1550–1850*, edited by H. V. Bowen, E. Mancke, and J. G. Reid, 1–11. Cambridge: Cambridge University Press.

Bowles, Samuel, and Herbert Gintis. 2011. *A Cooperative Species: Human Reciprocity and Its Evolution*. Princeton, NJ: Princeton University Press.

Braddick, Michael J. 1998. "The English Government, War, Trade, and Settlement, 1625–1688." In Canny 1998, 286–308.

Brewer, John. 1990. *The Sinews of Power: War, Money and the English State, 1688–1783*. Cambridge, MA: Harvard University Press.

Brown, Elizabeth Gaspar. 1963. "British Statutes in the Emergent Nations of North America: 1606–1949." *American Journal of Legal History* 7(2):95–136. https://doi .org/10.2307/844250.

Butler, Judith. 1989. *Gender Trouble : Feminism and the Subversion of Identity*. New York: Routledge.

Canny, Nicholas P. 1998a. "The Origins of Empire: An Introduction." In *The Origins of Empire: British Overseas Enterprise to the Close of the Seventeenth Century*, edited by N. P. Canny, 1–33. Vol. 1 of *The Oxford History of the British Empire*. Oxford: Oxford University Press.

———, ed. 1998b. *The Origins of Empire: British Overseas Enterprise to the Close of the Seventeenth Century*. Vol. 1 of *The Oxford History of the British Empire*. Oxford: Oxford University Press.

Chwe, Michael Suk-Young. 2013. *Rational Ritual: Culture, Coordination, and Common Knowledge*. Rev. ed. Princeton, NJ: Princeton University Press.

Clay, C. G. A. 1984. *Economic Expansion and Social Change: England 1500–1700*. Vol. 2, *Industry, Trade and Government*. Cambridge: Cambridge University Press.

Colomy, Paul. 1998. "Neofunctionalism and Neoinstitutionalism: Human Agency and Interest in Institutional Change." *Sociological Forum* 13 (2): 265–300.

Cordingly, David. 2006. *Under the Black Flag : The Romance and the Reality of Life among the Pirates*. New York: Random House.

Cormack, Bradin. 2007. *A Power to Do Justice: Jurisdiction, English Literature, and the Rise of Common Law, 1509–1625*. Chicago: University of Chicago Press.

Crump, Helen J. 1931. *Colonial Admiralty Jurisdiction in the Seventeenth Century*. London: Longmans, Green.

Davies, J. D. 1991. *Gentlemen and Tarpaulins : The Officers and Men of the Restoration Navy*. Oxford: Clarendon.

Davis, Ralph. 1954. "English Foreign Trade, 1660–1700." *Economic History Review* 7 (2): 150–66. https://doi.org/10.1111/j.1468-0289.1954.tb01521.x.

Deák, Francis, and Philip C. Jessup. 1933. "Prize Law Procedure at Sea—Its Early Development." *Tulane Law Review* 7:488–528.

———. 1934a. "Early Prize Court Procedure: Part One." *University of Pennsylvania Law Review and American Law Register* 82 (7): 677–94.

———. 1934b. "Early Prize Court Procedure: Part Two." *University of Pennsylvania Law Review and American Law Register* 82 (8): 818–37.

Dobbin, Frank. 1994. "Cultural Models of Organization: The Social Construction of Rational Organizing Principles." In *Sociology of Culture: Emerging Theoretical Perspectives*, edited by Diana Crane, 117–41. Oxford: Blackwell.

Douglas, Mary. 1986. *How Institutions Think.* Syracuse, NY: Syracuse University Press.

Downing, Brian M. 1992. *The Military Revolution and Political Change: Origins of Democracy and Autocracy in Early Modern Europe.* Princeton, NJ: Princeton University Press.

Elias, Norbert. 1969. *The Civilizing Process.* Vol. 1, *The History of Manners.* Oxford: Blackwell.

Elliott, John Huxtable. 2007. *Empires of the Atlantic World: Britain and Spain in America 1492–1830.* New Haven, CT: Yale University Press.

Erikson, Emily. 2014. *Between Monopoly and Free Trade: The English East India Company, 1600–1757.* Princeton, NJ: Princeton University Press.

———. 2021. *Trade and Nation: How Companies and Politics Reshaped Economic Thought.* New York: Columbia University Press.

Erikson, Emily, and Peter Bearman. 2006. "Malfeasance and the Foundations for Global Trade: The Structure of English Trade in the East Indies, 1601–1833." *American Journal of Sociology* 112 (1): 195–230. https://doi.org/10.1086/502694.

Ertman, Thomas. 1997. *Birth of the Leviathan: Building States and Regimes in Medieval and Early Modern Europe.* Cambridge: Cambridge University Press.

Evans, Peter B., Dietrich Rueschemeyer, Theda Skocpol, Social Science Research Council (US), Committee on States and Social Structures, Joint Committee on Latin American Studies, and Joint Committee on Western Europe. 1985. *Bringing the State Back In.* Edited by Peter B. Evans, Dietrich Rueschemeyer, and Theda Skocpol. Cambridge: Cambridge University Press.

Ford, Richard T. 1999. "Law's Territory (A History of Jurisdiction)." *Michigan Law Review* 97 (4): 843–930. https://doi.org/10.2307/1290376.

Foucault, Michel. 1977. *Discipline and Punish : The Birth of the Prison.* New York: Vintage Books.

Friedland, Roger. 2009. "Institution, Practice, and Ontology: Toward a Religious Sociology." In *Research in the Sociology of Organizations*, vol. 27, edited by R. E. Meyer, K. Sahlin, M. J. Ventresca, and P. Walgenbach, 45–83. Bingley, UK: Emerald Group.

Fukuyama, Francis. 2011. *The Origins of Political Order: From Prehuman Times to the French Revolution.* New York: Farrar, Straus and Giroux.

Garland, David. 1991. "Punishment and Culture: The Symbolic Dimension of Criminal Justice." *Studies in Law, Politics, and Society* 11:191–222.

Geertz, Clifford. 1973. "Religion as a Cultural System." In *The Interpretation of Cultures*, 87–125. New York: Basic Books.

———. 1977a. "The Impact of the Concept of Culture on the Concept of Man." In *The Interpretation of Cultures*, 33–54. New York: Basic Books.

———. 1977b. "Thick Description: Towards an Interpretive Theory of Culture." In *The Interpretation of Cultures*, 3–30. New York: Basic Books.

———. 1981. *Negara: The Theatre State in Nineteenth-Century Bali.* Princeton, NJ: Princeton University Press.

Gerth, Hans Heinrich, and C. Wright Mills. 1958. "Introduction: The Man and His Work." In *From Max Weber : Essays in Sociology*, 1–74. New York: Oxford University Press.

Go, Julian. 2008. *American Empire and the Politics of Meaning: Elite Political Cultures in the Philippines and Puerto Rico during U.S. Colonialism.* Durham, NC: Duke University Press.

Go, Julian, and George Lawson, eds. 2017. *Global Historical Sociology.* Cambridge: Cambridge University Press.

Goffman, Erving. 1990. *The Presentation of Self in Everyday Life.* New York: Doubleday.

Goodman, Nelson. 1983. *Fact, Fiction, and Forecast.* Cambridge, MA: Harvard University Press.

Gorski, Philip S. 2003. *The Disciplinary Revolution: Calvinism and the Rise of the State in Early Modern Europe.* Chicago: University of Chicago Press.

Gorski, Philip, and Vivek Swaroop Sharma. 2017. "Beyond the Tilly Thesis: 'Family Values' and State Formation in Latin Christendom." In *Does War Make States?*, edited by L. B. Kaspersen and J. Strandsbjerg, 98–124. Cambridge: Cambridge University Press.

Gosse, Philip. 1932. *The History of Piracy.* Mineola, NY: Dover Publications.

Gray, Charles Montgomery. 2004. *The Writ of Prohibition: Jurisdiction in Early Modern English Law.* Vol. 1, *General Introduction to the Study and Procedures.* University of Chicago Law School, Chicago Unbound series, Books section, 1066. https://chicagounbound.uchicago.edu/books/1066, accessed March 11, 2022.

Greene, Jack P. 1988. *Pursuits of Happiness : The Social Development of Early Modern British Colonies and the Formation of American Culture.* Chapel Hill: University of North Carolina Press.

Greimas, Algirdas Julien. 1983. *Structural Semantics: An Attempt at a Method.* Lincoln: University of Nebraska Press.

———. 1987. *On Meaning : Selected Writings in Semiotic Theory.* London: F. Pinter.

Gross, Neil. 2009. "A Pragmatist Theory of Social Mechanisms." *American Sociological Review* 74 (3): 358.

Hall, Michael G. 1957. "The House of Lords, Edward Randolph, and the Navigation Act of 1696." *William and Mary Quarterly* 14 (4): 494–515. https://doi.org/10.2307/1918518.

Hallett, Tim, David Shulman, and Gary Alan Fine. 2009. "Peopling Organizations: The Promise of Classic Symbolic Interactionism for an Inhabited Institutionalism." In *The Oxford Handbook of Sociology and Organization Studies: Classical Foundations*, edited by P. Adler, 486–509. Oxford: Oxford University Press.

Hallett, Tim, and Marc J. Ventresca. 2006. "Inhabited Institutions: Social Interactions and Organizational Forms in Gouldner's Patterns of Industrial Bureaucracy." *Theory and Society* 35 (2): 213–36. https://doi.org/10.1007/s11186-006-9003-z.

Harris, G. G. 2008. "Mainwaring, Sir Henry (1586/7–1653)." In *Oxford Dictionary of National Biography.* Oxford: Oxford University Press.

Hatfield, April Lee. 2005. "Mariners, Merchants, and Colonists in Seventeenth-Century English America." In *The Creation of the British Atlantic World*, edited by E. Mancke and C. Shammas, 139–59. Baltimore: Johns Hopkins University Press.

Hill, L. M. 1968. "The Two-Witness Rule in English Treason Trials: Some Comments on the Emergence of Procedural Law." *American Journal of Legal History* 12 (2): 95–111. https://doi.org/10.2307/844383.

Ikegami, Eiko. 1995. *The Taming of the Samurai: Honorific Individualism and the Making of Modern Japan*. Cambridge, MA: Harvard University Press.

Israel, Jonathan I. 1998. "The Emerging Empire: The Continental Perspective, 1650–1713." In Canny 1998b, 423–44.

Joas, Hans. 1996. *The Creativity of Action*. Chicago: University of Chicago Press.

Kelsey, Harry. 2000. *Sir Francis Drake: The Queen's Pirate*. New Haven, CT: Yale University Press.

King, Stephen. 2000. *On Writing: A Memoir of the Craft*. New York: Simon and Schuster.

Kinkel, Sarah. 2018. *Disciplining the Empire. Politics, Governance, and the Rise of the British Navy*. Cambridge, MA: Harvard University Press.

Kiser, Edgar. 1994. "Markets and Hierarchies in Early Modern Tax Systems: A Principal-Agent Analysis." *Politics and Society* 22 (3): 284–315. https://doi.org/10.1177/0032329294022003003.

Kiser, Edgar, and Yong Cai. 2003. "War and Bureaucratization in Qin China: Exploring an Anomalous Case." *American Sociological Review* 68 (4): 511–39. https://doi.org/10.2307/1519737.

Kiser, Edgar, and April Linton. 2001. "Determinants of the Growth of the State: War and Taxation in Early Modern France and England." *Social Forces* 80 (2): 411.

Kleiman, Mark, and Beau Kilmer. 2009. "The Dynamics of Deterrence." *Proceedings of the National Academy of Sciences* 106 (34): 14230–35. https://doi.org/10.1073/pnas.0905513106.

Lamont, Michèle. 2002. *The Dignity of Working Men: Morality and the Boundaries of Race, Class, and Immigration*. Cambridge, MA: Harvard University Press.

Lamont, Michèle, and Virág Molnár. 2002. "The Study of Boundaries in the Social Sciences." *Annual Review of Sociology* 28 (1): 167–95. https://doi.org/10.1146/annurev.soc.28.110601.141107.

Langbein, John H. 1983. "Shaping the Eighteenth-Century Criminal Trial: A View from the Ryder Sources." *University of Chicago Law Review* 50 (1): 1–136. https://doi.org/10.2307/1599383.

Leeson, Peter T. 2009. *The Invisible Hook: The Hidden Economics of Pirates*. Princeton, NJ: Princeton University Press.

Lewis, David. 1969. *Convention: A Philosophical Study*. Cambridge, MA: Harvard University Press.

Liszka, James Jakób. 1996. *A General Introduction to the Semeiotic of Charles Sanders Peirce*. Bloomington: Indiana University Press.

Lizardo, Omar. 2004. "The Cognitive Origins of Bourdieu's Habitus." *Journal for the Theory of Social Behaviour* 34 (4): 375–401. https://doi.org/10.1111/j.1468-5914.2004.00255.x.

Loveman, Mara. 2005. "The Modern State and the Primitive Accumulation of Symbolic Power." *American Journal of Sociology* 110 (6): 1651–83.

———. 2014. *National Colors: Racial Classification and the State in Latin America*. New York: Oxford University Press.

Mahoney, James. 1999. "Nominal, Ordinal, and Narrative Appraisal in Macrocausal Analysis." *American Journal of Sociology* 104 (4): 1154–96. https://doi.org/10.1086/210139.

———. 2000. "Path Dependence in Historical Sociology." *Theory and Society* 29 (4): 507–48.

———. 2010. *Colonialism and Postcolonial Development: Spanish America in Comparative Perspective.* Cambridge: Cambridge University Press.

Mancall, Peter C. 1998. "Native Americans and Europeans in English America, 1500–1700." In Canny 1998b, 328–50.

Mancke, Elizabeth. 1999. "Early Modern Expansion and the Politicization of Oceanic Space." *Geographical Review* 89 (2): 225–36.

———. 2005. "Chartered Enterprises and the Evolution of the British Atlantic World." In *The Creation of the British Atlantic World*, edited by E. Mancke and C. Shammas, 237–62. Baltimore: Johns Hopkins University Press.

Mann, Michael. 1986. *The Sources of Social Power: A History of Power from the Beginning to A.D. 1760.* Cambridge: Cambridge University Press.

Marley, David. 1994. *Pirates and Privateers of the Americas.* Santa Barbara, CA: ABC-CLIO.

Marsden, R. G. 1909. "Early Prize Jurisdiction and Prize Law in England, Part 1." *English Historical Review* 24 (96): 675–97. https://doi.org/10.1093/ehr/XXIV.XCVI.675.

———. 1910. "Early Prize Jurisdiction and Prize Law in England, Part II." *English Historical Review* 25 (98): 243–63.

———. 1911. "Early Prize Jurisdiction and Prize Law in England, Part III." *English Historical Review* 26 (101): 34–56. https://doi.org/10.1093/ehr/XXVI.CI.34.

———. 1916. *Documents Relating to Law and Custom of the Sea.* Vol. 2, *A.D.1649–1767.* [London:] Printed for the Navy Records Society.

Mattingly, Garrett. 1963. "No Peace beyond What Line?" *Transactions of the Royal Historical Society* 13: 145–62. https://doi.org/10.2307/3678733.

Mayrl, Damon, and Sarah Quinn. 2016. "Defining the State from Within: Boundaries, Schemas, and Associational Policymaking." *Sociological Theory* 34 (1): 1–26. https://doi.org/10.1177/0735275116632557.

McCusker, John J., and Russell R. Menard. 1985. *The Economy of British America, 1607–1789.* Chapel Hill, NC: University of North Carolina Press.

Mead, George Herbert. 2015. *Mind, Self and Society: The Definitive Edition.* Edited by C. W. Morris, D. R. Huebner, and H. Joas. Chicago: University of Chicago Press.

Merriman, John M. 1991. *The Margins of City Life : Explorations on the French Urban Frontier, 1815–1851.* New York: Oxford University Press.

Meyer, John W., and Brian Rowan. 1977. "Institutionalized Organizations: Formal Structure as Myth and Ceremony." *American Journal of Sociology* 83 (2): 340–63.

Mische, Ann. 2009. "Projects and Possibilities: Researching Futures in Action." *Sociological Forum* 24 (3): 694–704. https://doi.org/10.1111/j.1573-7861.2009.01127.x.

Moore, John Bassett, ed. 1931. *International Adjudications Ancient and Modern and Documents.* Vol. 4. New York: Oxford University Press.

Mukerji, Chandra. 2011. "Jurisdiction, Inscription, and State Formation: Administrative Modernism and Knowledge Regimes." *Theory and Society* 40:223–45. https://doi.org/10.1007/s11186-011-9141-9.

North, Douglass Cecil. 1990. *Institutions, Institutional Change, and Economic Performance*. Cambridge: Cambridge University Press.

North, Douglass Cecil, John Joseph Wallis, and Barry R. Weingast. 2009. *Violence and Social Orders : A Conceptual Framework for Interpreting Recorded Human History*. Cambridge: Cambridge University Press.

Norton, Matthew. 2011. "A Structural Hermeneutics of 'The O'Reilly Factor.'" *Theory and Society* 40 (3): 315–46. https://doi.org/10.1007/s11186-011-9143-7.

———. 2014a. "Classification and Coercion: The Destruction of Piracy in the English Maritime System." *American Journal of Sociology* 119 (6): 1537–75. https://doi.org/10.1086/676041.

———. 2014b. "Mechanisms and Meaning Structures." *Sociological Theory* 32 (2): 162–87. https://doi.org/10.1177/0735275114537631.

———. 2014c. "Temporality, Isolation, and Violence in the Early Modern English Maritime World." *Eighteenth-Century Studies* 48 (1): 37–66. https://doi.org/10.1353/ecs.2014.0044.

———. 2015. "Principal Agent Relations and the Decline of the Royal African Company." *Political Power and Social Theory* 29:45–76. https://doi.org/10.1108/S0198-871920150000029003.

———. 2017. "Real Mythic Histories: Circulatory Networks and State-Centrism." In *Global Historical Sociology*, edited by J. Go and G. Lawson, 37–57. Cambridge: Cambridge University Press.

———. 2019. "Meaning on the Move: Synthesizing Cognitive and Systems Concepts of Culture." *American Journal of Cultural Sociology* 7 (1): 1–28. https://doi.org/10.1057/s41290-017-0055-5.

Nutting, P. Bradley. 1978. "The Madagascar Connection: Parliament and Piracy, 1690–1701." *American Journal of Legal History* 22 (3): 202–15.

Owen, David R., and Michael C. Tolley. 1995. *Courts of Admiralty in Colonial America: The Maryland Experience, 1634–1776*. Durham, NC: Carolina Academic Press.

Pagden, Anthony. 1998. "The Struggle for Legitimacy and the Image of Empire in the Atlantic to c. 1700." In Canny 1998, 34–54.

Peirce, Charles S. 1978. *The Collected Papers of Charles S. Peirce*. Vol. 5, edited by C. Hartshorne and P. Weiss. Cambridge, MA: Harvard University Press.

———. 1990. "Charles S. Peirce on Objects of Thought and Representation," edited by H. Pape. *Noûs* 24 (3): 375–95. https://doi.org/10.2307/2215771.

Pincus, Steve. 2009. *1688: The First Modern Revolution*. New Haven, CT: Yale University Press.

Plank, Geoffrey Gilbert. 2001. *An Unsettled Conquest: The British Campaign against the Peoples of Acadia*. University Park: University of Pennsylvania Press.

Prichard, M. J., and D. E. C. Yale. 1993. *Hale and Fleetwood on Admiralty Jurisdiction*. London: Selden Society.

Raffield, Paul. 2004. *Images and Cultures of Law in Early Modern England: Justice and Political Power, 1558–1660*. Cambridge: Cambridge University Press.

REFERENCES | 215

Rediker, Marcus. 1987. *Between the Devil and the Deep Blue Sea: Merchant Seamen, Pirates and the Anglo-American Maritime World, 1700–1750*. Cambridge: Cambridge University Press.

———. 2005. *Villains of All Nations: Atlantic Pirates in the Golden Age*. Boston: Beacon Press.

Reed, Isaac Ariail. 2013. "Power: Relational, Discursive, and Performative Dimensions." *Sociological Theory* 31 (3): 193–218. https://doi.org/10.1177/0735275113501792.

———. 2019. "Performative State-Formation in the Early American Republic." *American Sociological Review* 84 (2): 334–67. https://doi.org/10.1177/0003122419831228.

———. 2020. *Power in Modernity: Agency Relations and the Creative Destruction of the King's Two Bodies*. Chicago: University of Chicago Press.

Reid, John Phillip. 2004. *Rule of Law: The Jurisprudence of Liberty in the Seventeenth and Eighteenth Centuries*. DeKalb: Northern Illinois University Press.

Reyes, Victoria. 2019. *Global Borderlands: Fantasy, Violence, and Empire in Subic Bay, Philippines*. Stanford, CA: Stanford University Press.

RHC. 1960. "The Rule of Law in Colonial Massachusetts." *University of Pennsylvania Law Review* 108 (7): 1001–36. https://doi.org/10.2307/3310210.

Ritchie, Robert. 1986. *Captain Kidd and the War against the Pirates*. Cambridge, MA: Harvard University Press.

Rodger, N. A. M. 1996. *The Wooden World: An Anatomy of the Georgian Navy*. New York: W. W. Norton.

———. 1998. "Guns and Sails in the First Phase of English Colonization, 1500–1650." In Canny 1998b, 79–98.

———. 2005. *The Command of the Ocean: A Naval History of Britain, 1649–1815*. New York: W. W. Norton.

Root, Winfred T. 1917. "The Lords of Trade and Plantations, 1675–1696." *American Historical Review* 23 (1): 20–41. https://doi.org/10.2307/1837684.

Runyan, Timothy J. 1975. "The Rolls of Oleron and the Admiralty Court in Fourteenth Century England." *American Journal of Legal History* 19 (2): 95–111. https://doi.org/10.2307/844801.

Ryle, Gilbert. 1968. *The Thinking of Thoughts: What Is "le Penseur" Doing?* Saskatoon: University of Saskatchewan.

Sahlins, Marshall. 1981. *Historical Metaphors and Mythical Realities : Structure in the Early History of the Sandwich Islands Kingdom*. Ann Arbor: University of Michigan Press.

Sainty, J. C., ed. 1974. "Council of Trade and Plantations 1696–1782." In *Office-Holders in Modern Britain*, 3:28–37. British History Online.

Schelling, Thomas C. 1960. *The Strategy of Conflict: With a New Preface by the Author*. Cambridge, MA: Harvard University Press.

Scott, James C. 1999. *Seeing Like a State: How Certain Schemes to Improve the Human Condition Have Failed*. New Haven, CT: Yale University Press.

———. 2010. *The Art of Not Being Governed: An Anarchist History of Upland Southeast Asia*. New Haven, CT: Yale University Press.

Sewell, William H. 1996. "Historical Events as Transformations of Structures: Inventing Revolution at the Bastille." *Theory and Society* 25 (6): 841–81.

—. 2005a. *Logics of History: Social Theory and Social Transformation*. Chicago: University of Chicago Press.

—. 2005b. "A Theory of Structure: Duality, Agency, and Transformation." In *Logics of History: Social Theory and Social Transformation*, 124–51. Chicago: University of Chicago Press.

Shapiro, Barbara J. 2003. *A Culture of Fact: England, 1550–1720*. Ithaca, NY: Cornell University Press.

Shoemaker, Robert B. 2002. "The Taming of the Duel: Masculinity, Honour and Ritual Violence in London, 1660–1800." *Historical Journal* 45 (3): 525–45.

Skocpol, Theda. 1979. *States and Social Revolutions: A Comparative Analysis of France, Russia and China*. Cambridge: Cambridge University Press.

Smith, Philip. 2003. "Narrating the Guillotine: Punishment Technology as Myth and Symbol." *Theory, Culture and Society* 20 (5): 27–51.

—. 2008. *Punishment and Culture*. Chicago: University of Chicago Press.

Spillman, Lyn, and Michael Strand. 2013. "Interest-Oriented Action." *Annual Review of Sociology* 39 (1): 85–104. https://doi.org/10.1146/annurev-soc-081309-150019.

Steele, Ian K. 1986. *The English Atlantic, 1675–1740 : An Exploration of Communication and Community*. New York: Oxford University Press.

Steinmetz, George. 2007. *The Devil's Handwriting: Precoloniality and the German Colonial State in Qingdao, Samoa, and Southwest Africa*. Chicago: University of Chicago Press.

Sterelny, Kim. 2012. *The Evolved Apprentice: How Evolution Made Humans Unique*. Cambridge, MA: MIT Press.

Thelen, Kathleen. 1999. "Historical Institutionalism in Comparative Politics." *Annual Review of Political Science* 2 (1): 369–404. https://doi.org/10.1146/annurev.polisci.2.1.369.

Thomson, Janice E. 1994. *Mercenaries, Pirates, and Sovereigns*. Princeton, NJ: Princeton University Press.

Thornton, Patricia H., William Ocasio, and Michael Lounsbury. 2012. *The Institutional Logics Perspective: A New Approach to Culture, Structure, and Process*. Oxford: Oxford University Press.

Tilly, Charles. 1975. *The Formation of National States in Western Europe*. Princeton, NJ: Princeton University Press.

—. 1990. *Coercion, Capital and European States: AD 990—1990*. London: Wiley-Blackwell.

Trumbull, J. Hammond, ed. 1859. *The Public Records of the Colony of Connecticut, May 1673–June 1689*. Hartford, CT: Case, Lockwood.

Wagner-Pacifici, Robin. 2000. *Theorizing the Standoff: Contingency in Action*. Cambridge: Cambridge University Press.

—. 2010. "Theorizing the Restlessness of Events." *American Journal of Sociology* 115 (5): 1351–86. https://doi.org/10.1086/651299.

Weber, Max. 1981. "Some Categories of Interpretive Sociology." *Sociological Quarterly* 22 (2): 151–80.

Williams, Daniel E. 1987. "Puritans and Pirates: A Confrontation between Cotton Mather and William Fly in 1726." *Early American Literature* 22 (3): 233–51.

Wilson, Nicholas Hoover. 2011. "From Reflection to Refraction: State Administration in British India, circa 1770–1855." *American Journal of Sociology* 116 (5): 1437–77.

Zahedieh, Nuala. 1990. "'A Frugal, Prudential and Hopeful Trade.' Privateering in Jamaica, 1655–89." *Journal of Imperial and Commonwealth History* 18 (2): 145–68.

———. 1998. "Overseas Expansion and Trade in the Seventeenth Century." In Canny 1998b, 398–422.

———. 2010. *The Capital and the Colonies : London and the Atlantic Economy, 1660–1700*. New York: Cambridge University Press.

Zerubavel, Eviatar. 1987. "The Language of Time: Toward a Semiotics of Temporality." *Sociological Quarterly* 28 (3): 343–56

Index

Page numbers in italics refer to illustrations

accomplice testimony, 120–21

Acemoglu, Daron, 12, 13, 16, 188n2

Act for Punishment of Pirates and Robbers of the Sea, 1536, 65, 114; and accomplice testimony, 120; common law procedures, 90–91, 108, 193n34; interpretive power limited to commissioned Admiralty court, 105–6, 107

Act for Restraining and Punishing Privateers and Pirates. *See* Jamaica Piracy Act of 1681

Act for the More Effectual Suppression of Piracy, 1700: acceptance of as legitimate interpretive power, 113; and cross-examination of witnesses, 115–16; death as only penalty, 116; elimination of indictment through grand jury, 121; as foundation of "transatlantic legal culture," 113; institutional framework for classification of pirates, 83–84, 99, 112, 116, 135; jurisdictional innovations, 107–9, 114, 117; jurisdictional limitations, 143–45; major legal changes of, 97–98; and meaning of piracy in relation to mutiny, 168; and option of using the provisions of the 1536 piracy law, 195n15; as permanent legal structure, 98–99;

and power of revocation over colonial charters, 193n27; and principal-agent relations, 137–39, *138*; and procedures for colonial courts, 114–15, 116–19; provisions for accessories to piracy, 194n7; and rewards for seaman who assist in defense of their ship, 168; and trial of pirates in the Bahamas, 132–33. *See also* piracy, post-1700 interpretive institutional infrastructure; piracy trials, by vice admiralty courts

admiralty law: basis in civil law, 89–90; and instance jurisdiction, 90; and piracy courts, 198n14; and prize law (*see* prize law); and Rolls of Oleron, 89

adventure capitalism, 3, 36, 38, 40, 43, 46. *See also* piracy, pre-1700; privateering

aesthetics: and pirates, 173–76; and state actions, 111–12, 139

Alexander, Jeffrey C., 32, 112, 113

Alexander VI, 41

Alford, Robert R., 30

Allein, Richard, 159–60

An Account of the Behaviour and last Dying Speeches of the Six Pirates, that were executed on Charles River, Boston Side (pamphlet), 145

INDEX

Anand, Alexander, 125
Andrews, Charles M., 38, 43, 54, 55, 78
Andrews, Kenneth R., 188n2
Anglo-Dutch War: First, 191n39; Third, 59
Anglo-Spanish War, 36–37, 38–39, 41, 54, 133
Anne, Queen, 98
Archer, John Rose, execution of, 140, 156
Arundel, 81
Atkinson, William, 176, 205n29
Atlantic culture, emergence of: information exchange through newspapers and packet mail, 47; multiple passages of colonists among colonies, 48; role of mariners in, 47; and transatlantic legal culture, 100–101, 113
Auchmuty, Robert, 126
Aurangzib, 63–64, 86, 95
Austin, John L.: and classification rituals, 25, 102, 112; theory of performative speech acts, 180–81; and verdictives, 73
Avery, Henry. *See* Every, Henry (Avery)
Ayres, Philip, *The Voyages and Adventures of Captain Bartholomew Sharp*, 147

Baer, Joel, 121, 128, 151, 194n13
Bahamas, and piracy, 129–35. *See also* Rogers, Woodes
Bank of England, creation of, 45–46
Bannister, Joseph, 67–69, 70
Baptist, John, Junior, 124
Basse, Jeremiah, 62
Batchelor's Adventure, 131
Beauchamps, Captain Robert, 132
Bellamy, Samuel, trial and execution of, 122, 141–42, 145, 153, 154, 172, 198n5
Benton, Lauren, 104, 193n32
Bilder, Mary, 47–48
Blathwayt, William, 52
Blumer, Herbert, 31

Board of Trade (Council of Trade and Foreign Plantations), 35, 62, 66, 68, 146, 194n11; creation in 1696 to coordinate trade and colonies, 86–87; efforts to transform piracy interpretive infrastructure, 86, 87–89, 96–97, 192n4; and Benjamin Fletcher, 136; and procedures for colonial courts, 117–19
Bonnet, Major Stede: execution of, *144*; trial of crew, 98, 125–26, 159–60
Bonny, Anne, 124
borders, and demarcations of differing rules, 11
border stories: and complexity, 13; and institutional analysis, 12
Boston News-Letter, piracy-related items, 147
boundary making, and inequality and hierarchy, 22
Bourdieu, Pierre, 22, 33–34
Braddick, Michael J., 48
British colonies, colonial governors, and state agents: ambiguity and legal complexity in attempts to deal with piracy, 58, 64–75, 81–86, 91–92, 104–5; and complicity with or support for piracy and privateering, 40, 51, 58–59, 61–64, 66, 76–77, 85, 91, 129–30, 135–39, 189n13; and Jamaica Piracy Act, 92–94, 97, 192n15; and repugnancy concept, 100. *See also* piracy trials, by vice admiralty courts in colonies; vice admiralty courts
British Empire, emergence and transformation: colonial society, transformation in, 46–48, 49; early colonial claims based on Protestant civilizing mission, 41, 52; emergence of hybrid British Atlantic culture, 47–48, 100–101; expansion of sociolegal order, and piracy trials, 142–43; "government by license," 42, 48, 49, 100; imperial governance, transformation of, 42–43, 48–49; privateering, importance of in financing coloniza-

tion, 38–43; trade, transformation in, 43–46, 49, 51–52; and transition from opportunistic plunder to merchant capitalism, 3, 36–37, 66, 153

British Empire, interpretive institutional infrastructure, and piracy. *See* piracy, pre-1700; piracy, post-1700 interpretive institutional infrastructure; piracy trials, by vice admiralty courts

British mariners: adjudication of violence against by ship captains, 169–70; and Atlantic culture, 47; and legal disputes over wages, 168–70; and pillage, 167–68; and practice of captains abandoning in distant ports, 151, 167; shipboard mutiny as point of entry into piracy, 157, 168; viewed as vulnerable to violence and exploitation, 150–51, 166–67

Broome, John, 80–81

Browne, James, capture, trial, and execution, 66–67, 69, 70, 91–92, 190n22

buccaneers of Caribbean, 57–60

Bumstead, Jeremiah, 140

Bunch, Phineas, 131–32

Burgess, Captain Josias, 132

Canny, Nicholas P., 47

Cape Coast Castle, Gold Coast of West Africa, mass trial and execution of pirates, 1–2, 4, 124, 144, 146–47, 175

Charles II, 65; and government control of customs revenue, 48; and privateering, 59, 60; and right to pillage, 167–68

classification rituals: and classification of pirates, 83–84, 99, 112, 135; and interpretive institutional infrastructures, 24–26; and legal hermeneutics, 101–2; and procedure, 23–25, 114, 116, 180; and propagation and ratification chains, 25, 116, 162, 180–81; and public moralism in regard to piracy, 156–57; and social and state power, 22, 24, 33–34

Clay, C. G. A., 45

Cockram, Captain John, 132

Coke, Edward, 102, 103, 193n30, 193n34, 198n3

Colman, Benjamin, 148–49

commission of oyer and terminer: common law procedures, 90–91, 108; only legal authority to hear cases of piracy, 74, 85–86, 91, 94, 107; reliance on juries to convict, 93; trial and conviction of Kidd, 69

Committee and Standing Council for Trade and Navigation, 86

common law: conflict with admiralty law, 8; and English subjects in colonies, 100; and 1536 piracy law, 193n34; and procedures for commission of oyer and terminer, 90–91, 108; and theory of the jury, 89

Connecticut Act of 1684, 107, 192n15

Cooley, Charles Horton, 31

coordination: and institutional order and power, 6, 14, 16, 19–22, 27, 111, 114, 129, 182–84; and interpretive infrastructures, 23, 64, 70–71, 138–40

Coote, Richard, 137

Council of Trade and Foreign Plantations. *See* Board of Trade

Courant, Captain Peter, 132

Courtney, Stephen, 164

Cromwell, Oliver, Western Design, 58

cultural theory: and institutional analysis, 13–14; other approaches to, 30–34; semiotic and meaning-centered approach, 17–22

Cunningham, David, 140

customs revenues, government control of, 48–49

Dampier, William, 147, 164, 203n8

Da Silva, Nuno, 56

Davis, Ralph, 43

Davis, Thomas, 127

Deák, Francis, 79

Deane, John, case of, 65–66, 91–92, 94, 104–5, 106

Delicia, 132
derrotero, 60
Douglas, Mary, 21
Dover, Thomas, 164
D'Oyley, Edward, 61
Drake, Francis, 158; pillaging of Spanish Empire, 38, 55–56, 57, 59; *World Encompassed*, 147
Dudley, Thomas, 146
Dutch independence, 50

East India Company, 42, 44–45, 69, 95, 99, 192n21
East Indies, cotton calico trade, 44
Elizabeth, 176
Elizabeth I, 38, 57; financial backing of English slave trade, 54, 55; knighting of Drake, 56
enforcement, and institutional order, 22–24, 30, 49, 182
European treaty agreements, and New World claims, 50–51
Every, Henry (Avery), 63–64, 71, 86, 95, 141, 192n13
Exquemelin, Alexandre, 58; *The Buccaneers of America*, 147

Fairfax, William, 132
Fine, Gary Alan, 31
flags: flown by pirates, and hourglass, 174; permitted to fly on merchant ships and by privateers, 81
Fletcher, Benjamin, 61, 63, 136–38
Fly, Captain William, capture and execution of, 126, 151, 155–56, 168, 175–76, 205n29
Ford, Richard T., 103
Foucault, Michel, 4
Franco-Dutch War, 59
François, 191n41
Friedland, Roger, 30
Fukuyama, Francis, *The Origins of Political Order*, 12, 17

Gale, Captain Wingate, 132
game theory, 8

Geertz, Clifford: analysis of Negara theater state, 20, 111–12, 139; and semiotic and meaning-centered approach to cultural theory, 17, 18, 21, 183
George I, 98, 128–29
Glorious Revolution, 69, 77; and end of Stuart absolutism, 99–100, 101
Goffman, Erving, 31, 182
Golden Fleece, The, 67
Golden Hind, 56
"government by license," 42, 48, 49, 100
Gray, Charles Montgomery, 101
Green, captain of *Elizabeth*, 176
Greimas, Algirdas, 171
Gunj-i-suwaee, 63–64, 95

Hakluyt, Richard, 38
Hallett, Tim, 31
Hannah, 169
Hawkins, John, slave trade in West Indian Spanish colonies, 54–55, 57, 59
Hedges, Sir Charles, 92, 96, 97, 191n40
Henry VIII, and 1536 piracy law, 65, 90–91
Herdman, Captain Mungo, 1
High Court of Admiralty, 66
Hipps, John, 133
historical institutionalism, 32–33
HMS *Shoreham*, 127
HMS *Swallow*, 1
Hornigold, Captain Benjamin, 129, 132, 172, 205n20
hostis humani generis ("enemy of mankind"), pirates defined as, 141–42, 146, 152–53, 173, 198n3
Houblon, Sir John, 71

incentives: and coordinated, meaningful action, 19; and institutional order, 14–16; and mechanisms of interests and meanings, 30; and piracy, dependence on state violence, 5, 34, 35
inhabited institutionalism, 31–33

instance jurisdiction, 90
institutional logics perspective, 30–31
institutional order: as collective world
making, 21; coordination and, 14,
16, 19–22, 27; cultural sources of, 16–
22; enforcement and, 22–24, 30, 49,
182; and interpretive institutional
infrastructures, 22–28, 182–84;
meaning as foundational source
of, 8
institutional scholarship: and cultural
theory, 13–14, 16–17; focus on incentive as central mechanism of power,
6–7; and interpretive aspects of
institutional orders, 7
institutions: defining, 12, 28–30;
instrumental, 30; and rules and
coordinated action, 6, 27; working of, 14–16. *See also* institutional
order; interpretive institutional
infrastructures
international relations: and control
of privateering, 51; transformation
of through treaties and shifts in
power, 50–52
interpretive institutional infrastructures: appearance throughout
all institutional orders, 28; and
classification rituals, 24–26; and
coordination, 23, 64, 70–71, 138–40;
and distinct mechanisms of social
meaning, 27–28; and enforcement,
22–23; and institutional order,
22–28, 182–84; legal system as, 24;
as metarules governing the making of meaning, 7; as network of
codified signifiers, 25, 26–27; and
social power, 24. *See also* piracy,
post-1700 interpretive institutional
infrastructure

Jamaica: English invasion of, 1635, 77;
support of privateering, 58–59, 61–
62, 85, 91, 189n13
Jamaica Piracy Act of 1681 (Act for Restraining and Punishing Privateers

and Pirates), 66, 92–94, 106–7, 114,
190n22; colonial passage of versions
of, 94, 192n15; piecemeal approach
to colonial piracy control, 93–94,
96–97, 108; reliance on jury to convict pirates, 93, 94
James I, efforts to control piracy, 39,
57–60, 86
James II, 49, 100; "Reducing and Suppressing of Pirates and Privateers in
America," 76
Jenkins, Leoline, 191n40, 192n15
Jessup, Philip C., 79
John Adventure, 65
Johnson, Captain Charles, *General
History of the Pyrates*, *144*, 147
joint stock companies, 45, 55
Jolly Roger, 174
jurisdiction: constitutive and limiting nature of, 102–3; innovations
in 1700 piracy act, 107–9, 114, 117;
instance jurisdiction, 90; and legal
hermeneutics, 102–5; limitations
in 1700 piracy act, 143–45; and
struggles over legal and interpretive
power, 103–5, 193n32

Kidd, Captain William: and commissions to attack French or pirate
ships in East Indies, 69, 178, 181;
indictment, guilty verdict, and
execution, 69–70, 86, 97, 141, 177–82;
trial of crew, 197n40
King, Stephen, *On Writing*, 177

Lamont, Michèle, 22
Lancaster, 131
La Paix, trial and execution of crew
members, 126–27
Larkin, George, and instruction of colonial courts in methods for trying
piracy, 117–19, 194n13
legal hermeneutics: and accomplice
testimony, 121; and classification
rituals, 101–2; and jurisdiction, 102–
5, 107; and 1700 piracy act, 135

legal performances, and meanings of piracy, 110, 118, 122; and coordination, 129; and executions, 143; and framework for moral transformation, 156–57; propagation and ratification chains, 112–15, 119–35, 178

letters of marque, 39, 51, 77, 191n41

letters of reprisal, 39, 76–77

Levant Company, 42, 45

Lloyd, Sir Richard, 65, 104, 106

Lords of Trade and Plantations, 65, 86, 94, 104, 106

Lounsbury, Michael, 30

Low, Edward: heinous acts of violence, 172; trial of, 152–53, 196n30

Lowther, commander of pirate ship, 126, 127

Lynch, Thomas, 59, 82–83, 85

Macarty, Dennis, 134

Mahoney, James, 12

Mainwaring, Henry, 39, 147, 160

Mancke, Elizabeth, 51

maritime insurance, 45

Markham, William, 71

Mary, 131

Massachusetts, passage of version of Jamaica Piracy Law, 94

Mather, Cotton, and sermons on piracy, 148–51, 153–56, 199n26

Mayrl, Damon, 188n5

Mead, George Herbert, 17, 21, 31, 183

Meinzies, James, 119, 120–21

merchant ships, flags permitted to fly, 81

Messon, Charles, 126

Meyer, John W., 22

Mi'kmaq and French pirates, trial and execution of in Boston, 124, 142–43, 195nn27–28

Modyford, Thomas, 58, 59, 62, 85

Molesworth, Hender, 68–69

moral discourse, and piracy: aimed at mariners considered vulnerable to pirate activities, 150–51; theme of obedience, 151–53; theme of pirate

wildness as threat to civilized order, 152–53, 173; theme of repentant pirate, 154–56

Morgan, Henry: published accounts of exploits, 147; as vice governor of Jamaica, 59, 171; violent and sadistic privateering in Spanish Caribbean, 41, 58–59, 85, 147, 158, 171

Mughal Empire, pirate voyages against, 63–64, 86, 95, 192n13

Myngs, Christopher, 58

Naval Stores Act of 1705, 188n8

Navigation Act of 1696 (Act for Preventing Frauds, and Regulating Abuses in the Plantation Trade), 78, 168; granting of jurisdiction of Navigation Acts to colonial admiralty courts, 95–96; lack of legal structure for trying piracy, 106

Navigation Acts: and customs service, 49; difficulty of enforcement, 189n9; and licensing system for ships, 49; and restructure of commercial system, 48–49; and statutory barriers around trade, 188n7

Newtown, Thomas, 119, 120–21

New York, as refuge for pirates, 61, 97

Nichols, Thomas, 125–26

Nicholson, Francis, 127–28

North, Douglass Cecil, 11, 16–17, 33; definition of institutions, 12, 28

Nuestra Senora de la Incarnacion Disenganio, 165

Ocasio, William, 30, 31

Ogle, Captain Chaloner, 1

Oort, Sarah Bradley Cox, 69

Owen, David R., 94, 169

Passenger, Captain William, and taking of the *La Paix*, 127, 196n37

Peirce, Charles S., and semiosis, 26, 188n7

pendants, 81

Pennsylvania, as refuge for pirates, 61

pillage, right to, 167–68

Pincus, Steve, 36, 43, 44, 52, 99–100

piracy, pre-1700: authorization by legitimate sovereign powers, 39, 40, 42, 51, 54, 56, 58, 59, 60; buccaneers of Caribbean, 57–60; challenges to by English political and merchant elites, 60–64; and death before capture trope, 175; as early technique for colonial expansion, 36–37, 38–43; and English hybrid ships, 41–42; high levels of, 97; historical importance of for long-distance trade, 4–5, 52; isolation of pirate encounters in remote places, 161–63, 203n4; maritime violence based in English colonies, 1–3; shipboard mutiny as point of entry into piracy, 157, 168; sociolegal ambiguity of, 9, 53, 54–57, 59, 60–64, 70–75; and Spanish New World colonies, 54–57; and summary justice, 68–69; supported by English colonial officials and subjects, 40, 51, 58–59, 61–64, 66, 76–77, 85, 91, 94, 97, 129–130, 135–139, 189n13; and tool for development of English maritime skills, 39, 40. *See also* privateering

piracy, post-1700 interpretive institutional infrastructure: and classification of pirates, 83–84, 99, 112, 135; coordination, and institutionalized power, 182–84; and decline of piracy, 141; effects of new infrastructure on privateering, 163–66; and fatalism and radicalism among pirates, 170–76; and idealized semiotic structure relating maritime violence and commerce, Greimas square illustration, 170, *171*; incentives dependent on state violence, 5, 34, 35; and insinuation of state power into mentalities of pirates, 163; and new temporality of piracy through retrospective trials, 158–63, 171–76; and performative ratification and propagation of meanings, 112–15, 119–35, 178; and pirate aesthetics, 173–76; and pirate executions, 141, 143–47, *144*; and pirates defined as wild beasts and enemies of mankind, 141–42, 146, 152–53, 173, 198n3; and procedure for legal performative action, 113 (*see also* piracy trials, by vice admiralty courts); and propagation through press and religious discourse, 147–56; and public display of pirate bodies, 146–47, 156; and remaking of social world of pirates, 156–57, 158; and social performances as communicative tableaux, 140–43, 175; and translation of semiotic structures into social performances, 110, 111, 112, 177; and violent turn of pirates against the British and their colonies, 172–73. *See also* Act for the More Effectual Suppression of Piracy, 1700

Piracy Destroy'd (anonymous treatise), 76, 151

piracy institutions, pre-1700, 1–3; Act for Punishment of Pirates and Robbers of the Sea, 1536, 37, 65, 90–91, 105–8, 114, 120; commission of oyer and terminer, 69, 74, 85–86, 91, 107; and conflict between common law and admiralty law, 8; and constitutional questions, 99; constraints of existing codes and procedures on reform, 83–89, 107; difficulties in defining piracy as social and legal category, 4, 5–6, 9–10, 37, 70–73, 78, 83–84, 99; efforts to build interpretive infrastructure, 24, 34, 75–81; and imposition of human order on the seas, 8–9; inadequate sixteenth-century interpretive infrastructure for defining and deterring, 64–75, 82; Jamaica Piracy Act of 1681 (Act for Restraining and Punishing Privateers and Pirates), 66, 92–94, 96–97, 106–8, 114; piracy tribunal, 1;

piracy institutions (*continued*)
prize law, 76–81; transformation of, and merchant capitalism, 36–37, 52, 66, 153; trials and errors in reform of, 89–92. *See also* Board of Trade (Council of Trade and Foreign Plantations)

piracy trials, by vice admiralty courts in colonies: and accomplice testimony, 120–21; acquittals based on pregnancy or age, 124–25, 195n27; acquittals for slaves and indentured persons, 128; and amelioration of piracy classifications, 123–29; amnesties, 128–29, 131; and *animo furandi* (intent to steal), 123; Cape Coast Castle, Gold Coast of West Africa, mass trial, 1–2, 4, 124, 144, 146–47, 175; civil law procedures, 121, 122; commutation of sentences, 123; as confrontations of state order with criminality, 142–43, 148; and cross-examination of witnesses, 115–16; departures from scripted procedures, 119–29; and differing levels of complicity of accused, 123–29; and efforts to control piracy in Bahamas, 129–35; and elimination of indictment through grand jury, 121; and expansion of empire's sociolegal order, 142–43; and eyewitness testimony, 194n53; and "forced man" arguments for acquittal, 125–27, 196n30, 196n35; pardons, 197n40; and principal-agent governance, 135–39; and questions about legal legitimacy of, 122; scripted procedures for, 114–15, 116–19; and signs as evidence of innocence or guilt, 123, 125–28; and silver oar, 145, 198n14; as symbolic public spectacles, 140–43, 145–46, 157; trial of Mi'kmaq and French pirates in Boston, 124, 142–43. *See also* piracy, post-1700 interpretive

institutional infrastructure; vice admiralty courts

pirate stories, 147

Plank, Geoffrey Gilbert, 124, 142–43

Popple, William, 62, 96

Porcupine, 173

privateering: and international relations, 51; Jamaican support of, 58–59, 61–62, 85, 91, 189n13; marginal legality in practice, 76, 163; and new temporality of through retrospective trials, 163–66; popularly defined as lawful form of private maritime violence, 75; and privateering commissions, 62–63, 77, 80, 82; and prize law, 76–81, 189n12; profitability, 188n4; sense of freedom of activities before 1700, 164; and 1694 proclamation on flags flown by, 81; Spanish Empire as target of, 2–3, 42, 50

Prize Act of 1692, 80

prize law, 76–81, 90, 190n33; adjudication by admiralty courts, 191n34, 191n40; and determination of legality of prize, 79, 191n41, 191nn35–36; and embezzlement, 204n15; inducement to violence, 204n16; and system of neutral passports, 191n39

procedure, as performance of legal authority and state power, 65, 90–91, 101, 108, 112–22

propagation and ratification chains: and classification rituals, 25, 116, 180–81; and institutional interpretive infrastructures, 23, 26, 76; and legal performances of meanings of piracy, 112–15, 119–35, 178; and principal-agent dynamics, 135; and rules, 29; through moral discourses, 141, 147–56

proprietary and charter colonies, 42

Quedah Merchant, 69, 178, 181

Quelch, Captain John, trial and execution of, 119, 120–21, 122, 145–46, 153, 154, 194n13, 195n16

Quinn, Sarah, 188n5

Rackam, John, trial of, 121, 124

Raleigh, Sir Walter, 43, 57

Randolph, Edward, 96

Ratchdale, Edward, 191n41

Read, Mary, 124

Reed, Isaac, 19–20

religion: and early colonial claims based on Protestant civilizing mission of Native peoples, 41, 52; importance of in Anglo-Spanish rivalry, 41

religious discourse, and propagation of pirate dramas, 148–56

Restoration: and regulation of privateering and prize taking, 77, 86–87, 94; and transition to imperial governance, 48

Rhode Island, as refuge for pirates, 61

Rich, Richard, 127

Ringrose, Basil, *Buccaneers Atlas*, 147

Roanoke expedition, 57

Roberts, Bartholomew: personal style at execution, 174; trials and executions of crew, 1, 121, 144, 172–73

Robinson, James A., 12, 13, 16, 188n2

Rodger, N. A. M., 41, 49

Rogers, Woodes: efforts to control piracy in Bahamas, 81, 129–35, 143, 197n46, 197n48, 205n20; lawfulness of 1708–11 privateering cruise, 164–66, 203nn8–9

Ross, George, 125

Rounsivil, George, 134

Rowan, Brian, 22

Royal African Company, 42, 45, 85, 124

Royal Fortune, surrender of and sentencing and punishment of crew, 1–2, 174–75

Royal Navy: reforms and involvement in customs enforcement, 49; response to piracy, 86

rule of law: and legal hermeneutics, 101–2; and struggles over English constitution and state power, 99–101

rules: as cultural models, 28–30; as incentivizing constraints, 29; and social coordination and control, 6

Ryle, Gilbert, on adverbs and thick description, 18, 178–81

Santo Rosario, 60

Schelling, Thomas C., 22–23

Select Council of Trade and Plantations, 87

semiosis, 26, 188n7

semiotic structures: idealized, relating maritime violence and commerce, Greimas square illustration, 170, *171*; and social performances, 33, 110, 112, 139, 156, 177

Sewall, Samuel, 145

Sewell, William H., 17

Shapiro, Barbara B., 113

Sharpe, Captain Bartholomew, 59–60, 164

Shulman, David, 31

silver oar, 145, 198n14

slave trade, 54–55, 57, 59

Smith, John, 126

Smith, Philip, 32

Snead, Robert, 71–75

social performances: as communicative tableaux, 140–43, 175; and semiotic structures, 33, 110, 111, 112, 156, 177; verdictive performances, 73–74. *See also* legal performances, and meanings of piracy

Spanish Empire: colonial claims based upon papal authority, 41; colonial demand for enslaved people and trade goods, 54; decline of by mid-seventeenth century, 40, 50; late sixteenth-century claim on all trade and navigation in West Indies, 40–41, 50; as target of privateering, 2–3, 42, 50

Staples Act of 1663, 188n8
state power: and classification rituals, 22, 24, 33–34; cultural forms of, 111–12; insinuation of into mentalities of pirates, 163; linking of symbolic and material dimensions of, 19–22; and procedure, 65, 90–91, 101, 108, 112–22; and rule of law, 99–101
Steele, Ian, 50–51
St. George's Cross, 81
structural hermeneutics, 27, 32–33
Swallow (Royal Navy ship), 174–75
Sweetser, Joseph, 127
symbolic interactionism, 31

Tallia, Richard, 64
Taylor, Nathaniel, 132
Teach (Thatch), Edward (Blackbeard), 205n20; attack on Charleston Harbor, 159, 172; and pardon, 197n40; personal style, 173–74
Tew, Thomas, 63, 95
theater state, 111–12, 113, 139
Thomson, Janice E., 190n32
Thornton, Patricia H., 30, 31
tobacco, import of from North America, 44
Tolley, Michael C., 94, 169
trade: importance of piracy in, 4–5, 52; slave trade, 54–55, 57, 59; transformation of in British Empire, 43–46, 49, 51–52. *See also* Board of Trade (Council of Trade and Foreign Plantations)
transatlantic legal culture, 100–101
Treaty of Madrid, 50, 59, 60, 77, 189n4
Treaty of Münster, 50–51
Treaty of Paris, 190n32
Treaty of Uppsala, 191n39
Tropic of Cancer, as line of demarcation in treaty agreements, 50
Trott, Nicholas, 61, 64, 195n15

Vane, Captain Charles, trial of, 130–31, 143

Vaughan, John, 3rd Earl of Carbery (Lord Vaughan), governor of Jamaica, 65–67, 91–92, 104–5
verdictive performances, 73–74
vice admiralty courts, 94–99; adjudication of violence against seamen, 169–70; advantages for seamen, 169, 204n17; and disputes over mariners' wages, 168–70; and granting of jurisdiction of Navigation Acts in 1696, 94, 95–96; lack of in colonies before 1696, 96; lack of power to try capital cases until 1696, 86, 95, 106; regulation of prize system, 78–81. *See also* piracy trials, by vice admiralty courts
Violence and Social Order (North, Wallis, and Weingast), 16–17

Wafer, Lionel, 147
Wager, Sir Charles, 204n15
Wagner-Pacifici, Robin, 21
Walker, Thomas, 132
Wallis, John Joseph, 16–17
Ward, Sir Edward, 197n40
Weingast, Barry R., 16–17
West Indian colonies: affluent planter class, 47; dependence on manufactured goods exported from London, 44; and privateering, 40; sugar trade, 44
White, William, execution of, 140, 155
William III, 62, 77–78, 87, 114, 179–80, 190n33
Willis, Robert, 127
Wilson, Nicholas Hoover, 32
Wittgenstein, Ludwig, 182
Woodward, Josiah, *Seaman's Monitor*, 150, 152, 200n32

Yanky, Captain, 164

Zahedieh, Nuala, 40, 45, 189n9